Advance praise for *The Global Politics of Interreligious Dialogue*

"Driessen has written a vital tour d'horizon of religious change sweeping across parts of the Middle East that could signal a new mode of global religiosity rooted in interreligious spirituality and solidarity. Responsive to a post-secular and radically plural social milieu, the growing network of Christian and Muslim councils as well as local religious communities, sects, foundations, and organizations, explored through a series of illuminating case studies, collectively represent a new moment of opportunity to realize the goal of inclusive citizenship grounded in human fraternity. It is a vision embraced not only by religious leaders like Pope Francis and Abdallah bin Bayyah, but also by state ministries across the Arab region. Scholars, religious practitioners, civil society, and government officials owe a debt to Driessen for the painstaking research and participant observation that enabled him to plot this roadmap to a more promising future."
—R. Scott Appleby, Professor of History and Dean of the Keough School of Global Affairs, University of Notre Dame

"This book sheds light on the ways Muslim majority countries have in the last decades engaged in interreligious dialogue. Driessen offers a fresh perspective beyond the state instrumentalization of religion and pays careful attention to the religious content of these initiatives. A much-needed addition to the existing literature on the topic."
—Jocelyne Cesari, Professor of Religion and Politics, University of Birmingham and Senior Fellow, Georgetown University's Berkley Center for Religion, Peace, and World Affairs

"Whether you agree or not with his postmodern and post-Islamist framing of the global politics of interreligious dialogue in the Middle East, you can't help but benefit from engaging with Michael Driessen's master analysis in this book and learn from evidence-based and mostly unseen facts about the surprising influence of the bottom-up dialogue on both theological and political narratives, which may also influence future democratic developments across the region."
—Fadi Daou, Executive Director of Globethics, Geneva

"Driessen's book is the landmark study that we were waiting for, and for a long time. For those who want to understand Catholicism and the papacy today, it is an indispensable key to interpret Pope Francis' outreach to Islam through trips in the Middle East and the participation in interreligious events organized by Catholic groups and movements. But the book is much more than that: it helps discern a certain romanticism of interreligious dialogue, analyzes the growth of interreligious dialogue

initiatives as a critical example of religion operating in global institutions today, and looks at interreligious dialogue in the Middle East in the context of geopolitics and global religious change and the response of religious traditions to liberal modernity."
—**Massimo Faggioli**, Professor of Historical Theology, Villanova University

"A well-written, cogently argued, and wisely described analysis of the political meaning of dialogue projects in the Arab region. Using the fields of inquiry of political science and religious studies, informed by the author's knowledge of Catholicism and Sunni Islam, this book analyzes the ideas certain interreligious efforts promote; the political context they have emerged from; the geopolitics that influence their form; the political theologies they imply and construct; the changing religious societies they respond to; and the challenges, risks, and unintended consequences which confront them. A must-read for anyone interested in learning about religious discourses and geopolitics in the Arab region—and globally."
—**Azza Karam**, Professor of Religion and Development, Vrije Universiteit Amsterdam and Secretary General, Religions for Peace

"With passionate erudition and a sharp post-secular gaze, Michael Driessen navigates the complex recent history of the new dynamics of interreligious dialogue—especially Islamo-Catholic—in the Middle East. It is a crucial prism through which the sociopolitical challenges and aspirations of the people living in the region resonate and are projected toward the future. A must-read for political scientists and policymakers, religious scholars, and activists interested in the Middle East."
—**Fabio Petito**, Professor of Religion and International Affairs, University of Sussex

"This book is a very important resource to understand the dynamics of interreligious dialogue in the MENA region, whether from a geopolitical perspective or from a faith-based perspective. It shows how interfaith dialogue is connected to the reshaping of religiosity, to a renewed sense of citizenship but also to political instrumentalization. It presents the readers with a grid by which they can analyze political and religious positions concerning dialogue, and identify those that actually do serve the values of inclusivity and solidarity."
—**Nayla Tabbara**, President, Adyan Foundation

"For roughly 20 years now there has been a growing debate over the global religious resurgence, or religion's 'return from exile' in International Relations. Driessen's *The Global Politics of Interreligious Dialogue* helps to reframe this argument by focusing on a variety of case studies in interreligious dialogue, often not well-known, and links them to some of the everyday policy issues confronting everyone in the region on education, citizenship, and development. In this way, the book contributes a religious dimension to the 'practice turn' in International Relations theory, and to understanding new, positive religious forms of institutionalization in International Relations in the twenty-first century."
—**Scott M. Thomas**, Senior Lecturer of International Relations, University of Bath, United Kingdom

The Global Politics of Interreligious Dialogue

Religious Change, Citizenship, and Solidarity in the Middle East

MICHAEL D. DRIESSEN

OXFORD
UNIVERSITY PRESS

Oxford University Press is a department of the University of Oxford. It furthers the University's objective of excellence in research, scholarship, and education by publishing worldwide. Oxford is a registered trade mark of Oxford University Press in the UK and certain other countries.

Published in the United States of America by Oxford University Press
198 Madison Avenue, New York, NY 10016, United States of America.

© Oxford University Press 2023

All rights reserved. No part of this publication may be reproduced, stored in a retrieval system, or transmitted, in any form or by any means, without the prior permission in writing of Oxford University Press, or as expressly permitted by law, by license, or under terms agreed with the appropriate reproduction rights organization. Inquiries concerning reproduction outside the scope of the above should be sent to the Rights Department, Oxford University Press, at the address above.

You must not circulate this work in any other form
and you must impose this same condition on any acquirer.

Library of Congress Cataloging-in-Publication Data
Names: Driessen, Michael Daniel, author.
Title: The global politics of interreligious dialogue : religious change, citizenship, and solidarity in the Middle East / Michael D. Driessen.
Description: New York, NY, United States of America : Oxford University Press, [2023] | Includes bibliographical references and index.
Identifiers: LCCN 2023004926 (print) | LCCN 2023004927 (ebook) | ISBN 9780197671672 (hardback) | ISBN 9780197671696 (epub)
Subjects: LCSH: Religions—Relations. | Dialogue—Religious aspects. | Religion and politics—Mediterranean Region.
Classification: LCC BL410.D75 2023 (print) | LCC BL410 (ebook) | DDC 201/.5—dc23/eng/20230206
LC record available at https://lccn.loc.gov/2023004926
LC ebook record available at https://lccn.loc.gov/2023004927

DOI: 10.1093/oso/9780197671672.001.0001

Printed by Integrated Books International, United States of America

For Silvia,
tutto

Contents

Preface	ix
Acknowledgments	xv
Introduction	1

PART I POLITICS

1. Geopolitics and Interreligious Dialogue	23
2. Political Theory and Interreligious Dialogue	40

PART II THEOLOGIES

3. A Brief History of Interreligious Dialogue	79
4. Catholicism and Interreligious Dialogue	89
5. Islam and Interreligious Dialogue	99

PART III PRACTICES

6. Comparative Contexts	129
7. The Focolare Community (Algeria)	137
8. The Adyan Foundation (Lebanon)	152
9. Interreligious Engagement in the Gulf: DICID (Qatar) and KAICIID (Saudi Arabia)	167
Conclusion: Interreligious Dialogue and the Future of Citizenship in the Middle East	185
Appendix	199
Notes	201
Bibliography	221
Index	245

Preface

I am not sure of the precise moment when I first read or heard about "interreligious dialogue," but I am pretty certain it was in the early days of the US wars in Afghanistan and Iraq and that it was connected to the work of the community of Sant'Egidio and their annual international (and interreligious) prayer for peace, which Pope John Paul II had charged them to conduct from 1986 onward "in the spirit of Assisi." Sant'Egidio organized the first iteration of their meeting in the United States in the spring of 2006 at Georgetown University, and my wife and I, along with a few other married graduate couples from Notre Dame, got the university to sponsor an old minivan to drive us from South Bend to DC for the event. I had come across the prayer of Christian de Chergé by then and had felt an instant tug toward the mystery of his words and the story of the monks of Tibhirine. In no small measure, Tibhirine inspired me to plunge deeper into the study of Islam, go to Algeria for my dissertation fieldwork, and come back to it again for this book.

At that time I was writing about religion, the state, and democracy in (predominantly) Catholic and Muslim societies across the Mediterranean, and in Algeria I spent most of my time interviewing Islamist or post-Islamist party members, government authorities, and religious authorities, both official and not. Like many scholars coming from abroad during that period, I was hosted in Algiers by les Glycines (through the Centre d'Études Diocésain), but because we came with a small child in tow, we arranged to be up the hill at the Maison Diocésain, where Henri Teissier was still an archbishop in residence, and we shared our daily meals with him and our son pawing around on all fours in the kitchen and soaked in his constant sharp, brutal yet hopeful reflections about Algeria, dialogue, democracy, peace, and Tibhirine. I interviewed Teissier twice for this book, once in Algiers and once at a Focolare meeting in Castel Gandolfo, before he died in 2020. When I did, it was as things falling into their order, and I hope this book does some service to his memory.

And so it was that as I walked about Algiers and Oran during those days, talking with post-Islamists about religion and democracy, I was also thinking about interreligious dialogue in Algeria, somehow smitten and wondering what the meaning of it all was. I began to have a notion that the two, dialogue and democracy, were somehow related and that both, together, had to do with the bigger global dynamics of religion-in-modernity. That inkling deepened in Doha, where my family and I relocated for a postdoctoral fellowship at Georgetown's Qatar campus in education city during the 2011–2012 academic year. Those were heady days to be in Doha, and I had to do my utmost to refrain from listening to *Al Jazeera* all day long in my office as everything unfolded in real time. I attended my first state-sponsored interreligious dialogue event there in 2012, held by the Doha International Center for Interfaith Dialogue (DICID), and wrote a short article about it with my good friend Brandon Vaidyanathan, which gave me a chance to start working out some conceptual categories to reflect on the politics of dialogue on display at the event and their connections to the Arab Spring.

About the same time, given my research exploring parallels between the experience of Christian democratic parties and Islamist or post-Islamist parties in the region, I was invited to a number of conferences across the Mediterranean which brought together scholars and legal experts who were thinking about the future of Muslim democracy and who were also mining the experience of Christian democracy to do so. This included a series of policy dialogues organized by Fabio Petito through the Italian Institute for International Political Studies (ISPI) and the Italian Ministry of Foreign Affairs' joint program on religion and international relations. Freshly elected Islamists from Tunisia, Egypt, Turkey, and Morocco also attended these conferences and seemed to scour the record to learn from the Christian democratic experience in Europe what institutional choices they had made, how far they had gone to combine religious ideals in democratic institutions, what compromises they had forged, where they had failed. The policy dialogues toggled between "democracy" and "peace," and a number of leading interreligious dialogue organizations were also invariably present at these conferences, including personalities like Paolo Dall'Oglio from Mar Musa in Syria, members of the Gülen community, the Royal Institute for Interfaith Studies (RIIFS), Muhammadiyah, Sant'Egidio, the Focolare, and the Adyan Foundation, and I sat at their feet and asked them what part they had to play in that moment of democratic hope and violent unraveling in the region. In the summer of 2014, just as ISIS took over Mosul, I went to Jordan to work on my Arabic and conducted a first set of interviews in Amman and Beirut with RIIFS and Adyan for a preliminary probe of my hypotheses, which I then wrote up for a paper for an Adyan conference in

Byblos in November 2014 and which would serve as a first draft of the theoretical chapter for this book.

I also began working more closely with the Adyan Foundation. I had first met Fadi at an ISPI conference in October 2012 in Trent, and then Nayla at an Adyan conference later in the same year. I helped Adyan draft the scientific prospectus for their 2014 Byblos conference on Islam and democracy, and then helped design a course with them titled Islam and Peacebuilding for a training program for young interreligious leaders in 2015 and 2016. We held another conference at the University of Notre Dame in Rome in 2016, together with Fabio Petito and Scott Appleby, called Democracy, Dialogue and Development, which presented and further explored the ideas of this book along with scholars from across Europe and the Middle East. Over the course of 2017 and 2018 I conducted summer fieldwork for the project with the Focolare community in Algeria and with Adyan youth participants in Lebanon and then traveled to Egypt, Qatar, and Vienna for further interviews in 2018 with the King Abdullah bin Abdulaliz International Center for Interreligious and Intercultural Dialogue (KAICIID), DICID, and other dialogue outfits operating in the region.

The following year I wrote a first draft of the book while in residence at the European University Institute (EUI) in Fiesole, where I enjoyed the good company of Olivier Roy and Georges Fahmi. While there, I got a call from Fadi, who asked me to join him for a project he had begun work on with the Forum for Promoting Peace in Muslim Societies (Sheikh Abdallah bin Bayyah's organization in the United Arab Emirates) and Wilton Park of the United Kingdom, together with a consortium of religious institutions and interreligious organizations active in the region, including the Muslim World League, the Middle East Council of Churches, the Pontifical Council for Interreligious Dialogue, KAICIID, and Kalam research, as well as a number of Yezidi, Druze, and Jewish participants from across the region. The intent was to write an interreligiously supported charter for inclusive citizenship that could be adopted and promoted by state ministries across the Arab region. Given the nature of my research, Fadi asked if I would participate in the project as the rapporteur and help write the first draft of the charter (which was originally mandated to be written in English) following the discussions and directions of the consortium. I said yes. What followed were three intense years of travel between Abu Dhabi, Wilton Park, and Lebanon, and difficult, revealing, high-level discussion around the themes of my research as well as close-up observation of a number of the key actors and institutions featured in this book, including Abdallah bin Bayyah, KAICIID, the Pontifical Council for Interreligious Dialogue, and Adyan Foundation. The process confirmed a number of research intuitions I had been writing about but inevitably scrambled many others, and I began the slow, painful process of rewriting the book.

Thus, on the one hand, and perhaps most important, the process confirmed for me the centrality of solidarity and citizenship as emergent ideals that were guiding interreligious efforts in the region, and in ways which directly responded to the hopes and anxieties, both religious and political, produced by the Arab Spring and the rise of the Islamic State. The unexpected visit of Pope Francis to the UAE in 2019 to sign the Human Fraternity Document with the Grand Imam of al Azhar, Sheikh Ahmed al Tayeb, as well as his subsequent visit with Ayatollah al Sistani in Iraq in March 2021, among other events, seemed to flow in that same direction. Out of the religious turmoil of the moment, interreligious actors and organizations had apparently assumed an important role in setting a postconflict vision for more inclusive political development in the region, one which was consistent, at least in part, with the religion-is-back mantra in international relations scholarship.

That vision was also clearly a postsecular one. In debates among participants in the consortium, nearly all of whom were from the Arab world, Habermas emerged unprovoked as a central figure of conversation. Many, including bin Bayyah, approvingly cited his writing on postsecularism, on that awareness of what is missing, as philosophical validation for what they felt they had discovered and what they knew was needed to respond to the moment of crisis, namely, to enable the fruitful dynamic positive role of Islam in the public sphere: that it was religion, "rightly understood," in a balanced partnership with reason and politics, which could create a better and more inclusive modern. "Thus, the theorem that only a religious orientation toward a transcendental reference point could help a remorseful modernity out of its impasse again finds resonance today," as Habermas put it in his debate with the future Benedict XVI In 2004 at the Bavarian Catholic Academy. It was not a surprise, therefore, when the UAE awarded Habermas its 2021 "Cultural Personality of the Year" prize. Habermas's acceptance and then about-face on the award was itself a mini-exposition of the sorts of mutual misunderstandings which have arisen around the new roles, norms, and institutional boundaries of religion being proposed in the post-peak-liberal public sphere, which this book tries to register and clarify. You said *post*secularism! No, I said post*secularism!*

Those misunderstandings were especially apparent in the discussions of the charter process around the question of religious freedom. While the term "democracy" was tabled rather quickly during the charter process, there was a strong desire to endorse a collective statement on religious freedom in the document, which, however, was difficult to agree upon. Some participants feared the extent to which endorsing religious freedom, particularly using language common in US and European policymaking circles, would open the doors in irreversible ways to liberal understandings of the individual over the community and create a line toward the breakdown of religious authority as well as that of the state. Others understood religious freedom as *the* central element of the charter. Fadi proposed the formulation "Religious Freedom and the Sanctity of Human Conscience" as a way to distinguish the language from that of Freedom of Religion or Belief (FoRB) discourses, and this seemed to garner general consent, including among the principal organizers of the charter, and it cleared the process over a hump. While the charter then came close to achieving a strong consensus, a number of events held it back from the full-throated and high-level endorsements it originally aimed to achieve. COVID intervened; Lebanon collapsed; the UAE and Israel established a new relationship—all of which shifted attention, priorities, and relationships. Nevertheless, the document was published, and the Forum for Promoting Peace in Muslim Societies made inclusive citizenship the central theme of their 2021 forum, issuing the "Abu Dhabi Declaration on Inclusive Citizenship" at the end of the conference, which confirmed the centrality of citizenship education and advocacy in their ongoing activity.

As this preface indicates, while I began this research project as a scholar guided by the methods and research aims of political science in the North American/European tradition, I am clearly not, simply, a disinterested, neutral observer of the interreligious engagement efforts that the book attempts to chronicle and analyze. Over time, especially through the Charter for Inclusive Citizenship process, I became an active participant-observer in the broader efforts to craft an interreligious response to political crises across the greater Mediterranean region and in ways which implicated my spiritual and religious life. This was the tug that drew me on throughout, which raised all the questions and troubles within, and fed the spark, the burning desire, to turn this thing over and over, to try to leave no stone unturned, no critique unconsidered. This book, then, is an attempt to come to terms with the political meaning of these dialogue projects in the region, using the fields of inquiry of political science and religious studies and continuing my comparative study of Roman Catholicism and Sunni Islam to name and analyze the ideas these interreligious efforts promote, the political context they have emerged from, the geopolitics that influence their form, the political theologies they imply and construct, the changing religious societies they respond to, the challenges and risks and unintended consequences which confront them, and the global politics and religious reconstruction which they may favor as a result.

Michael Daniel Driessen
August 6th, 2022
Rome, Italy

Acknowledgments

Many good colleagues have regaled me with comments and criticism on various drafts and chapters of this book over the years. I presented multiple versions of Parts I, II, and III at American Political Science Association and International Studies Association conferences, at ISPI's Religion and International Relations Policy Dialogues, at annual panels at the European Academy of Religion, at the European University Institute (EUI), at the European External Action Service, at a Religious Liberty conference at the UN in Geneva, at a Progetto Paolo Prodi conference in Bologna, at the Università Bicocca, at the Université de Genève, at the Istituto De Gasperi, at Leuven (online), at the G-20 Interfaith Forum in Bologna, and at a conference at Notre Dame in Rome, and I thank Fabio Petito, Scott Thomas, Melanie Barbato, Roberto Catalano, Paolo Frizzi, Jocelyne Cesari, Gregorio Bettiza, David Buckley, Ahmet Kuru, Sabri Ciftci, Nader Hashemi, Carlos Invernizzi-Accetti, Luca Ozzano, Alberta Giorgi, Bjorn Thomassen, Rosario Forlenza, Valentina Napolitano, Azza Karam, Jan Werner-Müller, Kristina Stoeckl, Simona Cruciani, Mahan Mirza, Ebrahim Moosa, Atalia Omer, Leonard Taylor, Nick Dines, Massimo Faggioli, Kathleen Cummings, Marcello Neri, Kurt Appel, Andy Bramsen, James Olsen, Lorenzo Malagola, Natascia Marchei, Stefania Ninatti, Katherine Marshall, Allison Hilliard, Mohamed Elsanousi, Peter Welby, Renee Hattar, Bob Dowd, Jeremy Menchik, Andrea Benzo, Martino Diez, Alberto Melloni, Cynthia Salloum, Merete Bilde, Piero Coda, and others for their comments and conversation and support. At Notre Dame, many thanks to Scott Appleby for criticism on parts of this draft, and for support for this project from the Contending Modernities program and the Ansari Institute. A special thanks also to Notre Dame's Rome Global Gateway, and to their incredible director, who hosted two major conferences linked to this project. I wrote a first draft of this book on sabbatical leave as a Jean Monnet fellow at the Robert Schuman Centre for Advanced Studies at the European University Institute in Fiesole and I thank the EUI for supporting me during that year. In Fiesole, I was especially grateful to spend time with Olivier Roy, who generously advised me throughout my stay, and Georges Fahmi, both of whom also helped organize panels for my project there.

At my academic home in Rome, John Cabot University, thanks in a special way to my colleague in joy and sorrow these long few years, Seth Jaffe. Thanks also to Pam Harris, Tom Bailey, and the interfaith initiative crew, and to Silvia Scarpa, Eszter Salgo, Diego Pagliarullo, Camil Roman, and everyone in the department who has made working at JCU so enjoyable. To all of my students, especially in the Religion and Global Politics seminars, who show up in this book more often than they will know. Finally, a special thanks to Vice President Mary Merva and President Franco Pavoncello at JCU for their support for this project, for cohosting and cofunding a number of workshops and conferences associated with it, and for enabling me the time to follow it through. In Rome, many thanks also to all of those from the interreligious community who have listened to me speak about too many versions of this project and offered their thoughtful comments and support in return, to Cenap at the Istituto Tevere, to Jason Welle and Diego Sarrío Cucarella at the Pontifical Institute for the Study of Arabic and Islam, to Samuele Sangalli and Antonella Piccinin at the Gregorian and LUISS, and Mohammed Hashas, Adnane Mokrani, Elena Dini, Khaled Akasheh, Riccardo Lufrani, Iain Matthew, Yayha Pallavicini, and many others.

In Lebanon, a dear special thanks to the whole Adyan team, to Ahmed Nagi, Wissam, Agapios, Mayssam, Eliza, Adriana, Nagham, Bernard, Adel, Christina, Dalia, and Elie, also to Ziad Fahed, and especially to Fadi and Nayla for their warmth and affection and friendship. In Algiers, a kind thanks to Pasquale Ferrara for inviting me to stay at Villa Hesperia and for all our conversations there together, and to Gesim and Amine as well. In Oran, a special thanks to Fayçal and his family and the Famille Korso, to both of their families for their hospitality, and to the inimitable Bob Parks, always with an open door, and to Karim Ouaras as well. In Tlemcen, thanks to Didier Lucas, Rassim, Gino, Matteo, Alex, and everyone at Dar es Salam. In Qatar, to Aisha al Mannai and Ibrahim al Naimi, and to John Fahy at Georgetown. In Cairo, thanks to Aliaa Wagdy, Jean Druel, Samira Luka, and especially cousin Paul for his hospitality. At KAICIID, many thanks to Patrice Brodeur, Mohammed Abu-Nimer, Waseem Haddad, and Faisal bin Muaammar. In Abu Dhabi, thanks to Zeshan Zafar, Al Mahfoudh bin Bayyah, and Sheikh Abdallah bin Bayyah for their hospitality and conversation. A very deep thanks to everyone I interviewed for this book, for pouring out their thoughts and allowing me to listen to their stories.

At Oxford University Press a great thanks to Angela Chnapko for her continued support and encouragement and Alexcee Bechthold, Preetham Raj, and the whole production team. A very special thank you to the Barjeel Art Foundation and, in particular, to the great Ismail al Rifai who has generously allowed his artwork to grace the cover of this book.

Always and especially to my family and friends, whose love made everything possible. To Therese, Christine, Mark, Molly, and Rebecca, to Jeff and Jerome for all of these years, to Massimo, Angelo, Andy, Tino, Xavier, and everyone at L'Arche. To my family in Italy, Lorenzo, Patrizia, and Marci, who are a firm foundation for making so many things happen. To my parents, whose boundless trust in my choices has been wholly unmerited but always lifegiving. And finally, and mostly, to Giacomo, Viola, and Bernardo, who are not bear cubs anymore but have been the best bears and blessing of my life, and of course most of all to Silvia, to whom this book is dedicated, who has shared everything written here with love and faith and oneness, even when we could not always travel across her beloved Mediterranean together.

I note with thanks that fieldwork in Lebanon, Algeria, Austria, the UAE, Qatar, Egypt, and Jordan was made possible by a grant from the Global Religion Research Initiative at the University of Notre Dame and to innumerable, generous faculty development grants from John Cabot University. If it were not for their aid, this book would not have been possible. I also note that I have drawn on a forthcoming article published with *CrossCurrents* (72:3) entitled, "Interreligious Engagement and Political Theory: Between Virtue Ethics and Religious Humanism," for parts of Chapter 3. Thank you to the Association for Public Religion and Intellectual Life for allowing me to reproduce some of that material here.

Finally, a small note on the transliteration from Arabic: I have favored common, simplified spelling of widely used Arabic terms (such as *sharia, hadith, dhimmi*) as much as possible, including proper names, and have avoided diacritical marks unless referencing works that include them.

Introduction

Over the past thirty years, scholars have observed the re-institutionalization of religion in global politics and documented the growing ways in which states have formalized new relationships with religious communities and individuals in their domestic and foreign policies (Huntington 1996; Thomas 2005; Petito 2011; Fox 2008, 2015; Toft, Philpott, and Shah 2011; Koesel 2014). As Jonathan Fox (2015) has chronicled, since the 1990s, across all major regions and including all the great powers of the world, governments have increasingly adopted legislative policies to accommodate, manage, discriminate against, regulate, communicate with, or support religious communities. While most scholars agree that evidence of this sort indicates the "return" of religion's importance to the study of global politics, there is little consensus about its meaning, exact shape, or future.

Thus, some scholars have read into this global re-institutionalization of religion the beginning of a post-Westphalian world order, in which religiously identified civilizational blocs overtake the nation-state as the most important organizing unit within global politics (Huntington 1996). This narrative might be termed the "Religion Is Back" story, with close links to what others have named the "Religious Resurgence" or "Religious Restoration" narratives in contemporary international relations studies (Toft, Philpott, and Shah 2011; Hurd 2007; Thomas 2005). Others contest these characterizations, arguing that new policies toward religions are fundamentally regulatory in nature and designed to reconsolidate state sovereignty and supremacy, further marginalizing or instrumentalizing religious communities in the process (Baskan 2011; Mahmood 2006, 2012; Künkler, Madeley, and Shankar 2018). This narrative might be termed the "State Supreme" story for the way it highlights the hegemonic power that modern states wield over religious spheres of life, employing both real and pseudo-ministries of religious affairs to domesticate, manage, and channel religious dynamics to serve their own interests.

This book contributes to this debate by analyzing the growth of interreligious dialogue initiatives as a critical example of religion operating in global institutions today. From the point of view of global politics, a number of states and international institutions have invested in interreligious dialogue initiatives over the past fifteen years. Since 2005, Saudi Arabia,[1] Qatar,[2] the United States,[3] the United Nations,[4] the European Union,[5] the Organization of Islamic Cooperation,[6] Turkey,[7] Indonesia,[8] Finland,[9] Germany,[10] and Italy,[11] among others, have all created or supported new institutions which conduct or fund interreligious dialogue efforts as well as other initiatives designed to engage religious communities (Petito 2018; Bettiza 2019). If "God is back" (Toft, Philpott, and Shah 2011) in global affairs, then the institutionalization of interreligious dialogue might be understood as concrete evidence of religious authority's global political reconstruction. Alternatively, state-sponsored interreligious dialogue efforts could also signify the re-instrumentalization, reappropriation, or further marginalization of religious identities, individuals, and ideas for political ends.

This debate is perhaps nowhere more pertinent than in the Muslim-majority world, which registers twice the amount of government involvement in religion of any other region and whose institutional entanglements with religion have also grown over the past decades (Fox 2015). At the same time, the Muslim-majority world is a global leader in the creation of state-sponsored interreligious dialogue initiatives (Pew Research Center 2013). In a major shift from previous decades, several of the most important interreligious dialogue initiatives of the past ten years have originated in the Middle East, as opposed to Europe or elsewhere. This includes international centers like the King Abdullah bin Abdulaliz International Center for Interreligious and Intercultural Dialogue (KAICIID), established through a Saudi Arabia–led initiative in 2012, and the Forum for Promoting Peace in the Muslim Societies,[12] established in the United Arab Emirates (UAE) by Sheikh Abdallah bin Bayyah in 2014, as well as major interreligious declarations like the Jordanian-led "A Common Word between Us and You" letter (2007), the Moroccan-hosted Marrakesh Declaration (2016), and the UAE-hosted Human Fraternity Document (2019). Especially given the backdrop of religiously expressed violence that has marked recent Middle East history and the attempts by various religious and political leaders to respond to it through interreligious dialogue forums, it is of particular importance to understand and contextualize the political meanings and consequences of these new forms of interreligious dialogue in the Middle East today.

As a result of the immediate policy context surrounding these initiatives, much recent scholarship on interreligious dialogue in the social sciences has tended to be in the fields of conflict resolution and international development, with scholars training their analyses on how to make these new forms of religious-political partnerships more effective in the pursuit of common and usually humanitarian-oriented policy goals, including on issues of global poverty, the sustainable development goals, immigration, human trafficking, and the reduction of violence and conflict (Bouta, Kadayifci-Orellana, and Abu-Nimer 2005; Abu-Nimer, Khoury, and Welty 2007; Shannahan and Payne 2016; Marshall 2017; Bamat et al. 2017; US Institute of Peace 2004). While this scholarship has yielded important insights on the functioning of interreligious dialogue in global and regional politics, its analytical lens has not been well-suited to pose the question of the deeper political meaning of interreligious dialogue, that is to say, not just what dialogue *does* or how *effective* it is but what dialogue *is* and what it *represents*.[13] In other words, why have states in the Muslim-majority world increasingly engaged in interreligious dialogue? What is the political appeal of dialogue as a specific form or idea? How do these interreligious dialogue initiatives impact the relationship between religious and political authority in the region? And what relationship, if any, does interreligious dialogue have with the evolving way in which religion is lived and practiced in Middle Eastern societies?

Through an exploration of a broad range of both state-promoted and civil society–directed interreligious dialogue initiatives in the Middle East, involving a variety of Muslim, Christian, and other religious actors, this book begins to respond to these questions. In doing so, it challenges the analytical frameworks which continue to dominate the study of religion in global politics, including various versions of the *God is Back* and *State Supreme* stories. While both narratives capture important dynamics animating the growth of interreligious initiatives in the Middle East, neither has adequately considered the larger ways in which states' institutional recognition of religious communities and elites affects the nature of contemporary religious authority as well as their political power within society, at both global and local levels. In the specific case of interreligious dialogue, both sets of scholarship have tended to ignore the ways in which new forms of religious authority supported by the state have been shaped and constrained by both the substantive ideas embedded within interreligious dialogue in the region *and* the new political roles asserted by religious citizens in countries of the Middle East and North Africa.

This book attempts to build a more comprehensive theory of interreligious dialogue in the region by contextualizing geopolitical accounts of its growth with a broader consideration of global religious change. In order to do that, the book adopts three levels of analysis to explain the (1) geopolitical, (2) ideational, and (3) social dynamics generating the growth of interreligious dialogue initiatives and to understand their political meaning and consequences. The book begins by mapping out the redistribution of political and religious authority facilitated by the growth of interreligious dialogue initiatives. It then considers the way these initiatives also reflect and institutionalize long-running changes and transformations in religious beliefs, structures of authority, practices, and worldviews both in the Middle East and across the globe. In doing so, the book complicates the political science account of interreligious dialogue in the region by emphasizing the specific sets of theological ideas and sociological practices which the growth of dialogue represents, both of which have independently shaped society's understanding of and demand for religious politics.

This substantive intrication of power, ideas, and social change at work in interreligious dialogue initiatives in the Middle East can be readily registered in the intellectual and policy production undertaken by organizations like KAICIID and the Forum for Promoting Peace in Muslim Societies. But it can also be registered in the experiences and ideals formulated by more independent and materially powerless religious and social actors, like the Adyan Foundation of Lebanon or the Focolare community in Algeria, which continue to produce and organize much of the dialogue activity in the region.[14] While their nature and goals might be quite different, the religious and spiritual dynamism of these nonstate dialogue actors has helped fuel the ambitious investment of religious and political authorities in interreligious dialogue. In often uncoordinated ways, therefore, all of these groups have contributed to an ongoing renegotiation of religion and state in the region, reshaping the ideals and authority that religious forces hold in state and society in the process. In part, that reformulation, and the sociological and theological shifts which it reflects, represents a response to a long-running crisis of religious authority in the Middle East and North Africa. This crisis, which catalyzed interreligious developments across the region, reached a critical moment in the Arab Spring uprisings[15] of 2011 and the religiously expressed violence which both preceded and followed in their wake. In their response to these crises and conflicts, interreligious initiatives in the region have advanced a distinct model of religiously friendly political development for both domestic and international politics. This model has grounded social support for citizenship and religious pluralism within the long history of theology and advocated for a strong public religious role to sustain political rights and freedoms. In doing so, these initiatives have also drawn on dynamic new experiences of religious pluralism and sought out alternative religious accounts of modernity. In this perspective, the book argues that the growth of interreligious dialogue initiatives in the region should also be understood as part of the broader, ongoing response of global religious communities to the challenges of modernization.

The next section briefly introduces the state-centered account of interreligious dialogue that is increasingly prevalent in political science literature. It then presents the theoretical framework adopted by the book to challenge and expand the analytical horizons of these accounts. The book builds this framework by drawing on recent scholarship on postsecularism and post-Islamism and connecting the growth of interreligious dialogue to larger debates about the evolving relationship of religion to global politics in late modernity. The rest of the introduction then discusses the methods, data collection, and case selection employed in the research and previews the rest of the book.

Interreligious Dialogue in the Middle East: States, Ideas, and Actors

Recent state-centered accounts of interreligious dialogue initiatives in the Middle East have identified various kinds of state interests that have driven investment in interreligious dialogue in the region. As Chapter 1 discusses, these accounts can be roughly categorized into three different but interlinked explanations for how state interests translate into support for interreligious dialogue. The first account emphasizes the way in which interreligious dialogue initiatives in the Middle East serve as a public relations strategy which allows states in the Middle East to signal to Western policymakers that they are responding to their security concerns about religiously expressed violence without, however, adopting what might be domestically interpreted as anti-Islamic or secularizing policy positions. The key to the appeal of interreligious dialogue in this narrative is that it allows states in the Middle East to propose themselves as simultaneously moderate, liberal, *and* religious. This account has tended to view interreligious dialogue as a largely top-down process with little "authentic" religious content or social resonance and has led several scholars to characterize state-based interreligious dialogue initiatives in the Middle East as "much ado about nothing" (Wolff 2017; Markiewicz 2018).

A second, linked way that scholars have approached interreligious dialogue initiatives in the Middle East is to characterize them as useful instruments for states to manage but also control domestic religious fields which have been disrupted and fragmented by globalization. In this account, scholars have emphasized how state-based interreligious dialogue initiatives endow specific religious actors with real authority and then channel that authority toward the specific needs of the state. Hence, in this account, interreligious dialogue platforms are interpreted to be part of the larger increase across the region of forms of religious regulation and part of state efforts to alternatively cultivate and coerce a national and "moderate" Islam which supports rather than undermines the legitimacy of the state and which more efficiently manages dynamics of social pluralism.

Finally, a third state-centered account of state-based interreligious dialogue initiatives in the Middle East has focused on the dynamics of regional geopolitical competition. In this account, scholars have paid attention to the shifting center of gravity of interreligious dialogue initiatives in the Middle East and the way interreligious dialogue seems to be used as an instrument of statecraft (Kayaoğlu 2010, 2015; Mandaville and Hamid 2018). Over time, as Chapter 1 develops in detail, a pattern emerges in which recent bids for regional leadership track with the promotion *or* demotion of interreligious dialogue as a foreign policy goal. In many ways this dynamic is captured by the stories of Saudi Arabia and Turkey. Saudi Arabia has only recently invested in interreligious dialogue after decades of support for a more exclusivist, conservative, global religious political project, which was employed, in part, as a counterweight to the forces of Arab nationalism in the postindependence years of the Middle East. The rise and success of reformist Islamist projects and the crisis represented by the Arab Spring has led Saudi Arabia to recalibrate its religious foreign policy. In this perspective, the kingdom's turn to interreligious dialogue could be understood as part of its ongoing strategic efforts to assert itself as the center of religious and political authority in the Sunni Middle East. In a reverse fashion, Turkey has dramatically reduced its support for interreligious dialogue after a decade in which dialogue initiatives were central to its domestic political vision and religious foreign policy. The importance of dialogue in the country was most visible in the close relationship that the ruling party, AKP, cultivated with the Gülen community throughout the early 2000s. The Gülen community was widely seen, especially abroad, as a leading dialogue actor in the Muslim-majority world and as an avatar for a new kind of Muslim democratic politics in the region. Turkey's stance toward dialogue and the community came undone following the 2016 failed coup attempt, which President Recep Tayyip Erdoğan has blamed on a decades-long project of political infiltration by the Gülen community. As a result, Turkey has criminalized Gülenists, reinterpreted interreligious dialogue as a hostile site of foreign manipulation, and largely shut down its support for dialogue activity accordingly.

All three of these accounts help establish the baseline political interests and geopolitical aspirations driving the growth of state-based interreligious dialogue in the Middle East. In all three accounts, however, the specific religious content of interreligious dialogue essentially washes out. Given their institutional origins and homes in the foreign ministries of the Middle East, and given the international pressure to do something about the security threat of Islam, analysts have tended to interpret interreligious dialogue initiatives in the Middle East not as representing meaningful ideational or religious change but as simple extensions of authoritarian state politics and their security strategies and national self-interest. Hence the swift reversal of Turkey's support for interreligious dialogue and the paradox of Saudi Arabia as its champion in the Middle East.

This book argues that such an analysis is incomplete. The specific religious content and practices that state-based interreligious dialogue initiatives in the Middle East represent and embody are, in fact, consequential. Underneath the geopolitics, interreligious dialogue initiatives represent a significant intellectual, theological, and sociological development in the region's politics and ideals which is linked to the longer term, complex, variegated attempt to construct an alternative, religiously infused model of modernity. In order to interpret the meaning of these developments and how they might impact the re-institutionalization of religion in global institutions, the book turns to theories of postsecularism and post-Islamism and the debates raised by them.

As their names suggest, the "post-" in either body of theory refers to very different circumstances and places: postsecularism contemplates religion and politics *after* a dominant period of secular ideas and politics in Western Europe; post-Islamism contemplates religion and politics *after* a dominant period of Islamist ideas and politics in the Middle East and North Africa. As such, post-Islamism does not seem to imply a period of secularization or thickly secular processes of transformation similar to that experienced in

Western Europe. It refers to states and societies which are still much more deeply religious than the West, broadly construed (Künkler, Madeley, and Shankar 2018). However, this affirmation is not quite accurate. Within the heart of Europe sociologists have long recognized that societies never fully secularized, at least not in a uniform, homogeneous way (Gorski and Altinordu 2008; Driessen 2014). The substantive democratic engagement by religious communities across contemporary Europe and the variety of religion-state-society arrangements sustained therein have led multiple scholars to theorize the new means and motivations that religious forces have discovered to reinterpret and to reassert their public presence (Casanova 1994; Berger 2014). Postsecularism, in this sense, recognizes both the continued vitality and the ongoing transformation of religious thought and practice in Western European societies and reflects on their political relevance for late modernity.

In a similar way, post-Islamism does not assume a uniform, homogeneous influence or dominance of Islamist politics or religious values throughout the Middle East and North Africa. Sociologists and political scientists, in fact, have long recognized the distinct varieties of religion-state-society arrangements across the region. This variety of models, which includes both aggressively secular political histories of modernization and more conservative religious ones, continues to underscore a diversity of religion-state interactions in contemporary Muslim-majority states (Kuru 2009; Driessen 2014; Fox 2015). Post-Islamism, like postsecularism, also contemplates the ongoing processes of religious transformation in societies and politics in the Middle East and theorizes about their political relevance for projects of democratization in the region.

Taken together, therefore, both theories have brought new attention to the dramatic sociological and intellectual developments in the way religion has been understood, practiced, and proposed by major religious traditions across the globe as they have struggled to position themselves with respect to secular liberal modernity. They have also brought attention to the impact of these developments on the aspirational boundaries and the actual presence and influence of religion in the public sphere. Importantly, both theories have linked macro-shifts in the ideas and goals of religious and political elites to the changing religious landscape inhabited by ordinary religious individuals both around the globe and within the Middle East. Critically, in their parallel theorization of these changes, both postsecularism and post-Islamism break from a classic, dominant way of conceptualizing the relationship between religion and political modernity along a continuum, with tradition, religion, and authoritarianism sitting on one end and rational, secular democracy sitting on the other. Instead, these theories conceive of the possibilities of multiple, religiously inspired matrices of modernity which draw on religious moral resources and patterns of social interaction to organize democratic politics and societies in distinct ways.

By building on both models of postsecularism and post-Islamism, the book adopts an explicitly comparative method of inquiry. In doing so, it seeks to theorize the recent evolution of dialogue in the Middle East as a process that is not unique to Islam but rather part of a global religious development in response to globally experienced dynamics of modernity. The comparative framework also explicitly addresses the presence and influence of another religious partner in the dialogue process, because it always takes two to tango and at least as many to start a dialogue. Alongside the recent experience of dialogue in the Muslim-majority world, therefore, the book also considers the historical development of interreligious dialogue in the Catholic world, which has oftentimes represented the religious "other" involved in dialogue efforts in the region.[16] This comparative approach enables the book to measure the extent to which interreligious dialogue initiatives in the region represent wider dynamics of political and social change which are connected to the global response of religious traditions to liberal modernity. This comparison also allows the book to register how the interplay between religious actors—which is intrinsic to interreligious dialogue—has impacted these responses. The historical trajectories of Sunni Islam and Roman Catholicism are particularly important in this regard. As I have argued elsewhere (Driessen 2014), dominant elements in both Catholicism in Europe and Sunni Islam in the Middle East responded with open hostility to early encounters with liberal modernity, and subsequently sought ways to construct counterprojects of modernity that better reflected the logics of their theological and historical traditions. Because of these marked trajectories, both traditions have been a central, although certainly not exclusive, focus of multiple modernities scholarship and other analyses of religious varieties of modernity (Eisenstadt 2000, 2003; Salvatore and Eickelman 2004; Katzenstein 2009; Salvatore 2007; Rosati and Stoeckl 2016). This book builds on this tradition and argues that the development of interreligious dialogue in Muslim and Catholic majority societies offers a privileged lens through which to study the ways that religious actors, communities, and traditions self-articulate or, as Saba Mahmood (2012:25) wrote, "co-imbricate" themselves in proximity to liberal, secular, and democratic modernity.

Two considerations are important in this regard. First, it is helpful to view interreligious dialogue as being closely connected to what might be termed the global democratization of religious authority, religious practices, and religious ideas, even in the authoritarian political settings which characterize many societies in the Middle East. As a political phenomenon, the book argues, interreligious dialogue builds on and continues to evolve out of new theological and practical commitments to citizenship and democracy assumed by religious authorities and religious individuals in both the Muslim and the Catholic world. Postsecularism and post-Islamism, in this regard, have articulated the gradual but persistent process of religious change in modernity which has made these commitments possible. With regard to social change, scholars have highlighted a general global increase in the individualization and personalization of religious practices which have endowed religious individuals with a larger voice in the determination of the form and content of religious and political authority in their societies (Roy 2010; Turner 2011). This shift, in turn, was made possible by increased access to religious choice and religious freedom, often through the growing recognition of the individual rights of citizens by states and religious authorities (Bayat 2013; Taylor 2007; Turner 2011). With respect to ideational change, scholars have also highlighted a general increase in religious self-reflexivity with regard to theological claims across religious traditions, in a way that has made mutual learning, and thus interreligious dialogue, with religious others possible (Habermas 2006; March 2013; Schmidt-Leukel 2017). In the West, Habermas (2006, 2008) and other scholars have argued that these changes have opened up new possibilities for a greater public participation and accommodation of religious actors in democratic decision-making. In the Muslim-majority world, scholars such as Bayat (2013) have also argued that these changes have increased the potential of everyday religious individuals and entrepreneurs to act as protagonists for democratization.

Second, the new attention paid to religious contributions to the public sphere in these and other accounts has often been underwritten by concerns about political fragmentation and social isolation. These concerns are driven by a fear that liberal democracy and the modern nation-state have made social cohesion and political cooperation more difficult to sustain over the long run (Habermas 2008; Bretherton 2014; Khan 2019). The religious changes described by theories of postsecularism and post-Islamism therefore help explain the new interest of states and policymakers to engage religious forces as a means to generate social solidarity and moral resources for the common national good at a time when both appear to be in decline (Bretherton 2014; Hallaq 2013; Khan 2019).

These dynamics of *religious change, citizenship,* and *solidarity* form the subtitle of this book. If, at any earlier time in Enlightenment history, most Western scholars understood the necessity of exiling religion from the public sphere, contemporary scholarship on religion and global politics, drawing on a greater plurality of historical religious experiences, points to new possibilities for public religious engagement in democratic or democratizing societies. As highlighted by post-Islamism and postsecularism, the contemporary transformation of religious thought and practice across modernization processes has made the religious generation of social solidarity in favor of citizenship more empirically possible and normatively appealing. While scholars working in both bodies of scholarship have tended, as a result, to view these developments in a positive light, they have also recognized that the very same forces which appear to favor this transformation, namely, social and political increases in individualization, freedom, and choice, themselves seem to eat away at the possibility of religious traditions to regenerate solidarity. The same changes also make religious forces more vulnerable to co-optation and appropriation by the state. In a widely held formula feared (or lauded) by many, participation in more liberal political processes in favor of pluralistic understandings of citizenship risks emptying religion of its specific content and the internal dynamism which it relies on to sustain social mobilization (Lilla 2008; Hallaq 2013; Deneen 2019). The capacity of liberal modernity to totally remake religion in its own image has led an increasing number of scholars working within the tradition of Islamic or Catholic political thought to forcefully reject its logic altogether and envisage a more fully Catholic or Islamic postliberal alternative (Hallaq 2013; Milbank and Pabst 2016; Deneen 2019).

In a similar vein, sociologists like Olivier Roy (2010) and Bryan Turner (2011) have highlighted how this emptying-out process and the freedom of choice which seems to underwrite it are closely connected to consumer market dynamics, themselves deeply inscribed in the liberal tradition. Consumeristic trends within religious practice, and the fragmentation of religious authority which accompanies them, also contribute to the loss of cultural mobilization capacity on the part of religious traditions. In this account, individualization and the quest for authentic, personalized religious experiences are at odds with the collective capacity of religion to construct social change. Partly as a result, as Roy (2004, 2010) argues, these same dynamics create the conditions for unmoored religious pathologies as much as they facilitate democratic religious worldviews and practices.

Hidden between the lines of this scholarship, the question of pluralism, including the response of religions to religious diversity and diverse claims to revealed truth, emerges as a central force that produces the tensions highlighted by scholars debating postsecularism and post-Islamism today. In an important sense, interreligious dialogue initiatives can be understood as addressing these tensions in ways that attempt to reconcile the dynamics of religious truth and religious pluralism and which seek to synthesize the social mobilizational capacities of organized religious authority with the protection of individual rights and freedom.

Parts II and III of the book trace the ongoing development of this synthesis by building an ideational and sociological account of interreligious dialogue initiatives in the Middle East over the past two decades.

To construct the ideational development behind the growth of interreligious dialogue initiatives in the Middle East, Part II analyzes the political worldviews, religious discourses, and political theology which have developed over the major recent declarations on interreligious dialogue in the region, including in the Amman Message, the "A Common Word" document, the Marrakesh Declaration, and the Human Fraternity Document. It also studies the network of official religious authorities who have authored and supported this bundle of declarations, which some have described as an "Islamic Vatican II." Across these documents and declarations, the development of a clear project of political and human development emerges which both draws on and constructs religious authority in the contemporary Muslim world. The worldview presented in these declarations has been increasingly codified through the language of "inclusive," "comprehensive," or "full" citizenship and represents a shift in intra- and interreligious relations in the region, as well as positions within official and influential Islam on questions of religious pluralism, religious freedom, the social aspirations of youth and spiritual solidarity with religious others. This project also has clear echoes of the reformist political project which key official figures of authority within Islam broadly share with a range of post-Islamist religious and political movements and personalities. It is an intellectual and theological project, therefore, that has been conditioned by religiously oriented political reform processes, and could be described as seeking an alternative political path in the region to support citizen rights and religious pluralism while avoiding both secular liberalism and closed forms of religious authoritarianism. At the same time, the nonantagonistic stance of cooperation assumed by various dialogue actors toward the state creates ambiguities about the long-term political impact of these visions on the authoritarian policies of states in the region.

Part III then analyzes four cases of interreligious dialogue in the contemporary Middle East. First it explores the practice and impact of interreligious dialogue among participants in the Focolare community of Algeria and the Adyan Foundation in Lebanon, two nonstate, interreligious dialogue movements in the region. It then explores the activities and goals of two state-based interreligious dialogue initiatives originating in the Gulf region, namely KAICIID and the Doha International Center for Interfaith Dialogue (DICID). These case studies give evidence that the shifts in ideas articulated through elite discourses on interreligious dialogue cannot be separated from the transformation of everyday religious practices—here, especially youth religious practices—to which these religious authorities must respond in order to reestablish religious credibility and authority. In various ways, interviews with participants in these initiatives reflect many of the expectations of religious change and dynamism highlighted by accounts of postsecularism and post-Islamism. Critically, these religious practices have also produced new political knowledge, from below, about how religious citizens can flourish in religiously diverse societies (Thomas 2019). The religious experience of various participants in the interreligious dialogue activities explored in this book, in fact, appear to combine sustained religious commitments, which were simultaneously oriented toward positive relationships with religious and nonreligious others, and which were also often accompanied by a release of dynamic social and civic engagement. In indicative ways, therefore, the profiles and stories of the participants surveyed in this research point to the lived experience of new religious syntheses in these societies in favor of religious pluralism which also contain the potential for social change beyond fragmented communities.

Reading the religious politics of state in light of this multidimensional analysis of interreligious dialogue in the region captures a complex reconstruction and reorientation of political and religious partnerships, ideas of political legitimacy, and social and religious interactions in which geopolitical interests combine with long-running religious developments.

Definitions, Research Methodology, and Case Selection

As scholars have recognized, there are a number of diverse activities which might fall into the category of "interreligious dialogue," including various activities which do not employ, or may even reject, that title. The book defines interreligious dialogue initiatives as activities which are intentionally constructed to include two or more different religious communities or individuals with the purpose of furthering collaboration, peaceful coexistence, or general knowledge between them. This definition recognizes the existence of a minimal normative framework that generally structures interreligious dialogue and which aims at creating nonantagonistic encounters between religious actors in order to increase social, religious, or political peace. The nature and extent of that normative framework, however, as various chapters will discuss, can differ considerably from one activity to another. Leonard Swidler (2013), one of the pioneers of the study of interreligious dialogue, has defined it as the act of "mutual learning," which is to say that the act of interreligious dialogue signifies that one religious actor has something to learn from the other religious actor. And yet the extent to which religious actors are open to learning through the practice of interreligious dialogue can vary a great deal.

In some contexts, "interfaith dialogue" is used instead of or interchangeably with "interreligious dialogue." In academic discourse on dialogue, some have argued that "interfaith" is less institutionally attached than "interreligious" as a term, and thus opens doors to include other, nonreligious systems of "faith" in dialogue activities.[17] Others have argued nearly the opposite.[18] While both the terms are used in English translations and titles in the Middle East, the Arabic does not distinguish between the two and either can be translated into Arabic as *hiwar al adyan*. In general, many interreligious and interfaith dialogue initiatives in the Middle East and elsewhere use the terms loosely and might include diverse forms of dialogue, including intrareligious as well as religious-secular dialogue, under that label.

In other contexts, "interreligious dialogue" has taken on a pejorative meaning, oftentimes for political, historical, or religious reasons, whether because of the instrumentalization of the term, the historical failure of dialogue activities to achieve peace, or its negative association with foreign groups or groups perceived to be hostile to the religious or political well-being of others. In some national and religious settings, therefore, as in the case of contemporary Turkey, groups interested in promoting the construction of peaceful communication and relationships between religious groups have avoided using the term and have opted instead to refer to their activities in different terms. Thus, various movements and organizations in the Middle East have described their activities as fostering "peaceful coexistence," favoring "inclusive religious societies," working for "multifaith friendship," striving to "live together peacefully in a diverse world," or fostering "intercultural communication," "multilateral religious collaboration," or "religious cosmopolitanism," among other monikers. This book considers interreligious dialogue activities to include a broad range of activities largely focused on facilitating, structuring, or encouraging interreligious relationships and action for a diverse array of goals. These dialogue activities may or may not be explicitly faith-based or faith-oriented in nature.

In this context it is useful to note that, despite sharing a minimal normative framework, interreligious dialogue activities are more properly understood as representing a means, an instrument, or a method whose end is either left undetermined or, more often, structured and shaped by the organizations, ideas, and personalities facilitating and participating in the dialogue activity. As such, the category of interreligious dialogue in the Middle East, as across the globe, includes an immense variety of actors, institutions, and philosophic and religious approaches. Recent studies have proposed a number of different typologies to highlight the different aims and natures of this variety of interreligious dialogue initiatives (Marshall 2017; KAICIID 2015; Abu-Nimer, Khoury, and Welty 2007; Lehmann and Koch 2015; Driessen et al. 2020). Some interreligious dialogue actors and institutions, for example, have been described as seeking transformative religious and political change, often linked to an emancipative vision of society and an ideal of interreligious collaboration in favor of social justice (Abu-Nimer, Khoury, and Welty 2007). Other interreligious dialogue actors and institutions have been described as "orthodox adapters" seeking more minimal political or religious goals (Rötting 2007; Lehmann and Koch 2015). Other actors and institutions might not be fundamentally oriented toward change at all and instead focus on the more contemplative dimensions of dialogue, as in intermonastic dialogue or the pursuit of increased knowledge production, among other things.

In this context, a number of scholars (Petito 2018; Petito, Daou, and Driessen 2021) have adopted the term "interreligious engagement" to describe the growth of policy-oriented interreligious initiatives which include states and international organizations, on the one hand, and religious and interreligious actors, communities, and platforms, on the other hand (Petito, Daou, and Driessen 2021). "Interreligious engagement," as a term, differentiates this form of religion-policy interaction from other forms of dialogue and links it to the broader efforts of states and international organizations to engage religious actors for both humanitarian projects and security needs (Appleby, Cizik, and Wright 2010; Marshall and van Saanen 2007; Bettiza 2019).

Despite the great variety of interreligious dialogue actors and projects, this book argues that a common thread unites many dialogue actors and activities in the Middle East and ties them together as diverse parts of a broader response to a historical process of religious, political, and social change. To construct and calibrate this thesis, the book analyzes a variety of interreligious dialogue initiatives, including both state- and non-state-sponsored dialogue initiatives inspired by and identified with a number of different religious traditions and communities. Although the central comparison in the book regards the development of interreligious dialogue within the larger traditions of Sunni Islam and Catholicism, the book adopts a multivocality perspective (Stepan 2000) with respect to those traditions. This means that while the book will often focus on ascendant theological positions within either tradition that are becoming official or semi-official discourses with legitimate claims to orthodoxy, the book also squarely recognizes the multiple, ongoing, internal debates, dissent, and contradictions which remain. These internal dialectics sometimes move forward toward something approaching a positive equilibrium in either tradition, but they can also lurch toward full-blown crises of religious authority. As I have argued elsewhere (Driessen 2014), this ongoing process of theological interpretation and reelaboration undertaken by religious traditions represents a complex, long-term process, one which contains fixed points and religious boundaries within which religious reasoning builds toward new syntheses while simultaneously reasserting familiar theological norms and practices (see also Toft, Philpott, and Shah 2011; Fadel 2012).

The book also takes the position that ascendant official discourses lay in an indeterminate relationship with religious believers themselves, who may or may not support such positions or may go about their lives unencumbered by the influence of that authority or may be trending toward other religious ideas, practices, and sensibilities. This indeterminacy, which is relative but not absolute, has increased in importance in late modernity, as argued in

Chapters 2 and 3. In this regard, one of the central theoretical aims of this book is to better incorporate the heightened influence of these social pulls from below into *state-supreme* and *religion-is-back* analyses of global politics. The political desires of religious believers, of course, are themselves also multivocal, but they can aggregate into larger positions which achieve wider or lesser support. As Chapters 2 and 5 spell out in greater detail, the widespread social aspirations expressed throughout the Muslim-majority world for both *sharia*-identified political norms *and* democratic rights and freedoms represent just such an influence from below. New practices of religious pluralism represent another. In this sense, the fact of religious multivocality, both internal and external, frames a central query of this book: How do religious traditions seek to regenerate religious authority and social mobilization in a context of deepening religious diversity? Does investing in interreligious dialogue and new models of citizenship enable them to do so?

Fieldwork was conducted for the book over a period of five years, as Part III discusses in greater detail. In order to analyze the political theology of interreligious dialogue, that is to say, to articulate the specific political meaning of interreligious dialogue's ideas and language in the Middle East, and to examine the extent to which this language influences state-sponsored platforms of interreligious dialogue today, primary sources were gathered on a range of initiatives operating in the region. These initiatives include the four case studies featured in Part III of the book: the Focolare community in Algeria; the Adyan Foundation in Lebanon; KAICIID, sponsored by Saudi Arabia; and DICID, sponsored by Qatar. It also includes a number of other initiatives which sponsored or led the key dialogue declarations analyzed in Chapter 5, including the Royal Institute of Interfaith Studies of Jordan and the Forum for Promoting Peace in Muslim Societies in the UAE. Visits were made to these organizations' principal centers; interviews were conducted with their leading members and executives; and publications, symposia, and conference materials were collected.

In order to measure the extent to which interreligious dialogue impacts or transforms the lived experience of everyday religious citizens and their relationship to religious and political authority, semi-structured, in-depth interviews were conducted with participants in the Adyan Foundation and Focolare interfaith activities, drawing on a survey instrument (included in the appendix) to do so. Chapter 6 describes the collection and analysis of these interviews in greater detail.

Structure of Book

The book is divided into three parts, which consider the political, religious, and social dynamics structuring the growth of interreligious dialogue initiatives in the region. Part I concentrates on the political dimensions of dialogue initiatives. Thus, Chapter 1 begins by mapping out the rise of state-sponsored interreligious dialogue initiatives in the Middle East and reviews state-centric theories of interreligious dialogue which scholars have developed to explain this growth. The chapter articulates the security needs, power dynamics, foreign policy, and domestic concerns which have driven state interest in dialogue activities. It also analyzes the geopolitical competition underwriting the growth of dialogue initiatives in the Middle East, especially in relation to the use of Islam as an element of foreign and regional policy positioning. In this analysis, geopolitical concerns mix with ideological needs as states attempt to reclaim a position of power and legitimacy following the show of strength of both democratic and Islamist-oriented political forces in the Arab Spring. As the chapter observes, the promotion of interreligious dialogue initiatives in the region can be understood as part of the search by states for a national narrative which responds to the social and religious aspirations involved in the Arab Spring, and in such a way that allows the state to manage those aspirations. At the same time, this ideological investment raises important questions about why the ideas reflected in these interreligious dialogue initiatives appear to be so attractive for states seeking to respond to social unrest and what, as a consequence, such an attraction might say about contemporary religious dynamics in the region.

Chapter 2 reviews theories of postsecularism and post-Islamism and the debates raised by each in order to build a theoretical framework for interpreting the religious and social dynamics at play in the global growth of interreligious dialogue. The chapter connects the growth of interreligious dialogue initiatives in the Middle East to longer-term processes of religious and political transformation both in the region and across the globe. It also raises questions about the capacity of these transformed religious and political forces to mobilize social solidarity in favor of citizenship in the Middle East and elsewhere. In doing so, the chapter articulates the ways in which the phenomenon of interreligious dialogue offers insight into broader debates in the study of religion and politics today, including the relationship of contemporary religious forces to liberalism and democracy, the impact of immanent frameworks on religion's social mobilizational capacity, and the challenges that religious pluralism poses to both religious and political authority.

Part II analyzes the religious meaning of dialogue as an idea in light of the theoretical framework built in Part I. Thus, Chapter 3 provides a global history of interreligious dialogue and reviews debates among scholars of religion about the problems posed by religious pluralism. Chapter 4 then considers the development of the Catholic Church's position on interreligious dialogue following the Second Vatican Council and their impact on dialogue initiatives in the Middle East and North Africa. Chapter 5 charts the development of theological positions within Islam in favor of interreligious dialogue and religious pluralism. It traces the impact of those positions on recent, major declarations in the Middle East, including the Amman Message, the "A Common Word between Us and You" letter, the Marrakesh Declaration, and the Human Fraternity Document. The chapter also analyzes the network of religious authorities and scholars who have authored these declarations and their social and political development across them.

Part III presents four case studies of interreligious dialogue initiatives in the Middle East. Chapter 6 introduces the data and methodology employed for the case studies and their comparative political and religious contexts. Chapters 7 and 8 study the Focolare community in Algeria and the Adyan Foundation in Lebanon, respectively. Drawing on fieldwork conducted in both countries, both chapters focus on the lived experience of youth participants in each organization's dialogue activities. The case studies consider the attractiveness of dialogue activity in contemporary Middle East societies and explore how participation in dialogue activities have both impacted individuals' religious and social lives and shaped their political worldviews and actions. Chapter 9 presents a case study of two prominent, state-based interreligious dialogue initiatives from the Middle East, KAICIID and DICID, and examines their goals and activities. Taken together, the case studies offer a broad portrait of interreligious dialogue initiatives in the Middle East and highlight the dynamics and desires which have enabled various actors and institutions to support common positions on religious pluralism, solidarity, and citizenship despite their myriad differences.

The book closes with a conclusion which draws on the insights offered by the case studies and reflects on the interplay of power, ideas, and religious change at work in these interreligious dialogue initiatives and their implications for global politics. The conclusion highlights the ongoing development of dialogue activities by states and civil actors in the region, considers the unresolved tensions they have produced, and reflects on how interreligious dialogue initiatives might continue to shape the future political development of states and societies in the Middle East.

PART I
POLITICS

1
Geopolitics and Interreligious Dialogue

Introduction

An important and growing body of scholarship has explored the global growth of interreligious dialogue initiatives as part of the larger shift in the openness of policymakers, particularly in the West, to partner with a range of religious actors for shared humanitarian goals. Much of this scholarship accepts some claim about the return of religion to global politics and advances an argument that religious actors possess unusual, if not unique, combinations of material and spiritual resources that make them especially well-placed to address common international development goals. Thus, scholars and policymakers have argued that more effective partnerships with religious actors can help states and international organizations to better achieve action on the environment (Sachs 2013, 2015), respond to political violence and discrimination (Appleby 1999; Shannahan and Payne 2016; Abu-Nimer, Khoury, and Welty 2007; Abu-Nimer and Smith 2016), mediate in civil wars and other contexts of political crisis (Omer, Appleby, and Little 2015; Petito 2018; Thomas 2010; Marshall 2017; Hayward 2016), provide aid for immigrants and refugees (Bretherton 2014), and help alleviate world poverty (Bamat et al. 2017; Marshall and van Saanen 2007). Within this scholarship, much attention has been paid to the capacity of interreligious dialogue initiatives to serve as a platform that makes such partnerships possible within a shared, normative framework which prizes development, pluralism, and international peace. This body of policy-oriented research has attempted to measure and qualify the extent to which interreligious dialogue initiatives have been effective at achieving these goals in order to recommend how states and the international community can better collaborate with religious actors for humanitarian ends (Vader 2015; Woodrow, Oatley, and Garred 2017; Joint Learning Initiative on Faith and Local Communities 2017). While the strategic impetus on the part of states to engage with religious actors greatly increased following the attacks of 9/11, it is important to recognize that this recent development of an "interreligious engagement"

The Global Politics of Interreligious Dialogue. Michael D. Driessen, Oxford University Press.
© Oxford University Press 2023. DOI: 10.1093/oso/9780197671672.003.0002

perspective (Petito 2018) among scholars and policymakers has been much influenced by the growing understanding of the positive force religious activity can play in the development of society and politics, after decades in which secularization was understood to be synonymous with both modernization and development (Thomas 2010; Appleby, Cizik, and Wright 2010; Hatzopoulos and Petito 2003).

An emerging body of scholarship, however, has challenged this narrative by highlighting the political interests which motivate states to invest in interreligious dialogue initiatives. This critical scholarship has articulated the tensions that exist between the humanitarian goals of many interreligious dialogue initiatives and the interests in security, survival, and power which animate both state and religious authorities. These tensions and interests strongly impact the outcomes of state-based interreligious dialogue platforms and their overall "success" or "effectiveness." This chapter reviews this set of geopolitical or state-centered critiques of dialogue initiatives in the Middle East which have gained ascendance within recent political science literature. The chapter argues that these accounts represent a useful starting point to consider the politics of interreligious dialogue, which is to say, the politics motivating state investment in dialogue initiatives and the policies and ideas both reflected in and produced by those investments. These accounts have effectively mapped out the major state-based interreligious dialogue initiatives in the region, analyzed their specific institutional forms, and established the basic geopolitical context and political interests which motivate states to pursue dialogue initiatives. In doing so, this body of literature has emphasized several overlapping logics driving state interest in interreligious dialogue in the Middle East. These include (1) the usefulness of interreligious dialogue as a form of public diplomacy over the international image of Islam, (2) the usefulness of interreligious dialogue initiatives as an instrument to manage and regulate domestic problems related to religious pluralism, and (3) the usefulness of interreligious dialogue as a means for asserting leadership and leverage in regional geopolitical competition. In highlighting these logics, this account forefronts the apparent paradoxes which attend state-based programs of interreligious dialogue in the Middle East and the interests of political power and regime survival which often accompany proclamations of pluralism, diversity, and tolerance in state-based interreligious dialogue platforms. Some scholars have argued that the contradictions between the rhetoric of interreligious dialogue and the state interests inherent in them cripple the social and religious credibility of interreligious dialogue platforms or weaken their effectiveness (Hunter 2018; Markiewicz 2018; Fahy 2018a). Others have argued that interreligious dialogue initiatives serve as an instrument for the state to neutralize threats, increase coercive power over its domestic religious field, and thereby strengthen authoritarian control over society and politics (Browers 2011; Gutkowski 2016; Mahmood 2012).

While illustrating the instrumentalist logic by which many states invest in interreligious dialogue, this account has its limits. As the following chapters will argue, analyzing interreligious dialogue simply through a measure of effectiveness or through a framework of power politics is both necessary but also insufficient for understanding the broader political meaning of interreligious dialogue activities in the Middle East. In particular, these analyses miss the ways in which interreligious dialogue efforts reflect and advance larger religious, ideational, and social transformations in the region beyond authoritarian and other traditionally conceived modernization projects.

State Strategies I: Interreligious Dialogue as International Public Diplomacy

A distinct and emerging literature within political science has begun to chart the institutionalization of interreligious dialogue initiatives across the Middle East and beyond and linked this institutionalization to the geopolitical challenges and political strategies of contemporary states in the Middle East. In these narratives, as in most analyses of interreligious dialogue, processes of globalization are understood to be a significant driver for the growth of interreligious dialogue. Interreligious dialogue initiatives, here, represent an important instrument constructed by the state for the purpose of managing religious diversity issues, both internationally and domestically, that are caused or accelerated by globalization. From an international perspective, this includes the increased potential for religious or identity-expressed conflict between states and regions. As a result, a number of scholars have categorized dialogue initiatives in the Middle East as international branding exercises on the part of Muslim-majority states in response to perceived Western security threats (Gutkowski 2016; Fahy 2018a). In this account, states have invested in interreligious dialogue initiatives in the Middle East as part of a public relations campaign aimed at securing continued partnership with the United States and its allies in their "war on terror." As scholars have emphasized, many of the important institutions of dialogue in the Middle East were constructed in the aftermath of international political violence that Western audiences associated in some form with Islam. King Abdullah II of Jordan, for example, recounts his decision to commission the Amman Message following the international reaction to the Beslan Theater attacks in 2004 by Chechen Islamists (Markiewicz 2019). Sheikh Abdallah bin Bayyah (2016) has similarly cited the sharp increase in violence against religious minorities following the Arab Spring and the growth of ISIS as inspiring the origins of the Marrakesh Declaration. For many of these initiatives, the 9/11 attacks, and policy responses to it which drew on "clash of civilizations" or "Islam vs. the West" frameworks, represented a watershed origin event (Gutkowski 2016; Wolff 2017; Markiewicz 2018). This was especially the case for Middle East states who sought to maintain a close financial and security alliance with the United States and Europe through trade, energy supplies, and military and intelligence cooperation (Fahy 2018a; Mandaville and Hamid 2018). These countries faced immense pressure to distance themselves from nationals who participated in these attacks, including in Jordan, Egypt, and, especially, Saudi Arabia.

Scholars have also pointed to the interest of all of these countries in changing the narratives adopted in the annual US Congress–mandated International Religious Freedom Reports, which had negatively profiled their religious policies, as well as other US intelligence reports which flagged concerns about their countries' soft approach to terrorism and religious extremism (Mahmood 2012; Wolff 2017; Fahy 2018a). The position of several of these states was complicated by domestic politics and the widespread social support in all of these countries for various Islamist movements and, often separately, Islam-friendly state policies. These policies, especially viewed through a clash-of-civilizations framework, were increasingly suspected by policymakers in the West to be linked to various Islamist movements' anti-Western rhetoric and goals. In this context, interreligious dialogue initiatives appealed to states in the Middle East as an instrument which could effectively signal to Western policymakers that they were not abetting or exporting extremist religious ideologies and, at the same time, do so without embracing what would appear to be unpopular and potentially destabilizing anti-Islamic or secularizing religious policies at home.

This appeal was heightened by the official foreign policy positions adopted by both the Bush and Obama administrations that they were not at war with Islam. In fact, reflecting the new, evolving recognition among the Western foreign policy community[1] of the importance of engaging religious communities abroad and establishing formal institutions to do so (Appleby, Cizik, and Wright 2010; Bettiza 2019; Mavelli and Petito 2012; Petito and Thomas 2015), the United States and other Western states increasingly sought to partner with moderate Muslim voices and authorities to win the war of ideas in the Muslim world. As various critical scholars have pointed out, the goal of these partnerships included not only outward forms of cooperation but the ambitious, and theologically ambiguous, project of modernizing or Westernizing the "modern Muslim consciousness" (Mahmood 2006; Cavanaugh 2009). The title of Gutkowski's (2016) article, "We Are the Very Model of a Moderate Muslim State," which describes the strategy behind the Jordanian-led A Common Word initiative, captures the pressures felt within Middle East states to prove their Western partnership reliability to international interlocutors, both political and financial. The primary audience of interreligious dialogue in this account, therefore, is a Western international audience. The close links of various leading interreligious dialogue initiatives to their home departments of foreign affairs, including the DICID and the KAICIID, or to the personal projects of heads of state such as the A Common Word initiative and the Marrakesh Declaration, offer evidence in this regard. As a result, interreligious dialogue initiatives appear to be employed primarily as a form of diplomacy which seeks to recast or rehabilitate a national Islamic identity for Western governments anxious about Islamic political threats.

State Strategies II: Interreligious Dialogue as Domestic Religious Regulation

Interreligious dialogue initiatives thus respond to the developing recognition among Western policymakers, states, and international institutions in a post-9/11 security environment of the need to partner with faith-based organizations, movements, and leaders to counter violent extremism identified with Islam. Interreligious dialogue platforms offer an institutional mechanism through which to organize religious leaders around the developmental goals of these states and allows Muslim-majority state leaders to propose themselves as the moderate partners required by the West to effectively block extremist ideologies.

If interreligious dialogue is primarily a state-led branding exercise, as several scholars point out, the credibility of such a move is thin, and the potential for authentic religious change, the kind that might effectively counter extremist ideologies through its rooted social credibility and attraction, is low (Markiewicz 2018). Thus, several scholars have used the epigram "Much ado about nothing" (Wolff 2017; Markiewicz 2018) to describe projects like the Jordanian-led A Common Word initiative, or pegged interreligious dialogue as a passing fad, belonging to a category of rhetoric that developing states adopt in response to international prompts to attract investment and the good political graces of the international community (Fahy and Haynes 2018). King Hamad bin Isa al Khalifa's 2017 Kingdom of Bahrain Declaration on Religious Freedom, which was signed and launched in a hotel in Beverly Hills, California, instead of Manama, Bahrain, would seem to be a case in point (Abdulla 2017). The end result is to retrench the power and authority of the state which is enabled to use these institutions for their own benefit, making the exercise of interreligious dialogue by states another form of authoritarian state learning (Browers 2011; Mahmood 2012). Rather than "sportswashing," interreligious dialogue in these accounts is presented as a form of "religionwashing" that aims to cleanse away doubts and attention from otherwise repressive politics.

Here, oftentimes, but not without some intellectual tension, accounts of an empty religious state go hand in hand with accounts of the all-powerful management of religion by the state. Interreligious dialogue, in these accounts, ultimately retrenches the power of the state, which is simultaneously presented as a noncredible source of religious authority within society *and* its most powerful arbiter. Thus, the growth of interreligious dialogue in the Middle East also fits into a pattern which many scholars have articulated as the natural drive of modern states to organize their religious fields (Griera and Nagel 2018; Wainscott 2017). By convoking religious authorities as privileged interlocutors through interreligious dialogue initiatives, states recognize, but also construct, those same authorities' social, political, and religious power for both domestic and international audiences. The preoccupation with who has religious authority in the Middle East and "who speaks for Islam" has been a concern of states and religious elites alike in recent decades (Hallaq 2001; Krämer and Schmidtke 2006; Esposito and Mogahed 2007; Zaman 2010). In this perspective, the construction of interreligious dialogue platforms can also be understood as part of a larger attempt to create a more effective form of governance and management between states, the international community, and religious authorities in Islam. The creation of interreligious dialogue platforms composed of networks of religious authorities across the Muslim world, it is often reasoned, can facilitate a more coordinated religious response to religious problems in the region, in collaboration with the state. Thus, as regional religious leaders stated in the 2018 founding document of KAICIID's "Interreligious Platform for Dialogue and Cooperation in the Arab World," "We, the leaders and religious institutions from all over the Arab World . . . in our belief and awareness of . . . [t]he urgent need for a regional mechanism to coordinate efforts, develop action strategies and programs that promote a culture of dialogue and a moderate religious discourse which advocates coexistence and openness and instils values of pluralism and diversity."[2]

Critics, however, have observed that the creation of these initiatives, and the logic underlying them, impose a form of hierarchy and control over their respective religious fields (Mahmood 2006; Cavanaugh 2009; Griera and Nagel 2018). This is especially the case in state-based dialogue efforts aimed at domestic audiences, including the Amman Message, Saudi Arabia's National Dialogue process, and Doha's early dialogue outreach efforts, which often accompany or are housed by the same institutions tasked with conducting interreligious dialogue internationally. Like their international counterparts, scholars have perceived the undertaking of these domestic or intra-Islamic initiatives as part of an effort by Middle East states to reassert authority over the religious field as a response to internal security threats and to increase their political and social legitimacy in the process (Fahy 2018b). In this sense, the increase of religious regulation across the Middle East during this period is striking (Fox 2015; Driessen 2014, 2018) and suggests that dialogue efforts in the region could be effectively understood as one activity among others that the state employs to tame, domesticate, channel, and organize religious dynamics in order to deal with political problems, both old and new, arising from the presence of religious diversity. This includes finding new state mechanisms to manage Christian minorities in Egypt and Jordan (Omer 2017), guest workers and Shia minorities in the Gulf (Fahy 2018a, 2018b), and dissenting Islamists across the region (Lacroix 2011). In this perspective, states seek to effectively assert control over their religious fields through a combination of coercion (by monitoring sermons and jailing dissenting imams), inculcation (by controlling religious education and formation institutes), and attraction (by celebrating national festivities, building centers for religious dialogue, or signing onto interfaith declarations of tolerance).

In all these activities, state agendas are entangled with an outward appearance of intent to "moderate Islam," promote "peaceful Islam," encourage "moderate religious behavior," or combat "religious extremism." As such, some scholars have categorized these forms of religious regulation, including interreligious dialogue, as a constitutive part of secularization, where secularization is understood not primarily as a decline of religious authority or religiosity but as the expansion of bureaucratic state power and its ability to penetrate, organize, and direct religious and other spheres of life (Mahmood 2006, 2012; Zeghal 2008; Cesari 2014; Wainscott 2017).

State Strategies III: Interreligious Dialogue as Regional Competition

So far this chapter has described some of the basic security challenges that motivate states to invest in interreligious dialogue, including the prevailing international environment of the post-9/11 era, which has been marked by the US war on terrorism, the growth of Al Qaeda, the Arab Spring, the Islamic State, fears of Islamic immigration, and the strategic search for a moderate Islam which could serve as a counter to these dynamics. For many analysts, the growth of interreligious dialogue represents a response to these security challenges by states seeking better solutions to manage their religious fields. From the perspective of national state interests, interreligious dialogue efforts represent a useful instrument for meeting the narrative needs of international partners. Dialogue initiatives also respond to the internal needs of states to manage new forms of domestic religious diversity as well as religiously expressed threats to their political legitimacy. A similar logic also makes interreligious dialogue important in regional geopolitical dynamics.

This last section explores the rise of interreligious dialogue in the context of regional political competition among Middle East states. Geopolitical competition among Muslim-majority states can also be understood to be a driving force in the creation of today's interreligious dialogue map in the Middle East. The nature and form of that competition also begins to raise questions about the ideological content of interreligious dialogue and its implications for the reformulation of religious authority in the region,

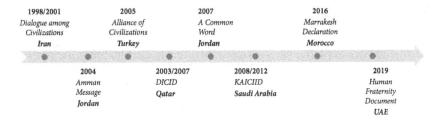

Figure 1.1 Timeline of State-Sponsored Interreligious Dialogue in the Middle East

as well as its relationship to the activities and desires of everyday religious individuals that the rest of the book will highlight.

Figure 1.1 maps out a number of the most important state-based or state-promoted interreligious dialogue initiatives and declarations in the contemporary Middle East. The timeline helps chart some of the important contours of regional political competition motivating and constraining states' engagement in interreligious collaboration. To that end, it is useful to begin by observing which states are not on this timeline, namely, Algeria, Iraq, Tunisia, and Syria, all of whom, to varying degrees, could be described as exemplars of former Arab nationalist states. At least in a broad sense, state-based interreligious dialogue initiatives appear to map fairly well onto secular-religious state identities in the Middle East.[3] Conservative state monarchies, like Jordan and Morocco, that have asserted a historical role as protectors of the Islamic faith and whose political legitimacy, in part, draws from claims to religious legitimacy, have been early and steady promoters of interreligious dialogue. As with the monarchies of the Gulf (leaving aside Saudi Arabia for the moment), Morocco and Jordan have also historically sought to project a moderate image of Islam as they have pursued partnership and mediation with the West. It is important to observe the religious logic embedded in this decision. Interreligious dialogue appeals, in part, because it reconciles these states' needs to credibly project religious legitimacy domestically as the defender or commander of the faithful—Amir al-Mu'minin[4]—and simultaneously position themselves as a reliable partner with the secular West. Interreligious dialogue allows Jordan, Morocco, and Qatar to do both and has led some scholars to characterize such attempts as a ploy, as in, again, "We are the very model of a Muslim moderate state" (Gutkowski 2016).

From this same perspective, the development of interreligious dialogue initiatives in the Middle East can be placed within a longer historical dynamic of regional religious-political competition. This includes the competition between states in the Middle East over claims to religious legitimacy and leadership. It also includes the competition between state rulers and domestic, religiously expressed opposition movements that have staked claims to political legitimacy by questioning the religious legitimacy of these very rulers. In this longer historical arc, the shifting, postindependence dynamics between Arab nationalism, conservative Arab monarchies, and Islamist political movements become important keys to interpret the geographical growth and political meaning of interreligious dialogue in the Middle East.

Following the rise of Arab nationalism in the 1950s and 1960s, conservative monarchs found themselves on the defensive and sought various means to counter secular pan-Arab and Arab nationalist discourse in order to shore up their own political legitimacy and the religious justifications that legitimacy drew upon. The rise of political Islam further challenged the religious legitimacy of these rulers and led to the adoption of new (and ambiguous) religious strategies. The contemporary history of Saudi Arabia is both instructive and enigmatic in this sense. Throughout the mid-twentieth century, the kingdom of Saudi Arabia sought ways to neutralize the threat of Arab nationalism to its legitimacy at home, which had inspired successful, secularizing revolutions against Arab monarchs in Iraq, Egypt, and Syria (Mouline 2015; Baskan and Wright 2011; Farquhar 2016). In order to do so, the kingdom financed and constructed what amounted to a counter-ideological project based on a conservative understanding of global Islam. By creating institutions like the Muslim World League (MWL), the International Islamic Relief Organization, and the International University of Medina; through its influence in the Organization of Islamic Cooperation; and by leveraging its position as the custodian of the two Holy Mosques, the Saudi state promoted a transnational project of Muslim unity, guided by Saudi-based institutions, grounded in a conservative Islamic ideology, and under the patronage of Saudi leadership (Lacroix 2011, 2015; Farquhar 2016; Mandaville and Hamid 2018). In this early phase, secular Arab nationalism was understood to represent the main threat and competitor to the Saudi project; this perception amplified Saudi Arabia's promotion of a more exclusivist understanding of Islam, in which *dawa*, Islamic apologetics, and resistance to conversion (as opposed to interreligious proclamations of pluralism) were central. Mandaville and Hamid (2018) have described this project as part of Saudi Arabia's strategic use of Islam as both soft power and statecraft to pursue its international geopolitical goals and best its political rivals.

In this competition with Arab nationalism, the Saudi government attempted to variously partner with and co-opt Islamist movements that also saw secular Arab nationalist states as a threat and that were also committed to a global political project rooted in the revival (and reform) of an exclusivist understanding of Islam. The political theology, social analysis, forms of religious exclusivism, and model of an Islamic state held by conservative monarchies and Islamists differed considerably. Nonetheless, they partnered together throughout the 1970s and, though with more difficulty, the 1980s (Lacroix 2011, 2014; Haykel, Hegghammer, and Lacroix 2015). These strategies of partnership and cooptation had evident parallels to the efforts of secular authoritarian regimes elsewhere in the region to hold off threats from more left-leaning, Marxist revolutionary groups by reaching out to Islamist movements and actors, including in Egypt, Mauritania, Algeria, and Turkey (Buehler 2018). As the revolutionary goals and potential of the project of political Islam became clear, both Arab nationalist states and conservative monarchies readjusted their relations with it, even as Saudi Arabia and the Gulf monarchies found ways to work together with Islamists on some common religious-political goals (Steinberg 2014; Hedges and Cafeiro 2017; Lacroix 2011).

From the perspective of the institutional management of Islam and the accounts of a strong religious state adopted by some scholars featured in the preceding sections, it is useful to recall here the scholarly emphasis on the weak capacity of many states during this period to co-opt and regulate religious movements which they had in part financed or enabled as a counterweight to either Arab nationalism or leftist-Marxist movements (Burgat 1997; Driessen 2014). In countries as diverse as Turkey, Morocco, Algeria, and Kuwait, the state proved to be neither a fully empty religious actor nor the final arbiter of the national religious field. It is also important to note that, like their host states, the first wave of Islamist movements did not feature interreligious dialogue as a central theme in their politics or social analysis, as the next chapter will examine.

Partly as a result of a string of failures and conflicts associated with political Islam in the 1980s and 1990s, in addition to a combination of pragmatic experience, learning, and ideational and sociological change (Roy 2004; Schwedler 2006; Tezcür 2010b; Hashemi 2009; Driessen 2014), leading protagonists within a variety of Islamist movements assumed a new reformist position toward democracy in which interreligious dialogue began to feature more prominently. Thus, as the timeline in Figure 1.1 also indicates, President Mohammad Khatami in Iran and Prime Minster Recep Tayyip Erdoğan in Turkey took on ambitious international dialogue projects in the early 2000s. These projects were linked to the attempt to refashion their state's relationship with the West and, at the same time, to reformulate the political project of Islamism (Kayaoğlu 2012, 2015; Yilmaz and Barry 2018). Parallels can be drawn to the roles played by Islamist movements during the *reformasi* period in Indonesia, especially with respect to the Muhammadiyah and Nahdlatul Ulama movements (Burhani 2011; Barton 2014), and in Malaysia, particularly through the leadership of Anwar Ibrahim (Esposito and Voll 2003; Dickinson 2010; Kayaoğlu 2012). Reformist trends in these movements also brought a new awareness of and attention to interreligious dialogue in these countries. The subsequent development of dialogue initiatives by Qatar (2003), Saudi Arabia (2008), and the UAE (2014), in this perspective, can be read as bundled into a significant evolution of these countries' strategies to adjust to the success of the reformist Islamist positions and to balance against them in complex and divergent ways (Lacroix 2014; Baskan 2014; al Azami 2017).

In many ways, the struggles and contradictions in both Qatar's and Saudi Arabia's efforts to establish centers of dialogue in the early 2000s capture these dynamics well. Thus, on the one hand, Qatar's and Saudi Arabia's sponsorship of major international conferences on interreligious dialogue in the 2000s can be interpreted as a shift away from the more exclusivist Islamic rhetoric espoused by both the global Wahhabi project and at least parts of the Muslim Brotherhood. At the same time, the difficulties these initiatives faced in convincing other religious authorities in the region to participate in, promote, or simply recognize the legitimacy of interreligious dialogue betrays just how much interreligious dialogue represented a break from past rhetoric and practice. These struggles, including boycotts of dialogue events by high-profile religious figures like Yusuf al Qaradawi, have strengthened the perception of dialogue as a product of a top-down political strategy rather than an organic religious development (Fahy 2018a; Markiewicz 2018). As Chapter 9 details, however, the investment of Qatar in interreligious dialogue was closely connected to its support for the *wasatiyya* school of thought, or "moderate Islamic knowledge," which was also directly linked to the work of al Qaradawi and parts of the Egyptian

Brotherhood (Gräf and Petersen 2009). The commitment of Qatar to the *wasatiyya* school, including through its establishment of the Qaradawi Center for Islamic Moderation and Renewal (2008), begin to offer a sense of the substantive intellectual aspirations wrapped up in Qatar's investment in dialogue, as Chapter 9 explores in more detail. These aspirations linked Qatar to the evolving democratic orientations of the *wasatiyya* school and the political projects of various reformist Islamist movements. The success of Islamist-inspired political parties across the region in the early years following the 2011 Arab Spring seemed to confirm the political ascendance of these movements and opened the door to a plausible future in which Islamist-inspired political parties dominated elections and public support in Morocco, Tunisia, Egypt, and Turkey. Prime Minister Erdoğan, who many saw as the leader of this trend, made triumphant visits throughout 2011 and 2012 to Egypt, Tunisia, Libya, and Qatar,[5] and Doha offered enthusiastic backing for the new regimes, including for Mohamed Morsi and the Muslim Brotherhood in Egypt.

As much as the 2011 Arab Uprisings buoyed Qatari politics, which found new political leverage as it mediated between the Islamist-inspired forces then at play in regional politics (Roberts 2012, 2014; Dorsey 2013), it rattled both the UAE and Saudi Arabia, which viewed the Arab Spring as a threat to their political stability. This suspicion was strengthened by the Bahraini uprising in 2011, to which both Saudi Arabia and the UAE sent troops in defense of the Bahraini government; the subsequent metastasizing of the Syrian conflict with violence in Iraq; the rise of the Islamic State; and the civil war in Yemen, which also prompted military interventions by Saudi Arabia and the UAE and mired both deeper in a proxy war with Iran. Following the Egyptian coup in 2013, in which President Abdel Fattah al Sisi jailed a number of prominent *Al Jazeera* journalists and accused Qatar of supporting terrorism, Iran and the Muslim Brotherhood, Saudi Arabia and the UAE joined Egypt in formally breaking diplomatic ties with Doha in 2017[6] and closing their borders to the movement of Qatari products and citizens. In the process, the three countries sought to build a political alliance around their shared interests to strengthen their regimes against Islamist-inspired movements and counter the regional assertiveness of Iran (Steinberg 2014; Baskan 2014; Lynch 2017).

In the pursuit of these policies, all three countries sought religious legitimacy for their projects and in ways that shifted the regional center of gravity of state-sponsored interreligious dialogue *away* from Turkey, Iran, and Qatar and *toward* Saudi Arabia and the UAE. In a particular way, and with echoes to Saudi Arabia's promotion of global Salafism as a counterweight to Arab nationalism in the 1960s, the policies associated with the ascent to power of Saudi Arabia's Crown Prince Mohammad bin Salman[7] could be interpreted in this light. In an evident push to respond to the domestic roots fueling the Arab Spring protests as well as preemptively thwart any dramatic political reversal of the ruling regime, bin Salman attempted to claim the reform mantle from Turkey and the Muslim Brotherhood, with all of its social, political, and international appeal (Lacroix 2019).

At the same time, also in response to the post–Arab Spring context, both Iran and Turkey have largely scuttled their international dialogue projects as the parties and movements they had championed failed (as in Egypt) and international partners (including the European Union and the United States) evolved in their openness to their policies (Yilmaz and Barry 2018; Kayaoğlu 2015). In 2010, Prime Minister Erdoğan replaced the dialogue-friendly president of Turkey's Directorate of Religious Affairs (Diyanet), Ali Bardakoğlu, with a new president, Mehmet Görmez, who would go on to declare that "dialogue between religions is impossible" and that Western states had supported interreligious dialogue with the aim of "antagonizing Muslims in the international arena" (quoted in Yilmaz and Barry 2018:8–9). The reversal of Turkey's support for dialogue has been especially dramatic following the acrimonious split between the Erdoğan government and the Gülen movement, which the government has relabeled and banished as the Fethullah Gülen Terrorist Organization (FETO) for its support of the 2016 coup attempt in Istanbul.[8] The Gülen movement had enjoyed a close relationship with the AKP in the early 2000s and was internationally acclaimed as both a major global dialogue actor and an embodiment of the new Turkish Islamic-democratic synthesis (Yilmaz 2011; Kayaoğlu 2010, 2012; Michel 2005). The reasons for the subsequent split between Gülen and Erdoğan's AKP were complex but swift, with many scholars dating the breakup to a 2013 corruption investigation against AKP members which Erdoğan saw as influenced by the Gülen movement and evidence of their threat to his power and narrative of political legitimacy. Through important associations like the Journalists and Writers Foundation, the Gülen movement had advocated for interreligious dialogue throughout the early 2000s, at home and abroad, tied it to a new vision of Islam and democracy in Turkey, and involved a number of high-profile AKP members in a public conversation on dialogue through events like the Abant meetings.

Saudi Arabia, on the other hand, has more fully embraced dialogue projects since the Arab Spring through its deepening support for the growth and influence of KAICIID, which formally opened its doors in 2012 and whose secretary general, Faisal bin Muaammar, has progressively taken on institutional roles linked to dialogue in the UN and other international organizations, as Chapter 9 details more extensively. Saudi Arabia has also promoted dialogue through its leadership in the MWL, which it has argued is the natural institution through which to coordinate dialogue efforts in the Arab region (Kayaoğlu 2015). The MWL's current secretary general, Mohammed al Issa, who was formerly the kingdom's minister of justice, has made dialogue a priority since taking office in 2016.

Likewise, the UAE has recruited some of the region's most influential religious authorities to Abu Dhabi, including Abdallah bin Bayyah, who broke with al Qaradawi in 2013 and founded his Forum for Promoting Peace in the Muslim World in the UAE with major financial backing from the state. In 2014, the UAE also created the Council of Muslim Elders, an international union of religious authorities from across the region which is formally headed by the Grand Imam of al Azhar, Sheikh Ahmed al Tayeb. The Council of Muslim Elders helped organize and host the 2019 Human Fraternity Conference in Abu Dhabi, which ended with a meeting between al Tayeb and Pope Francis during which they signed the Human Fraternity document.[9] For his part, bin Bayyah has had success partnering with American Evangelical, Jewish, and Muslim communities, as well as the US State Department under President Donald Trump. Bin Bayyah was a featured participant at the 2018 and 2019 US Ministerial to Advance Religious Freedom sponsored by the US secretary of state Mike Pompeo and, together with Sheikh Hamza Yusuf, was instrumental in the creation of new networks and declarations of religious leaders in support of religious freedom, including the Marrakesh Declaration (2016), the Washington Declaration (2018), and the New Alliance of Virtue (2019). All of these initiatives have embraced the language of religious freedom and inclusive or full citizenship as central to their projects and have strengthened ties with European and American policymakers in the process, who touted Saudi reforms (prior to the 2018 murder of Jamal Khashoggi) and heralded the UAE as a "trailblazer for freedom of religion in the region," in the words of President Trump's ambassador-at-large for international religious freedom, Sam Brownback.[10]

Why Interreligious Dialogue?

This chapter has introduced an emerging scholarly account in political science which interprets the growth of interreligious dialogue in the Middle East as the result of strategic decision-making on the part of states in response to geopolitical dilemmas. States variously invest in interreligious dialogue as a response to perceived security threats; as a branding exercise created for foreign consumption; as an attempt to manage, organize, and channel religious diversity and contentious religious politics both abroad and at home; and as linked to bids to assert leadership in the Middle East. These dynamics follow a long history of Middle East regimes employing Islam as statecraft (Mandaville and Hamid 2018) in the post-Ottoman and postcolonial phases of state-building in the region. By adopting dialogue strategies as integral parts of their political strategies, these states have constructed new institutions and instruments to govern their religious fields and align them with their foreign-policy-making goals. These policies have also formalized new positions for religious authorities in the region designed to be more in tune with what these regimes perceive as the political and religious dynamics of a post–Arab Spring society in the Middle East.

While this account is useful, it also tends to lead to foregone conclusions about the ineffectiveness of interreligious dialogue. This account assumes, for example, that the entanglement of these dialogue projects with questions of instrumentalization, religious regulation, and state control make them merely extensions of authoritarian projects in the Middle East which lengthens, rather than shortens, the asymmetry of power and capabilities between states and religious communities and institutions. Ultimately, in this account, the state powerfully shapes the religious field and it does so in the interests of the state above all else. While the immediate strategies and policy concerns of states are well articulated in these analyses, they offer little insight into why religion is important for these geopolitical struggles in the first place; what contentious religious politics claim within them; why interreligious dialogue is specifically adopted and attractive as a practice, idea, network, or institution; or how those ideas and practices might shape and orient the future of politics and society in the region.

In other words, the geopolitical narrative does not seriously consider the specific religious or political content of interreligious dialogue efforts in the region. The next two parts of the book argue that interreligious dialogue initiatives, as developed recently in the Middle East, incorporate specific theological, ideational, and sociological content, and that this content matters for politics and society in the region. The evolving discourses and practices promoted by interreligious dialogue initiatives in the Middle East make important claims about the way religious authority, communities, and values organize and undergird political and social life. These claims are reflective of larger shifts in the self-understanding of religious elites and communities in the Middle East of the place of religion in a post-Ottoman, postwar, postcolonial, late liberal world order. As such, the growth of interreligious dialogue initiatives, practices, and thinking is bound up with larger questions about the global roles played by religious actors in secular liberal modernity, which interreligious dialogue platforms in the Middle East invariably define themselves against. The growth of interreligious dialogue in the Middle East, therefore, cannot simply be understood as an isolated or technical tool to manage local and global encounters with religious diversity and insecurities; it is also linked to this broader construction of a religiously expressed project of political development for modernity.

The growth of state-sponsored interreligious dialogue in the Middle East cannot be separated from the political strategies of regime survival and the power politics which have animated, at least in part, their birth. And yet it is reductive to end the analysis here, for the state is neither the final arbiter of the religious field that it seeks to control nor fully in charge of the ideas and practices produced by interreligious dialogue. Dialogue processes, in this sense, possess an internal political and religious logic of their own which also shapes religion-state interactions that rely on dialogue strategies. The next chapters seek to qualify the geopolitical assessment of this chapter accordingly and place it into productive tension with the various sociological and ideational dimensions of interreligious dialogue in the Middle East and formulate a more comprehensive understanding of the politics of interreligious dialogue in the region today.

2
Political Theory and Interreligious Dialogue

Introduction

The previous chapter reviewed a series of state-centered accounts of interreligious dialogue that highlight the geopolitical strategies which have led many states in the Middle East to invest in interreligious dialogue projects. These analyses effectively map out the institutionalization of interreligious dialogue over time in the Middle East and provide a basic political context for understanding where, when, and which states adopt interreligious dialogue initiatives in the region. At the same time, however, these analyses offer little insight into the specific religious and ideational content of dialogue initiatives and tend to imply that the content does not really matter or is subsumed by more dominating state interests. In the standard geopolitical account of these initiatives, a basic realist theory of politics holds sway: states concern themselves with self-preservation and security and instrumentalize religious forces when it serves that end.

This chapter introduces a theoretical framework to better understand the religious content and practice of these interreligious dialogue initiatives and why they matter for politics. In doing so, it argues that interreligious dialogue efforts reflect significant religious, political, and social developments in the region. The chapter connects these developments to the long-running efforts by religious communities across the globe to construct religiously expressed forms of modernity. The very idea and construction of religious modernities, which this chapter will attempt to calibrate, qualify, and register, is itself closely linked to the broader story of the construction and crisis of liberal Western secular modernity and the types of universality many scholars attached to it. In this story, the crisis of liberalism at a domestic level of politics implies a crisis of liberalism at the international level of politics and in those models of international cooperation which are based on assumptions of shared liberal, democratic values. Connecting the crisis of liberalism at both domestic and international spheres of politics, in turn, prepares the ground for the conceptualization of a postsecular account of global politics. This postsecular account helps decipher the declarations of recent interreligious engagement initiatives in the region more clearly as well as the religiously rooted models of political development and international cooperation which they propose. By articulating interreligious dialogue's political, social, and religious meaning in this way, the chapter recalibrates the geopolitical account of interreligious dialogue offered in Chapter 1 and reveals how interreligious dialogue efforts in the region represent larger religious and social shifts beyond the political calculations of states alone.

The chapter begins with a brief review of Huntington's "Clash of Civilizations" thesis and the attempt of various scholars to redefine a counterthesis, the "Dialogue of Civilizations," in which the construction of alternative projects of religious modernity, including, especially, Muslim and Catholic projects of modernity, features prominently. The chapter then considers recent work on theories of postsecularism and post-Islamism and what might be termed the democratizing religious changes that both highlight in contemporary Muslim and Catholic societies. These theories offer a useful theoretical framework for considering the origins, growth, and development of interreligious dialogue as an idea and as a practice, and for evaluating the efforts of interreligious dialogue initiatives to stimulate social and political change. Both theories link religious changes in contemporary Muslim and Catholic societies to public religious support for citizenship rights and social solidarity. In doing so, both posit a certain modernization of religious consciousness and personalization of religious practice, even as, critically, collective religious intuitions, identities, and institutions continue to ground and orient these same societies or important movements within them.

The second half of the chapter outlines two critical reflections on the limits of these theories and the challenges faced by interreligious efforts in the region to sustain religiously inspired projects of development. The first reflection focuses on the tension inherent in projects which attempt to combine an internal acceptance of pluralism with the generation of external forms of solidarity, as various interreligious dialogue initiatives try to do. Recent scholarship on the Axial Age and postliberal virtue politics highlights this tension. Scholars in both traditions have questioned whether the modernization of religious mentalities (which seems to be tied to some acceptance of religious pluralism) is compatible with religion's capacity to generate communal solidarity (which seems tied to the recognition of some transcendent truth claims). The second reflection focuses on the social effects of the personalization of religious practice, as especially highlighted in consumer market accounts of contemporary religiosity. Working in this scholarship, sociologists like Roy (2004, 2010), Miller (2003), Haenni (2005), Turner (2011), and others have questioned whether religious consumerism renders religious forces incapable of mobilizing in favor of societywide transformations, democratic or not. The chapter ends by responding to these criticisms, both of which question the sustainability of interreligious dialogue initiatives in the Middle East and elsewhere.

Religion, Dialogue, and Civilizational Discourses

In order to place interreligious dialogue within a broader context of global politics, and in order to understand many of the motivating narratives that interreligious dialogue entrepreneurs themselves adopt to explain why they do dialogue, it is necessary to briefly revisit the theses of Samuel Huntington (1993, 1996) on civilizational conflict. In a sense, Huntington reverses the analysis of the scholars reviewed in Chapter 1 (or really, they try to reverse him) by positing a present and future in which the geopolitical strategies of religiously denominated civilizational blocs outpace single states as the most determinative feature of world politics. If the previous chapter was mostly a *State Supreme* account of religion and politics in the twenty-first century which reaffirmed the Westphalian narrative, Huntington's thesis is decidedly a *Religion Is Back* account. When Huntington first made his claims in 1993, they appeared bold and out of tune with world developments which, in the early 1990s, seemed to give evidence of the global and universal triumph of liberalism, capitalism, and democracy, as described by Fukuyama (1989) and others. For Fukuyama, drawing on Hegel, Weber, and Marx, the events of 1989 consolidated a fundamental, cumulative shift in human history away from a religious and authoritarian-based model of legitimizing and organizing power and toward a secular, rationalist, democratic, and capitalist one.[1] At what seemed to be the cresting peak of global democratic expansion and international cooperation, therefore, Huntington called into question the universality of democracy as a global political project which was available to all states and societies.

For Huntington, the limits of democratic expansion and secular liberalism were in large part defined by religious history and theology. Distinct and religiously encoded ideas, values, and technologies which were forged over centuries to respond to local social and political problems distinguished civilizational blocs from each other. Those modes of ruling, molded over long historical periods, inevitably resurfaced in determinative ways as these blocs refashioned themselves in new political contexts. Specifically, for Huntington, the combination of secular liberal democracy, capitalism, and Westphalian nation-states which seemed to mark the 1990s did not represent a universal model of political modernity. Rather, they were the products of the particular history and theology of the Judeo-Christian (and largely Prostestant) West. As a result, other civilizational cultures, which did not share the history and values which made liberal democracy possible in the West, were unlikely to adopt it as a regime type. They would either stumble in their attempts to embrace democracy or reject it as a foreign imposition.

On account of these deeply entrenched religious and civilizational modes of organizing politics, Huntington predicted that the intensification of globalization would worsen rather than overcome the difficulties of managing pluralism. Globalization would simultaneously clarify the incommensurability of civilizational differences and heighten feelings of uprootedness, as well as the consequent need for individuals to reattach to identities and values, especially those provided to them by their religious civilizational pasts. All of this, for Huntington, made conflict along the lines of civilizational differences more probable and the need to seek balancing strategies to avoid them more necessary. Although he extended his analysis to the Sino and Eastern Orthodox–Russian civilizations, Huntington was perhaps most famous for his claim that the history and theology of the Muslim Middle East were fundamentally at odds with liberal democracy. As a result, the successful construction of international cooperation or an international order based on shared democratic values and institutions was unlikely. Instead, drawing on Bernard Lewis's (1990) analysis, Huntington predicted future global conflicts in the borderlands between the Islamic world and the West.

It is possible to interpret the growth of interreligious dialogue initiatives within Huntington's theoretical framework. The promotion and institutionalization of interreligious dialogue by states and the international community, in fact, might be understood as a concrete step toward the construction of a post-Westphalian world order in which real political power is transferred to transnational religious authorities. In this perspective, interreligious dialogue initiatives could be seen as a restoration or reproposal of classic institutions of community governance present throughout the long history of multireligious, imperial rule in the Middle East. Some scholars, in fact, see echoes of the Ottoman millet system in the construction of interreligious dialogue (Kayaoğlu 2015; Baskan 2014), the defining arrangement adopted by the Ottoman Empire to manage its "capacious system of difference" (Barkey 2008). The millet system worked in large part by decentralizing rule, institutionalizing religious autonomy for recognized religious communities, and relying on religious leaders as formal mediators between religious communities and the empire. In a similar way, states and international organizations have turned to interreligious dialogue initiatives as a means to organize religious diversity within regional and international politics, and they have formally institutionalized new forms of religious authority in order to do so.

There have been various schools of scholarly response to Huntington,[2] including those who contest the essentialist nature of his claims, particularly with respect to the Muslim-majority world (Said 2001), those who challenge his predictions about the future of the nation-state and the prominence of civilizational conflict (Fox 2002, 2019; Haynes 2018a), and those who critique the Western, Christian-Protestant identification he gives to secularism and liberal democracy (Ajami 1993; Norris and Inglehart 2004, 2011). Most of these academic responses are in the business of rejecting Huntington's claims.

Within the religion and global politics literature, however, there is an important alternative trend, one which simultaneously challenges Huntington's essentialist portraits, his narrowly defined particularism, and his predictions of inevitable clash among civilizations, while simultaneously adapting and modulating aspects of the religious and civilizational lens of his analysis.

The work of Petito (2011, 2016), Bettiza, Petito, and Orsi (2018), Thomas (2003, 2005, 2010), Katzenstein (2009), Mavelli and Petito (2012), Mavelli (2012), Barbato (2012, 2020a), Barbato and Kratochwil (2009), and Dallmayr (2012) is important in this respect. In general, these scholars have deployed a much looser conceptualization of civilization, employing insights from discourse analysis, constructivist logic, and poststructuralist thinking to define civilizations as broad groups of worldviews that bundle together evolving sets of values and identities that have been shaped by shared historical experiences. Thus, Katzenstein (2009:5) has defined civilizations as "loosely coupled, internally differentiated, elite-centered social systems that are integrated into a global context." Redefining civilization this way has enabled these scholars to question the rigid lines that Huntington used to mark off different civilizations and the inevitability of civilizational conflict associated with those differences. It simultaneously enables these scholars to recognize real differences that accumulated religious and theological lines of thinking, experience, and institutions hold over political cultures. Such an analysis also recognizes the hybridity of civilizations, what Katzenstein refers to as forms of "contaminated cosmopolitanism," and the role that human agency, especially through elite discourse formation, has in shaping their forward-moving forms.

By rethinking the nature of civilizational discourse, these scholars make the case that the religious resources which Huntington identifies as necessarily leading to international conflict have been and can become resources for the construction of a more cosmopolitan global society (Petito 2016; Mavelli and Petito 2012; Hatzopoulos and Petito 2003; Thomas 2005; Casanova 2011). Several of these scholars (Petito 2016; Mavelli and Petito 2012) have argued specifically that new forms of interreligious collaboration could offer a formal basis for a dialogue among civilizations rather than a clash of civilizations.

In order to make this argument, these scholars have engaged in what has been a major intellectual shift over the past thirty years to rethink what is particular and accidental about the development of modernity in the West and what might be universal and more widely adopted by other civilizations and cultures. Drawing on some of the most important scholarship on religion and contemporary society and politics, these schools have sought to decouple secularism and liberalism from the concept of modernity by exploring other models of religious moderns, including within the secular West itself. In this analysis, the institutionalization of interreligious dialogue offers evidence of a shifting international system in which transnational religious authorities have become an integral part of a new, complex web of non-state actors that have gained power beyond the nation-state in contemporary global politics, as expected by Huntington. At the same time, however, and contrary to Huntington, the development and discovery of interreligious dialogue in this story also represents an instance of religious change and adaptation to modernity in which religious resources are employed for social and political renewal and toward emancipatory and cooperative international ends (Thomas 2005, 2018; Petito 2011, 2018). The embrace of interreligious dialogue in both dialogue of civilization initiatives and the foreign policy strategies of states and international institutions, finally, gives voice and influence to the ideas and practices that these new religious syntheses represent and champion. In this approach to global politics, ideational and social changes combine with geopolitical dynamism to determine the possibility of international cooperation and conflict.

In making these arguments, this group of scholars has critically employed the concept of postsecularism (Mavelli and Petito 2012; Barbato 2010, 2012; Wilson and Steger 2013; Dallmayr 2012). Theories of postsecularism and, in a parallel way, this book argues, theories of post-Islamism offer a useful starting point for constructing a sociologically grounded political theory of interreligious engagement, one which is capable of articulating its political and social meaning, its normative goals, and the people, projects, and values it captures and represents. Critically, both sets of theories carefully consider the social and intellectual transformations wrought within Christian and Muslim societies in relation to their encounters with liberal modernity (Hatzopoulos and Petito 2003). As the multiple modernities scholarship has also argued (Rosati and Stoeckl 2016), rather than Huntington's implication of civilizational incommensurability, these encounters created new possibilities for combining traditions of religious authority, knowledge, and practices with more democratic systems of political organization and development in potentially organic and sustainable ways. The transformations named by postsecularism and post-Islamism explain, in part, the resilience and even growth of religion as a public force across contemporary Christian and Muslim societies and the renewed interest of political philosophers and policymakers in engaging religious forces for more democratic, humanitarian, and cosmopolitan projects.

At the same time, however, the persistence and growth of religiously expressed violence and extremism in the Middle East and other forms of religious exclusivism in Europe and North America, including, particularly, the return of strong forms of Christian Nationalism,[3] have led scholars to cast new doubts on the sustainability of religious projects in favor of democracy and their capacity to adequately deal with questions of pluralism. They also raise renewed (*state-supreme*-account) concerns about the way in which states might appropriate these religious projects of reform for their own ends. Scholarly debates on both postsecularism and post-Islamism have also highlighted the various limits of transformed religious dynamics to mobilize for political and social change. A close study of interreligious dialogue in the Middle East thus can help scholars better approach these questions and better register the complex ways in which both phenomena—religious violence and religious dialogue—are themselves linked together.

Postsecularism and Catholic Modernity in Europe

Postsecularism, as Habermas (2006, 2008), Barbato and Kratochwil (2009), Rosati and Stoeckl (2016), and others have articulated, advances both an empirical claim about the changed sociological conditions for religious belief in the contemporary era as well as a normative project that reinterprets the ideal relationship between religion and politics in liberal democracy.

As a normative project, postsecular political philosophy has generally enlarged the ideal space for religious voices and insights to participate in and contribute to the democratic public sphere. In doing so, postsecularism has readjusted or reinterpreted earlier iterations of liberal political thought, particularly with respect to the ideal democratic practices for positively managing religious diversity. In this respect, Habermas (2006) has argued that the types of restrictions that Rawls's work seems to place on religious actors and communities to translate their religious language, motivations, and political goals into secular ones for the sake of democratic consensus-making in a plural society represents an unfair burden placed on religious individuals. For Habermas, insofar as liberal politics aims to treat equally "all cultural sources upon which the consciousness of norms and solidarity of citizens draw" (2006:258), asking individuals to keep their religious motivations out of public reasoning—essentially requiring religious citizens to check their religious selves at the door of the public sphere—would seem to represent an illiberal proposition. Other scholars have made similar claims (Weithman 2002; Eberle 2002; Wolterstorff 1997; Taylor 2007; March 2013) and have either rejected (Bradley and Forster 2015) or reinterpreted Rawls's work (Bailey and Gentile 2015) to formulate a more inclusive understanding of religious discourse and action in plural liberal societies.

The normative claims at work in postsecularism and other parallel trends in the scholarship on religion, politics, and democracy draw on a dramatically revised sociology of religion. Postsecularism, as a result, revisits secularization as a sociological process as much as it revisits secularism as a political philosophy. The enlarged space given to religious actors in the public sphere, particularly by Habermas, is made possible by new assumptions about the changed conditions of religious belief in the contemporary West. Thus, empirically, postsecularism recognizes the various ways in which the contemporary religious landscape in the West is neither privatized nor ever-only-diminishing, as classic forms of secularization theory expected, nor is it simply representative of a "return" to a more traditional religious age. Rather, for postsecularism, religious individuals in the West have, by and large and over time, internalized what could be labeled more democratic forms of religious beliefs, practices, and commitments. These new commitments, as Charles Taylor's (2007) work has described, have been deeply influenced by the institutionalization and availability of religious choice and religious freedom that were made possible through the construction of democratic modernity over the centuries (see also Joas 2014; Halík 2011). In general, the rise of choice in religious affairs has meant less uncritical obedience to traditional forms of religious authority and the personalization as well as hybridization of new forms of religious belief and practice.

Taylor's work, and reflected in Habermas's analysis, has focused on the ways in which the decline of dogmatic religious authority in contemporary systems of religious belief, as the result of the prevalence of religious choice, has given rise to a kind of religiosity characterized by authenticity, an awareness of the limits of truth claims, and one that is tailored to the flourishing of specific individuals' life paths. Much contemporary religiosity, as a result, has tended to be less absolute or relentlessly centered on values such as self-sacrifice for the good of the religious community and loyalty to religious authorities.

This sociological narrative emphasizes the historical development of what might be described as the emancipated religious individual who has been empowered by political, economic, and intellectual choices. The new religious dispositions assumed by these individuals are more open to mutual learning between themselves and unreligious and otherly religious citizens. For postsecularism, this orientation makes it possible, but not inevitable, for these individuals to act as democratic religious citizens who advance religiously expressed public discourse and action. As theorists like March (2013) have argued, in an ideal liberal society the real distinction governing the role of religion in democracy is not *whether* public reasoning is done in religious language but *how* religious language is employed. For March, religious language which is spoken with "epistemic humility" (made possible by the forms of religiosity and religious reasoning highlighted in Taylor's work) is a language that is acceptable in the democratic public sphere. Epistemic humility about one's truth claims allows mutual learning to take place between religious and nonreligious citizens and makes it more likely that each can appeal to and advance commonly held moral sensibilities among citizens who do not share the same religious beliefs. Religious language which is dogmatic, on the other hand, and which attempts to impose its strictures on other citizens regardless of their belief system does not allow consensus or learning to occur and can lead to a tyranny of the majority. As Habermas (2006: 258) writes in this respect, "in post-secular society, the realization that 'the modernization of public consciousness' takes hold of and reflexively alters religious as well as secular mentalities in staggered phases is gaining acceptance. If together they understand the secularization of society to be a complementary learning process, both sides can, for cognitive reasons, then take seriously each other's contributions to controversial themes in the public sphere."

As other scholars have observed (Areshidze 2017), this altered sociology which underwrites the normative shifts taken by postsecularism implies the transformation not only of individuals' religious behavior and attitudes but of their theology as well. This is particularly important in the case of the European Catholic world, which significantly and formally altered its theological position on democracy and religious freedom in the 1960s at the Second Vatican Council. The new theological orientations adopted by the official institution of the Catholic Church at the Council significantly empowered the Catholic laity, that is to say, ordinary, everyday religious citizens, and both reflected and advanced their democratic religious dispositions, highlighted above.

The new theological elements integrated into the documents of the Second Vatican Council, in particular its 1965 declaration on religious freedom, *Dignitatis Humanae* institutionalized an idea of human freedom as the privileged means by which human beings advance toward truth in both politics and spirituality. This shift enabled the Catholic Church to consolidate its move beyond a defense of conservative and authoritarian politics in favor of traditionally organized societies in which the Church held significant political and spiritual authority (Huntington 1991; Philpott 2004; Driessen 2014). While some scholars have argued that the Catholic Church accepted democracy primarily for strategic reasons (Kalyvas 1996; Warner 2000; Chamedes 2019), by giving democracy a theological foundation within its own tradition the Second Vatican Council also enabled the Church and its believers to make democracy their own.

In the process of making democracy its own, the Catholic Church did not adopt wholesale secular liberal philosophy. Instead, the Church embarked on a major theological process which reformulated the idea of political freedom within Catholic thought and in the process placed its support for political freedom and democracy within a different metaphysical orientation than that of liberalism. The Church therefore carried forward its earlier critiques against the materialism, secularism, and individualism that it associated with liberalism, even while it incorporated those critiques into a more explicitly religious and humanist framework for political action (Müller forthcoming; Acetti 2019). Rather than view Christian democracy and midcentury Catholic political thought as a compromise position which served as a prelude and transition to a broader secularization of society and politics, therefore, a number of recent works have reevaluated the distinct and determinative project of Catholic political modernity on its own terms, as a generative set of ideas and policies, imbued with both religious and political dynamism, that deeply marked the reconstruction of European political institutions and nation-states and which oriented societal preferences in powerful ways (Moyn 2015; Chappel 2018; Forlenza and Thomassen forthcoming; Driessen 2014; Taylor 2020a, 2020b; Vatter 2013, 2020). The internal Catholic reformulation of modernity also influenced Catholic support for regional and international politics, from the construction of the EU to the "Catholic wave" of democracy in the 1990s (Huntington 1991; Philpott 2004; Driessen 2014, 2021). Chappel (2018) has referred to this synthesis as the "Catholic modern," a political approach to democracy that Moyn (2008:2) has described as the "spiritualist and communitarian search for a third-way alternative to the rival materialisms of individualist liberalism and totalitarian communism."

The work of Catholic philosophers and theologians, like John Courtney Murray and Jacques Maritain, were critical in the formulation of this new approach to democracy. Maritain ([1936] 1996: 211), for example, whose work inspired many of the founders of Christian democrat parties in Europe and South America, embraced democracy as the most fertile grounds for building up what he saw as a new, more fully humanist Christendom, one which represented the "veritable socio-temporal realization of the Gospel." Christian humanism, or what Maritain defined as "integral humanism," represented an important effort to develop a Christian approach to political modernity which could provide a compelling political vision in favor of individual rights, social justice, and freedom while remaining in the service of Christian truth claims and the theological tradition of the Catholic Church. Religious pluralism, choice, and freedom, in this vision, were to be protected for the sake of the common good, to safeguard the human dignity of all individuals, but also to enable them to freely recognize the truth of the Gospels. The opening lines of *Dignitatis Humanae* reflect this understanding and link religious freedom to the obligation of "all men to seek the truth."[4] In *Dignitatis Humanae*, freedom creates the conditions necessary for the discovery of truth, as well as the construction of a political and social order which reflects it. As Vatter (2013:337) has written,[5] Maritain sought to defend persons and communities from the totalitarian state by conceiving of a new "cosmopolitan democracy" whose foundation rested on recognition of the God-given dignity of all human beings, a recognition which Maritain saw as protecting individuals and communities from the totalizing claims of sovereign states.[6] *Dignitatis Humanae*, as a result, also links religious freedom to religious flourishing, as well as to the creation of social values which favor democratic solidarity and a just political order. As the declaration states, "Government is also to help create conditions favorable to the fostering of religious life, in order that the people may be truly enabled to exercise their religious rights and to fulfill their religious duties, and also in order that society itself may profit by the moral qualities of justice and peace which have their origin in men's faithfulness to God and to His holy will" (*Dignitatis Humanae*, §6).[7]

Perhaps not surprisingly, Dignitatis Humanae therefore also recognizes the historical legitimacy of religious establishment. Murray, however, who participated in the drafting of the text, has noted that this recognition was conditional and that the final text of the document reflected a clear agreement among Council participants that the Church did not hold a preference for religious establishment in the contemporary context (Murray 1966). At the same time, for Murray, the declaration's support for human freedom in both legal and theological terms was *not* conditional and represents the fundamental thesis of the document. Murray argued that the primary way states should show favor to public religious life was by providing religious individuals and communities with freedom (as opposed to institutional establishment). As Murray writes, "Government . . . must somehow stand in the service of religion, as an indispensable element of the common temporal good. This duty of service is discharged by service rendered to the freedom of religion in society. It is religion itself, not government, which has the function of making society religious" (14).[8]

For Maritain ([1936] 1996: 258), the end of politics was therefore "the perfection of natural law and Christian law," as it had been for centuries in Catholic political thought. However, as Dignitatis Humanae expressed, the means and reasons for achieving this perfection, through and for the spiritual and political emancipation of individuals and in recognition of their innate dignity as created in the image and likeness of God, had dramatically changed. On this point there is an important tension between Maritain's and Habermas's approach to religious pluralism, one that captures a more general tension characterizing contemporary debates about liberalism and public religion. On the one hand, the political vision adopted by the Church at Vatican II represents an important epistemological shift in the Church's self-understanding, one which effectively sanctioned as well as taught religious individuals an idea of how to flourish as a public religious citizen in plural religious and political settings. This vision significantly altered the place of the religious other in the ideal Christian polis. On the other hand, in Maritain's approach, and the position taken by the Catholic Church at Vatican II, epistemic humility does not imply the relativization of specific, absolute, revealed Christian truth claims. In other words, the "modernization of public consciousness," which Habermas posits as a condition for religious participation in the public sphere, does not signify the relinquishment of dogma for Maritain and the Church, nor the defense of revealed truth claims, nor the belief that the Catholic Church continues to represent the "one, true religion" (*Dignitatis Humanae*, §1). Religious reasoning processes remain governed by appeals to revealed truth and the authority of scripture and the Church, not, as Habermas and Enlightenment thinkers argued, by autonomous reasoning processes and scientific consensus.

Thus, for Maritain and mainstream theology within the Catholic Church, the acceptance of external pluralism does not necessitate the adoption of internal pluralism, or at least not to the degree that Habermas would seem to suggest. This tension foreshadows a similar tension in theories of post-Islamism and forms the basis of one of the major criticisms of both sets of theories which, as Part II of this book will illustrate, has major implications for interreligious dialogue.

Although Chapter 4 will consider the Catholic Church's evolving position on interreligious dialogue more closely, it is important to note here that the Church's new approach to religious freedom was closely connected to its new positions on religious and political pluralism. This was expressed in an important way in the positive statements made at the Second Vatican Council on interreligious dialogue in the Council's *Nostra Aetate: Declaration on the Relation of the Church to Non-Christian Religions*. In particular, *Nostra Aetate* proclaimed that the Catholic Church rejected "nothing of what is true and holy in these religions" and urged "its members to enter with prudence and charity into dialogue and collaboration with members of other religions ... preserving and encouraging the moral truths found among non-Christians as well as their social life and culture" (*Nostra Aetate*, §2).

In this declaration, interreligious dialogue can be read as a meaningful extension of the Church's new claims to religious freedom and a heightened awareness of the human dignity, which is to say, the image of God present in all individuals regardless of religious belief. As a result, *Nostra Aetate* encouraged the Church to more positively recognize and value the presence and meaning of this dignity among those who were not Christian. By accepting the duty to politically protect individual choice and freedom, the Church also accepted that it had something to gain from its interactions with unbelievers and other-believers and that it must create a space to preserve these interactions. While a full theology of dialogue or pluralism was not formulated at the time of the council, as Chapter 4 explores, these statements opened up new orientations for the study and practice of interreligious dialogue within the Catholic tradition, and the new relationship struck between laity and clergy enabled the experience and intuitions of everyday religious individuals to become protagonists in the further development of interreligious dialogue.

Everyday Religious Citizens and Informal Religious Politics

So far I have described how postsecularism has enlarged the space for public religious action and discourse and done so on the basis of a new sociological reading of religiosity in Europe, one that highlights the rise, particularly in Catholic European countries, of new types of democratic religious citizens *and* religious political movements, which were oriented by a new political theology of freedom. Distinguishing between democratic religious politics on the one hand and democratic religious citizens on the other can help make sense of the apparent secularization of formal religious politics across twentieth-century Europe as well as the relative resilience of religious dynamism in many European societies. While secularization accounts help make sense of much of the postwar history of Christian democracy (Kalyvas and van Kersbergen 2010; Diotallevi 2016; Ignazio and Wellhofer 2013), the weakening of Catholic party politics did not cause or parallel either the evaporation of religious life or the disappearance of religiously inspired public action in Catholic European countries, but rather the transformation of both. The new sociology adopted by postsecularism helps us to trace the ways in which individual religious actors remain deeply embedded in the political and social life of the polis even as they do so in remarkably changed ways and in different formats, mostly outside of the channels of formal party politics. In this reading, everyday religious citizens remain key generators of civic life and leadership, particularly in the spaces of informal politics.

Thus, across Europe, in the postwar, post–Vatican II environment, lay Catholic elites who had made democracy their own both sociologically and theologically consolidated or constructed a plethora of new lay-based movements which functioned outside of Christian democratic parties. These new associations and movements flourished in the maturing democratic environments of their nations, which offered them new opportunities for growth and relevance throughout civil society. The social persistence of religious civic activism embodied by these religious democratic actors increasingly came to be seen by both scholars and the actors themselves as essential sources of associational life, moral energy, and social capital in a fragmenting political landscape. Important to this story, several of these Catholic lay movements, including the community of Sant'Egidio and the Focolare community, which had internalized the "spirit of Vatican II," dedicated themselves to developing interreligious dialogue activities at various levels of society. It is only after the democratic turn of the Catholic Church and its legitimization of religious freedom that such thick and autonomous forms of religious civic activism in favor of religious others could fully develop and explore what it meant to "enter with prudence and charity into dialogue" and to preserve and encourage "the moral truths found among non-Christians," as *Nostra Aetate* urged them to do.

It is important to emphasize that it is exactly because of this combination of social capital qualities and informal political standing that postsecularism opens the door, so to speak, to religious individuals in the first place. As Habermas (2006, 2008) argues, explaining his change of thought on religious discourse in the public sphere, religious insights and motivations (whose mentalities have sufficiently modernized) might actually be necessary for the foundations and future of liberal democracy in Europe and the regeneration of its moral and civic sources, loyalties, and solidarity, *as long as* they stay in the realm of informal politics and do not pursue exclusivist, dogmatic religious policies in the formal political sphere. Commenting on the Böckenförde paradox, that "the liberal, secularized state is sustained by conditions it cannot itself guarantee,"[9] Habermas (2006, 2008) suggests that religious communities might respond to this dilemma by working to repair the unseen moral foundations which guard political freedom from excesses of individualism, isolation, and loss of meaning. In this way, Habermas (2006:257) writes, the intuitions "buried" in religious traditions might be brought to bear on new political and social problems facing contemporary political life that secular reasoning alone had failed to come to grips with and, at the same time, create more meaningful ways for religious individuals to invest themselves full-heartedly in the common good of the whole of their societies.

In the early 1990s, therefore, the vitality of religious communities living seemingly at ease within liberal democratic environments in Europe beckoned to a number of political philosophers as a source for renewing social solidarity in liberal democratic societies. This trajectory from public religious political parties to informal religious associational life, however, also raises questions about the capacity of religious democratic citizens and movements to mobilize social capital and solidarity over the long run.

Post-Islamism and Religious Modernities in the Muslim-Majority World

"Post-Islamism" is the term coined by Asef Bayat to identify the substantial change in goals, discourses, and practices of Islamist parties and individuals in the 1990s and 2000s that, over time, as Chapter 1 began to describe, dropped their revolutionary project of state capture and opted for pursuing religious goals through more democratic means.

The origins, meaning, and future of post-Islamism were widely debated, particularly within francophone academic circles throughout the 2000s (Roy 1994, 2004, 2012; Lauzière 2005; Zeghal 2008; Lacroix 2011; Bayat 2013). In order to highlight its sociologically innovative similarities with postsecularism, it is useful to contrast the post-Islamism debate over the evolution of Islamist parties with the parallel one that unfolded in North American political science circles and which largely centered on what Schwedler (2006) termed the "inclusion-moderation hypothesis." In scholarship dominated by North American political science methods and concerns, writers[10] debated the extent to which Islamist political parties moderated their religious goals and ideas given the dynamics of electoral democracy. The inclusion-moderation hypothesis emphasized the impacts of institutional mechanisms of democracy to explain changes in Islamist goals and practice, highlighting how the logics of electoral strategies and practical governance favored pragmatic Islamist politicians over ideologues in the parties that adopted less radical (read: less religious) platforms to win over voters. This scholarship, similar to the political science accounts of Christian democracy described above, more or less explicitly adopted a sociological narrative of secularization. In this reading, individuals over time in a democratizing setting, as happened in Europe, became less interested in pursuing religious politics and less integrally religious themselves, forcing Islamist parties to water down their religious message and become more moderate and politically secular in order to sustain winning electoral coalitions (Schwedler 2006; Tezcür 2010b).

Post-Islamism adopted a different sociology for its account. Similarly to the inclusion-moderation hypothesis, for scholars like Roy (2004) and Bayat (2013), the evolution of political Islam had much to do with the historical failure of its earlier self, which had produced undesirable authoritarian regimes like Iran and Sudan, or precipitated mass violence, as in Algeria and Afghanistan, and turned away potential constituents in the process. Like postsecularism, however, for post-Islamists this undesirability shown toward 1980s-style political Islam was also propelled by a dramatic religious shift in Middle East Muslim-majority societies. Like postsecularism, thus, for post-Islamism the evolution of Islamist politics does not mean that Muslims have become less religious, but they have become religious in profoundly different and less traditional ways. Post-Islamism as a phenomenon responds to this change and signifies, as Lacroix (2011:263) has emphasized, the attempt of Islamism to reinvent and redefine itself for a new social and political arena which has rejected the authoritarian fusion of religion and politics.

Understanding these shifts in contemporary religiosity in the Muslim-majority world and their relationship to encounters with Western modernization has been a central question for much scholarship on contemporary Islam and politics beyond the post-Islamism debate and has critically informed it. The sections that follow therefore draw parallels between post-Islamism and the multiple-modernities literature as well as the broader scholarship developed on contemporary Islam and politics in the Middle

East. It highlights the work of various scholars who have sought to articulate the complex and nuanced ways in which contemporary Muslim individuals, communities, and states define themselves as creating and building an Islamic modern other over and against Western secular liberalism. A key theme in many of these studies has been the way these projects assume forms and ideas of Western secular modernity through the very process of articulating themselves against those forms and ideas, even as they make them their own and resignify them through specific rituals, practices, and language (Deeb 2006; Mahmood 2012).

Many scholars of contemporary Islam, therefore, have also traced the impact of individualization on contemporary Muslim religiosity in the Middle East and elsewhere. Increases in individual agency and self-reflexivity in the determination of religious beliefs and practices, including beyond elite scholarly circles alone, it has been argued, have transformed contemporary religiosity in the Muslim-majority world (Deeb 2006; Salvatore 2016; Mahmood 20012; Hashemi 2009; Tobin 2016; Fealy and White 2008). In this perspective, and in a way which parallels the descriptions and analysis of Taylor's (2007) *Secular Age* in the West, Deeb's (2006) work defines this process as the drive to construct and live an "authenticated Islam," in which individuals embrace Islamic beliefs and practices which they have independently deliberated over and consciously chosen. Deeb describes authenticated Islam as the pursuit of a "purposeful and knowledgeable Islam," as opposed to what could be described as traditional, conformist, or "unthinking" Islam (113).

While these descriptions of authenticated or "expressive" Islam (Fealy and White 2008) clearly recall the emphasis placed on increased agency and the construction of a culture of authenticity in the West by scholars like Taylor, this same group of scholars has also emphasized how such agency has been tied to a very different understanding of self-realization in the Muslim-majority world and within a very different religious context. In describing the "politics of piety," for example, Mahmood (2012) highlighted how the individualization of religiosity in the Middle East cannot be understood primarily as an emancipation of the individual self's desires, as typically assumed by liberal Western scholarship. Rather, many Muslim individuals consciously reintegrate that self into a pious Muslim community, through, especially, the adoption of outward religious practices which signify and reinforce the authenticity of one's inner religious commitments and beliefs (see also Deeb 2006). In making this argument, Mahmood has outlined how the creation of the modern pious self in the Middle East is built on alternative historical, cultural, and theological pasts from the West.

Salvatore (2016) and others have explored how these alternative cultural practices and institutions, which were produced within the historical matrix (or ecumene) of Islam, might combine with other dynamics of modernity to create distinct political and social equilibria in Muslim-majority countries today. For Salvatore, these new equilibria are likely to be sustained by a combination of religious piety and modern, rational political organization which do not necessarily end in Weberian forms of religious disenchantment. To make his case, Salvatore focuses on what he terms historical patterns of "Islamic civility" that synthesized the ideals and practices of egalitarianism and cosmopolitanism which have distinguished Islamic civilizations. Salvatore explores these patterns through the practices of *tariqa* brotherhood associations, the production of *waqf* institutions, and the moral idiom given by the *hadith* (154ff.). The form and nature of these Islamic social institutions guard against disenchantment and keep these cosmopolitan and egalitarian projects more closely linked to the norms and practices of the *sharia* in the contemporary imagination of much of Muslim-majority societies. Even scholars like Wael Hallaq (2013) who mount stronger criticisms of the political project of liberalism and its corrosive impact on Muslim-majority societies have often done so by returning to a lost Islamic past to recuperate distinctly Islamic moral sources in order to imagine a better project of modernity for both domestic and international politics. In focusing on "sharia-mindedness" and premodern norms of Islamic governance, for example, Hallaq has argued that "the Shari'a ... represented and was constituted by a moral law, hence its significance for us as a moral resource for the modern project (equivalent to Aristotle and Aquinas in the MacIntyrean proposal)" (10).[11]

Some scholars have argued that the "post-" in post-Islamism signifies that Islamist political projects are no longer distinctively Islamist in their orientation or goals (Roy 2004, 2010). Post-Islamist political parties may retain an emphasis on promoting piety or religiosity, but by accepting the logic of individual agency and choice, especially with respect to religious beliefs and practices, they have largely given up on a collective Islamic project of capturing and remaking the state along integrally religious lines. For other scholars working in this vein, however, the increase of agency and subjectivity in contemporary Islamic religiosity in the Middle East has neither stripped it of its religious specificity nor shorn it of its political character (Salvatore

2016; Mahmood 2012; Bayat 2013). With respect to politics, post-Islamism understands religious activity as representing a dynamic, recurring source of vitality in contemporary Muslim-majority societies. Thus, as Mahmood (2012:xi) defines it, the politics of piety "transforms the very ground on which nationalist, statist and other kinds of secular liberal projects can be envisioned and practiced."

In Bayat's (2013) analysis, the individualization and personalization of religiosity in the Muslim-majority world, including its emphasis on choice and freedom from religious compulsion, has largely represented a democratizing dynamic which has had substantive consequences for post-Islamist parties and politics. For Bayat, thus, shifts in Islamist-oriented parties over the 1990s and 2000s reflected important changes in both political strategy and ideological thinking. In Bayat's account, post-Islamist parties and their constituents recognize, to greater and lesser extents, that democracy represents both a normatively good form of governance as well as a pragmatically useful political regime desired by Muslim citizens. Democracy in particular allows post-Islamists to institutionalize religious freedom as a good in and of itself, allowing Muslims the right to practice their religious beliefs free from the interference of the state and, at the same time, to pursue religiously informed political policies. Echoing the dynamics on postsecularism and Catholic politics described earlier in this chapter, post-Islamism also identifies the evolution of more democratically oriented theological dispositions assumed by both religious authorities *and* religious individuals in the Muslim world. These new religious orientations are diverse in their structure and inspiration and, as Catholic politics and theology did after Vatican II, have led post-Islamist actors to continue to mount robust critiques of secular liberal modernity. Democracy, citizenship rights, and some measure of religious freedom are nonetheless recognized as essential for preserving the dignity of Islam from political corruption and restoring its credibility for public action (Lauzière 2005). This altered sociology forms the background for understanding shifts in official religious discourse across the Middle East on ideas like citizenship, religious freedom, and dialogue, as Part II explores.

It is worth quoting Bayat's (2013: 307–308) description of post-Islamism at length to capture this full portrait of post-Islamism:

> [Post-Islamism] is neither anti-Islamic nor un-Islamic or secular, but represents a critique of Islamism from within and without, an attempt to transcend the duty-centered and exclusive Islamist politics towards a more

rights-centered and inclusive outlook. Post-Islamism signifies an endeavor to fuse religiosity and rights, faith and freedom, Islam and liberty. . . . Post-Islamism is expressed in acknowledging secular exigencies, in freedom from rigidity, in breaking down the monopoly of religious truth. In short, whereas Islamism is marked by the fusion of religion and responsibility, post-Islamism emphasizes religiosity and rights, even though the latter's relationship with liberalism remains tense, for the ethical sensibilities of the post-Islamist constituency may come into conflict with individual liberties and expressions.

These sensibilities are reflected in the results of multiple surveys across the first two decades of the 2000s which show that a majority of individuals living in the Muslim-majority world simultaneously support democracy *and sharia* law, but not necessarily post-Islamist political parties (Ciftci 2010; Driessen 2018; Teti, Abbott, and Cavatorta 2019). These large sectors of Middle East society, anywhere between 40% and 75% of the population, depending on national contexts, largely view *sharia* law as a normative force for good in their societies and as generating essential, ideal-orienting values which make society and politics work, including in democratic settings (Pew 2012, 2017; Driessen 2018).

Post-Islamism thus posits a real change in the democratic goals and ideals of Islamist-oriented political parties and the religious and social landscape in which those parties are embedded. These new dispositions, in turn, have led post-Islamist parties and scholars to focus on religious change from below, that is to say, from within culture and civil society, in response to the new political importance acquired by the public or democratic religious citizen in the Muslim world. The strategies, goals, and ideas of post-Islamist parties show an increasing awareness of the public authority that religious individuals possess to steer political as well as religious projects in substantive ways. It is partially for this reason that Bayat (2013) and others[12] pay so much attention to the role of large, often marginalized groups within many Muslim-majority societies and the impact that their collective actions have on Islamist parties and the state, including the poor, women, and the youth. The political and religious importance of these groups seemed to be confirmed in the 2011 Arab Spring and the subsequent response by states and religious authorities.

This scholarly attention to the collective religious activism of religious citizens in civil society, outside of party politics, as generating consequential post-Islamist religious-political dynamism can also be seen in recent work on religious movements such as the Gülen movement in Turkey (Ozzano 2014; Ciftci 2010; Catalano 2015), the Justice and Charity movement in Morocco (Lauzière 2005), and Muhammadiyah and Nahdlatul Ulama (NU) in Indonesia (Luissier and Fish 2012; Menchik 2016; Arifianto 2017). Once again, paralleling similar dynamics in postsecular Catholic Europe, several of these religious movements in the Muslim world, including Gülen, Muhammadiyah, and NU, have been central protagonists in the development of interreligious dialogue discourse and practice in the Muslim-majority world (Burhani 2011; Catalano 2015; Barton 2014; Arifianto 2013), as Chapter 5 explores in more detail. Dialogue initiatives have been employed to respond to domestic political struggles and to orient international political outreach by these groups. In all three cases, the embrace of interreligious dialogue as a religious and political goal has been closely linked to the development of a more democratic discourse on individual freedom and rights by these same movements and even the explicit recognition of the roots of both projects in a shared religious humanist tradition, as in the case of NU.[13]

Much post-Islamist scholarship, therefore, recognizes a shift in the locus of religious authority and political action away from religious elites and political parties and toward the everyday religious citizen, who, as Bayat (2013) argues, through the very art of their presence, through their "quiet encroachment of the ordinary" or their "everyday cosmopolitanism," constrain and steer and shift the spectrum of what is politically possible and desirable for religiously inspired politics. Once again, it is revealing to observe the parallel here to postsecular trends in political Catholicism. Post-Islamism, too, moves political attention away from the political party and formal politics and toward the realm of civil society and informal politics as a primary arena in which religious citizens contribute to politics and democracy construction. As in postsecular Catholic settings, both scholars *and* practitioners of post-Islamist politics have defined their contribution to democracy in terms of their investment in civil society. In these accounts, Islam, everyday democratic religious citizens, and movements help provide the glue, or discipline, as Salvatore (2016) writes, that underpins the civic and moral order of the nation-generating social solidarity in distinctively Islamic ways. At the same time, the nature of this informal associational life and the patterns of religiosity it builds on also raises serious questions about its sustainability over time as a dynamic force holding social and political equilibria in place. The next section reflects on these tensions in more detail.

Critical Reflections: Immanence and Consumer Religiosity

The analysis above has highlighted how both post-Islamism and postsecularism describe processes of democratizing religious and social change which involve some transformation of political theology (the modernization of religious consciousness) and religious practice (the individualization of religiosity). Both theories, at least in some form, tend to view this process as desirable, which points to a new possible synthesis of the religious and the political for overcoming forms of political and social fragmentation often associated with secular and liberal modernity. Authenticated Islam, self-reflexive Christianity, and the rise of religious citizens who combine love for piety, freedom, and humanitarian action beckon as a model capable of overcoming secular-traditional-restoration struggles. In this narrative, interreligious dialogue initiatives, and the way they try to balance openness, pluralism, and religious truth claims, could be interpreted as a distinctively postsecular/post-Islamist endeavor, made possible by the religious transformations either theory describes and which is linked to the active construction of some form of religiously rooted project of democracy and development. And yet, religiously expressed violence and exclusivist projects of religious nationalism persist, both of which have underwritten strong criticisms of postsecularism as an approach to global and domestic politics. This section considers two of these criticisms, both of which are skeptical about the sustainability of postsecular or post-Islamist projects on account of the dynamics of either "immanence" or "consumer religiosity." Responding to these critiques will help clarify the limits and possibilities of interreligious engagement efforts to catalyze alternative modes of political development and their effectiveness in responding to patterns of religious violence and conflict.

Reflection I: Immanence and Religion's Lost Social Mobilizational Capacity

The first reflection regards criticism about the secularity that remains inherent in Habermas's understanding of postsecularism (Pabst 2012) and the avenues it offers to states to instrumentalize religious resources for political ends. As articulated above, for Habermas, March, and others, legitimate democratic religious discourse in the public sphere or political arena is postdogmatic religious discourse. Postsecular religion is more humble about its truth claims, places greater emphasis on individual freedom and choice, and is open to "mutual learning" and correction by others, including nonreligious sources. A similar description can be offered about theories of post-Islamism, in which the individualization of religious belief, through the internalization of religious deliberation processes, skepticism, choice, and the recognition of another's religious validity, is often presented as the first step toward a more democratized Islam. Bayat's (2013:307) description of post-Islamism as the "breaking down the monopoly of religious truth" parallels Habermas's description of postsecularism as the development of a "postdogmatic" modern-religious mentality. Within this framework, the persistence of dogmatic religious reasoning and insistence on unquestionable truth claims is viewed as democratically problematic.

Some scholars, in this respect, have argued that there is still something instrumental and insufficient in Maritain's vision of democracy or, in a parallel way, post-Islamist visions of democracy. As long as building up a Christian society remains the ideal for a political movement or ideology, it has not fully accepted the duty to practice or promote democratic pluralism. Even an implied dogmatic worldview is not really open to mutual learning or correction, in Habermas's terms, and does not fully recognize the legitimacy or spiritual equality of other religious (and nonreligious) individuals. In this perspective, deliberative democracy cannot function if one side is not open to learning from the other. Similar criticisms have been made of a range of Islamist thinkers who often explicitly embrace democracy or dialogue not as an enterprise in mutual discovery but as a way of better presenting Islam to a skeptical audience.[14] In this criticism, the promotion of dialogue or religious freedom is seen to be an insufficient or disingenuous position on the part of religious individuals, something that might be accepted as an act of religious charity or as a means to better recruit religious adherents, but not for the sake of learning from the other nor for the intrinsic value of freedom itself.

Scholars have responded to this criticism in a number of ways. First, they have argued that by requiring the modernization of religious consciousness, the assumption of postdogmatic forms of religious belief, or the adoption of moderate religious positions, postsecularism continues to set a high price of entry for religious individuals and traditions to participate in the public sphere (Areshidze 2017). These requirements also work to reify the state as the adjudicator of theological claims. As Mamdani (2002), Mahmood

(2006), Cavanaugh (2009), and others have pointed out, especially with respect to fostering moderate Islam, such projects amount to a more or less explicitly coercive project of religious engineering from above. The wholesale change of rationality associated with the construction of moderate Islam or postdogmatic religious democratic citizenship has been used to justify forms of public marginalization against those whom the liberal state defines as illiberal religious others (Mahmood 2006; Mavelli 2012; Massad 2015),[15] a trend various authors have argued is also underway in the formerly Christian West (Milbank 2009; Dreher 2017; Deneen 2019).

On a second, related level, these same theories appear to vastly underestimate the extent to which the social dynamism of religion might itself be predicated on (untransformed) transcendent truth claims. If this is true, then there is a basic contradiction to the theory of postsecularism, with parallels to post-Islamism, and with major implications for state-promoted interreligious dialogue initiatives throughout the Middle East. Policymakers and scholars have increasingly turned their attention to religion because of its capacity to build solidarity and social community. Yet, at the same time, they have sought to strip religion of the very thing that makes it capable of doing so, namely, its authority to make and defend truth claims which put exigent demands on believers to deny, rather than affirm, the individual self, as in the call to take up one's cross or to submit oneself entirely to the will of God. In this perspective, postsecular and post-Islamist religious developments and the projects they make possible, including interreligious dialogue initiatives, are likely to work to the advantage of the modern state and its interests in domesticating religious forces in ways which complement the geopolitical analysis of interreligious dialogue from Chapter 1. Griera and Nagel (2018:20) have noted with respect to the growth of the interreligious sector in Europe that the perception of religion as simultaneously a problem to be managed *and* a social-capital-rich resource has led states to instrumentalize interreligious dialogue initiatives in order to "advance hegemonic agendas on social cohesion."

As Moyn (2015) and Vatter (2013) point out, and as eventually adopted in the Catholic Church's declaration on religious freedom, it is partially out of fear of this possibility of state instrumentalization that Maritain insisted on defining human rights as the result of the God-gifted dignity of human being's nature, as opposed to being created, provided, or defined by the state. Human rights in Maritain's account are divine rights placed beyond the state (Vatter 2013, 2020; Taylor 2020). This order puts religious traditions in a privileged and autonomous position to criticize and demand change of the state, rather than simply act as social organs which are managed by it. Maritain asserts that once religions lose this capacity to criticize the state (as a result of their commitment to transcendent truth claims), they lose their ability to demand and enact progressive social change of those same states.

This tension—between the proposed need for religious authorities, mentalities, and patterns of behavior to transform themselves in order to sustain human rights, equality, individual freedom, and pluralism, on the one hand, and the seemingly untransformable sources which make those same religious communities capable of creating the social solidarity necessary for upholding those same values, on the other hand—is played out across several of the dominant debates about religion in sociology and political theory today. In particular, recent attention to Axial Age dynamics can be understood in these terms as well as recent criticisms of liberalism by scholars working on a new politics of virtue. As the next part of the book will highlight, both Axial Age framings and virtue politics framings have explicitly influenced contemporary interreligious dialogue scholarship and policy content.

The Axial Age Debates: Transcendence and the Production of Civilizational Progress

Recent Axial Age scholarship (Wittrock 2005; Salvatore 2007; Bellah 2011; Bellah and Joas 2012) recognizes a decisive shift across multiple human societies around the middle of the first millennium BCE toward what could be described as an epochal increase in humans' realization of their agency, self-understanding, and reflexivity. Wittrock (2005:72) explains that the Axial Age represents the "increasing reflexivity of human beings and their ability to overcome the bounds of a perceived inevitability of given conditions in temporal and social orderings."[16] For Axial Age theorists, the articulation of a higher ideal, the good, or a transcendent order was the motor that powered civilization-wide leaps in individual agency and criticism. Once they recognized and named a higher ideal, human beings could then criticize lower states of reality and prophesy that such states were not inevitable and must be worked against, overcome, and bettered. In Wittrock's (2012) articulation, by placing the realm of gods (i.e., the good and ideal) far outside that of human beings, the Axial Age made it difficult for kings to claim to be gods themselves (as they had in pre-Axial societies). As a result, prophets, preachers, and philosophers were enabled to criticize the human actions of kings and hold them to a higher standard of justice. This dynamism, it is argued, the forces unleashed by the development of criticism, self-reflection, and human agency made possible by the discovery and construction of higher ideals, became a key engine for human flourishing, progress, and civilizational building throughout history, including in both Christianity and Islam (Salvatore 2016).

In part, the renewed interest in the Axial Age is a function of scholarly reflection on the meaning of liberal, secular modernity. Scholars have asked whether the dramatic process of secularization in the West, what Taylor has described as the Secular Age of Immanence, is evidence that human civilizations are entering into a new Axial Age, in which societies break free of the need for transcendent ideals and faiths (Armstrong 2006; Bellah 2011; Casanova 2012).[17] If the basic dynamism animating civilizational progress was the positing of a transcendent ideal as a means to social and self-criticism, then perhaps that self-criticism can be progressively spun forward even without that narrative. In other words, if, in the Axial Age, humanity invented a new idea of god in order to liberate themselves from the old gods, then in a progressive next step, humans might simply get rid of ideas of god altogether and liberate themselves to their full subjectivity and the emancipatory agency that accompanies it. Within a certain theological perspective, in fact, as Chapter 3 presents, the development of a shared, global ethic which is capable of operating independently of any particular sacred narrative has become the end point of important interreligious dialogue efforts.

While some scholars have welcomed this development, others have read it as a typical chimera of liberal political theology which, various political theorists have argued, produces a self-defeating and unsustainable religious project. The suggestive title of Mark Lilla's (2008) book, *The Stillborn God*, captures this criticism. Lilla sees an unsurpassable gulf between a secular liberal political order and one based on some form of religious revelation. This gulf renders attempts to ease the transition from the latter to the former, as liberal Protestantism did in its eventual embrace of the ideals of the Enlightenment, a self-emptying act. Once the "Great Separation" is made, as Lilla names it, once political legitimacy rests on a self-evident, rational-legal basis stacked for the rights of individuals and faith is made into a strictly individual matter between the believer and God alone, any external religious authority over the lives of individuals is put into question, and eventually the whole edifice falls. This includes any claims that religious authorities might make over the justice and legitimacy of political rule or the private lives of citizens. In this way, liberal Protestantism and, by extension, all epistemically timorous political theologies, dissolve into the secular project of emancipating individuals from the need of God, the sacred, and the transcendent, whether that is their intention or not.[18]

Virtue Ethics and Postliberal Politics

A number of scholars working in the tradition of virtue ethics have made similar claims. Scholarship on virtue ethics emphasizes that social coordination in favor of the common good requires widespread habits of cooperation and moral virtue which, like the common good, are not readily apparent or acquired by individuals on the basis of their free, independent capacity to reason alone, as liberalism would believe. Rather, as MacIntyre (1981) and others claim, recognizing and acquiring moral virtue depends on knowing something about the purpose of human beings, their telos, what humans were made for and why they exist. The answers to these teleological questions are typically provided by tradition and religious narrative which conserve stories about the good over time (Murphy, Kallenberg, and Nation 1997; Thomas 2004, 2005). For virtue ethics, therefore, a strong concept of the good is necessary to orient the individual rights and freedom provided by a democratic regime toward the construction and preservation of a common political welfare.

These criticisms have strengthened the intuitions of very diverse scholars that such projects of dialogue may be complicit with secularism in ways which parallel the charge of liberal Protestantism emptying itself from the inside. Thus scholars from either end of the debate have questioned the possibility of a religiously expressed middle way between secular liberalism and religious authoritarianism.[19] For exclusive secular humanists, the religious hold left over from the religious roots of modernity must be overcome. The hope of getting out of the contemporary crisis of liberalism, therefore, is not to be found in a return to or reliance on religious resources in public, even seemingly democratized ones, but to see the emancipatory logic of self-revealed human rights through to its end (Moyn 2015; Lilla 2008,; Urbinati 2010; Rorty 1994).

Moyn's (2015) work on the Christian origins of the contemporary human rights framework is illustrative in this regard. Maritain, he argues, and the project of Christian democracy adopted human rights discourse as a bulwark against the power of the secular state over the religious field, on the one hand, and as a safeguard against religious authoritarianism, on the other hand. Moyn goes so far as to describe the Universal Declaration of Human Rights, which Maritain worked on and influenced in its early stages, as a "profoundly communitarian document—precisely a moral repudiation of dangerous individualism" (98).[20] These essentially conservative Christian legacies, however, continue to restrain the progressive possibilities of secular emancipation projects, and he argues that it requires an ongoing rewriting of human rights principles in secular terms. As Moyn writes with normative urgency, "Christianity is the global faith that many would like human rights to become" (174). These concerns mirror the suspicions of scholars and policymakers leveled at Islamist political projects which combine Islamic norms and parliamentary politics and the fear that these projects license illiberal and repressive religious projects.[21]

For the new traditionalists, on the other hand, both conservative and progressive, the task is the opposite: to shore up the transcendent roots of civilization. In concrete terms, this means more explicitly recognizing Christianity in the West or Islam in the Middle East as the real breakthrough, that which is capable of providing a lasting, meaningful source of human dignity and, thus, rights. A number of scholars working on a "postliberal" politics of virtue could be described in these terms. Indeed, many virtue ethics scholars are skeptical of liberalism's long-running capacity to regenerate public moral resources in favor of solidarity, human dignity, and rights without appealing to some sort of religious tradition. In doing so they criticize liberalism's claims to a more radical autonomy of individual agency within the political community, and they appeal to the moral force of religious tradition to guide and limit public reason and its defense of rights. As Deneen (2019) argues, liberalism has been able to flourish for so long in large part because it has relied on a moral stock of virtue provided in the West by the Christian tradition. And yet, he writes, "liberalism has drawn down on a preliberal inheritance and resources that at once sustained liberalism but which it cannot replenish" (29).[22] These criticisms are shared outside the West. In its searing critique of the modern liberal state, Hallaq's (2013:5–6) work is expressive in this sense and explicitly draws on MacIntyre to assert the need to recuperate public moral sources—which he looks to in the premodern paradigm of the *sharia*—in order to rehumanize political development: "[T]he relegation of the moral imperative to a secondary status . . . has been at the core of the modern project, leading us to promote or ignore poverty, social disintegration, and the deplorable destruction of the very earth that nourishes humankind, in terms of both material exploitation *and* value. . . . The continuing deep effects of [the classic Muslim] tradition on modern Muslims lends credence to MacIntyre's critique of the Enlightenment concept of autonomous rationality, where ethical values are assumed to issue from noumenal reason."[23]

Projects intent on recuperating these moral sources can take the form of circling the wagons to protect Islam or Christianity from the religiously destructive logics of liberalism and seek to renew from within (as projects like Dreher's 2017 Benedict Option and various Islamist projects propose). It can also mean pursuing public projects which more fully recognize transcendent logics as necessary orienting principles for progressive politics (e.g., Milbank and Pabst 2016). Here, as Milbank (2009:33) puts it, drawing explicitly on the language and debate of the Axial Age, particular narratives of transcendence are "actually less dangerous to politics because it opens up to a realm that is continuously self-critical . . . but with a positive exit."

On account of these critiques, a number of scholars in both the Muslim and Christian worlds have tended to view postsecular scholarship and interreligious dialogue efforts with suspicion, as belonging to part of a broader accommodationist trend in which religious leaders and theologians become "chaplains" to secular modernity (Reno 2016) or traitors to their faith, as *Al Jazeera*'s Ahmed Mansour recently described Mohammed al Issa, the general secretary of the Muslim World League, for his outreach efforts to Jewish communities.[24] Milbank (2009: 111), for example, refers to "all those craven, weak, sentimental theologians, doused in multiple tinctures of *mauvaise foi*, who claim to believe in some sort of remote, abstract, transcendent deity and who yet compromise the universal claims of Christianity in favor of mystical relativism, glorification of hypostasized uncertainty, and practical indulgence in the malignly infinite air-shuttle of mindless 'dialogue.'" For Milbank and others, interreligious dialogue, in what seems to be its acceptance of pluralism and its tendency to downplay exclusive and transcendent truth claims in favor of shared ethical commitments, appears to give away too much and to fold itself into the logic of liberal Protestantism and liberal modernity.

The multiple-modernities scholarship, and to some degree Habermas's turn to postsecularism, challenge such a proposition by recalling the role that religious traditions and practices played in the construction of agency, subjectivity, and rights in both the West and other Axial and post-Axial civilizations. In this perspective, as Turner (2011), Salvatore (2016), Eisenstadt (2000), Turner and Forlenza (2016), Deeb (2006), and other sociologists argue, decentering Western understandings of modernity through the study of the experience of other civilizations and religious systems points to ways in which they may combine specific social practices and ideals of religious authority to build "successful institutions of control and discipline as well as the liberation of modern creative forces in the economy and within cultural production [that] do not necessarily require the adoption of package like notions of modernity based on one, stereotypical and largely mythical ... European model" (Salvatore 2016:292).

These perspectives, particularly in Catholic and Muslim traditions, in critical development alongside liberal modernity, open up new horizons for transcendent worldviews to orient everyday political and social struggles toward novel, cosmopolitan syntheses which more explicitly build on the social and political institutions of their religious past. Thomas (2005), who also draws on virtue ethics in his work, refers to these syntheses as forms of "rooted cosmopolitanism." He writes, "I have called for a 'deeper pluralism' between different cultures and civilizations, and have argued for a 'rooted cosmopolitanism,' one which sees that a genuine dialogue between religious traditions and civilizations can only take place within the virtues and practices of particular religious traditions among the real existing communities that make up world politics" (248).

This recognition of the positive role that religious dynamism plays in sustaining democratic and cosmopolitan projects of modernity, especially through the long-term generation of forms of society-shaping practices of solidarity, explains Habermas's turn to religion. It also explains the search by Joas (2014), Taylor (1996, 2007), Casanova (2012), March (2009), Turner and Forlenza (2016), and others to rethink secularism and dialogue-friendly religious projects as foundational sources for dealing with the difficulties of religious and social pluralism in contemporary societies in both the West and elsewhere. The next chapter takes a closer look at the theological dimensions of these efforts.

Reflection II: Consumer Religiosity

In the discussion outlined above, which links debates on postsecularism and post-Islamism to the Axial Age, virtue ethics, and the multiple-modernities literature, much scholarship has focused on the evolution of philosophical worldviews over several generations following the Enlightenment and the encounter of diverse religious systems with those changes. For many of these scholars, modernization does not signify the decline of religion, but it does entail a process of transformation, here in the realm of religion's own self-understanding regarding its truth claims and the role of the individual in adjudicating those truth claims. This transformation process gives rise to authenticated and more democratically expressed forms of religiosity and entails an increased legitimacy and presence of religious plurality. For secular humanists, this largely represents a progressive move toward individual emancipation (and away from various forms of implicit and explicit authoritarianism and oppression) and the institutionalization of stronger individual rights. Many neotraditionalists find this move problematic and probably self-defeating, endangering the sources of civic solidarity and ideas of the good beyond the self. Others, like Taylor (1996:37),[25] find the same process creates equal doses of admiration and unease.

This account, of course, is not simply (or even primarily) a story about contemporary changes in philosophical foundations or the emancipated religious practices individuals assume in secular or post-Islamist societies. It is also closely connected to the rise of capitalism and consumer culture and their worldwide dominance through globalization. Hence, for many sociologists of religion (Turner 2011, 2013; Roy 2004, 2010; Berger 2014; Bellah 2011; Miller 2003), the rise of what Bellah et al. (1985) named as expressive individualism has been magnified and driven as much by market dynamics as by emancipatory individual projects in politics and life.

For a variety of sociologists, market dynamics have shaped a distinct consumer culture of religiosity which prioritizes individual personalization of choices, products, and lifestyles. Better and more religious products are sold in order to cater to personal needs and desires and to construct a more comfortable, pleasing, fulfilling, pain-free life path. Rather than declining as change in economic means and structures made nonreligious products which seemed to also meet those desires available on a mass basis, this scholarship has argued that religions have adapted to fit the increasingly plural expressions and desires of the consuming masses.

This narrative of the commodification of religion has also emphasized the degree to which turn-of-the-millennium religious beliefs and practices across the globe had become individualistic, subjective, expressive, and postinstitutional. Bryan Turner (2011) developed the term "low-intensity religion" to describe this adaptation of religious belief and authority to contemporary societies defined by freedom of expression and consumer capitalism. Rather than hewing to orthodox practices, which would necessitate the loss of members who choose other life paths which are more attractive to their self-fulfillment, religions made themselves competitive on the market by making fewer demands on their congregants, allowing for greater personalization of belief, and reformatting religious services as forms of entertainment, lifestyle choices, and individual therapy. Like the term "expressive individualism," many recent categorizations of contemporary religious practices and identifications, including "moralistic therapeutic deism" (Smith and Denton 2005), "spiritual but not religious" (Putnam and Campbell 2010), and "believing without belonging" (Davie 1990) could all be read as indicating signs in this direction. Critically, while market strategies have allowed for a greater presence (and diversity) of religious individuals in contemporary societies, low-intensity religious practice made adherents undermotivated and ill-equipped to mobilize for any coherent, religiously inspired political project (Turner 2011; Diotallevi 2016).

Turner (2011), Roy (2010, 2020), and others have argued that the commodification of the religious market is a global phenomenon, and various theorists have outlined its impact in Muslim-majority societies (Roy 2004; Haenni 2005; Cesari and McLoughlin 2005; Fealy and White 2008; Tobin 2016). Thus, as happened to Christian citizens elsewhere, Roy (2004) observed that Muslim citizens have also become religious consumers, personalizing their religious experiences in multiple and less holistic or communal ways. The weakening of clear sources of religious authority and the plural forms of religiosity that are the result of this change work against the mass mobilization of Islamist politics or any other religious movements seeking society-wide change. For Roy (2012), the end result has been the creation of Islamism-lite and the growing probability that Islamism, as a political project, will not have an overwhelming religious impact in those Middle East regimes where Islamists might be elected. From this perspective, the religious transformation described by post-Islamism has much to do with the personalization (and consumption) of Islam by everyday Muslim citizens in response to market dynamics, as opposed to, primarily, an authenticated process of belief or practice. Alongside processes of authentication of belief, the emancipation of individual religious projects, and the internalization of a socially relevant, Islamically pious lifestyle, therefore, there has also been the *Islamification* of a consumed lifestyle. Listening to contemporary Islamic music and telepreachers, seeking a fashionable but modest Islamic dress, and investing in a safe Islamic banking portfolio are all analogous to the pleasing and positive and entertaining religiosity commodified in the West and elsewhere. Higher levels of public piety in Muslim-majority countries may be favored by state policies in favor of Islam and driven by the availability of Islamic institutions (Driessen 2014; Künkler, Madeley, and Shankar 2018). Such piety, however, does not signify the surpassing of secularization but rather confirms a religious shift toward an expressive, more personalized public religious norm.

Many of these scholars therefore argue that by adapting to the demands of the market and adopting a low-intensity religion market strategy, new or evolved religious authorities have forfeited much of their capacity to transform society, even as religious societies seem to be flourishing. Echoing Axial Age discourses, as Turner (2011:227) puts it, a religion which poses as entertainment rather than salvation, with all of its demands for self-denial, discipline, obedience, and submission, can no longer sustain the division between the sacred and the profane, this world and its alternative. As a result, contemporary religiosity no longer contains the socially transformative potentialities of organized religions of an earlier epoch. This has led to what Turner describes as an elective affinity between passive citizenry and modern spirituality, which further weakens the roots of solidarity in late modernity.

In a similar vein, Roy (, 2010, 2020) has argued that the decoupling of individual religiosity from institutional religion has resulted in a state of "Holy Ignorance" in both Muslim and Christian societies. Roy is referring to the wholesale forgetting of territory-specific religious traditions and knowledge which were born of religious reflection and social accommodation over long periods of time. Such reflection and accommodation enabled religious authorities to address whole and diverse peoples of a larger national community and bind them together for a common ideal of justice. In this perspective, the emphasis of contemporary forms of spirituality, both Muslim and not, on lifestyle and personal consumption habits (veiling, banking systems, Christian rock music, etc.) is itself evidence of the loss of religious authority's capability to direct, shape, and transform culture and politics, of social life writ large, in a more substantive, serious, other-worldly, and communal way.

For Roy (2004, 2010), Turner (2011), and others, Holy Ignorance helps explain why there is a rise and extension of low-intensity religiosity in all of its plural, individualized forms and, at the same time, new and more violent forms of religious fundamentalism. In some ways, both low-intensity religion and religious fundamentalism are two sides of the same coin, what Appleby (1999; Almond, Appleby, and Sivan 2003) has described as resulting from forms of "weak" religion. Both are made possible by the dramatic crisis of institutionalized, society-wide forms of religious authority structures and the increased possibility modernity offers for an individual to make claims to religious authority and declare who is a truly believing or authentic religious individual and who is not. By embracing and defining a pure (and simple) Islam, Roy (2004) argues, Islamic fundamentalism is well-suited to globalization, as it connects pure, individual believers across the globe in the pursuit of pure Islam without the need for any cultural accommodations which might make it relevant for a geographically defined plural society as a whole. At the same time, the appeal and political sustainability of such projects are limited. As a revolutionary movement it either exhausts itself in violence once the initial explosion has faded (Front Islamique du Salut-FIS, Al Qaeda, ISIS); transforms into a more ordinary and secular-looking party in either authoritarian (Erdogan) or democratic (Ghannouchi) guise, or retreats into a quietist isolationist stance. The same logic extends to other denominational forms of religious fundamentalism (Roy 2010).

In any case, we are left living in what Roy (2004) has described as archipelago societies, in which few churches or religious movements, including those in favor of interreligious dialogue, appear to have the capacity or enjoy the sociological conditions that would allow them to make and sustain demanding claims on a pluralistic society as a whole and orient it toward a higher ideal.

Thus, various sociologists (Berger 2014; Roy 2004; Turner 2011) point to an increase of religious plurality as opposed to a decline of religious practices as the real outcome of processes of modernization, globalization, and democratization which have institutionalized individual political, economic, and religious choices. Interreligious dialogue movements might seek to respond to, diffuse, or manage the conditions of this religious plurality, but the very nature of plurality makes it difficult for these same movements to represent more than localized incidents of religious change. It also entails that there is a certain futility on the part of states to use interreligious dialogue as a way of arbitrating religious pluralism and that attempts by states to reassert credible religious authority over pluralized, individualist-oriented religious societies will be a difficult process at best.

Postsecularism, Post-Islamism, and Interreligious Dialogue

This chapter has reviewed theories of postsecularism and post-Islamism and the way both sets of theories articulate global changes in religious worldviews and practices which are outside and beyond the matrix of secularism and secularization or Islamism and Islamification. Postsecularism and post-Islamism highlight the role that religious forces continue to play in the development of alternative, religiously rooted projects of modernity which attempt to combine freedom, citizenship, religious piety, and public narratives anchored in transcendent ideals and values, as well as the reconstruction of forms of religious authority which are in equilibrium with these new religious social forces. Postsecularism and post-Islamism also highlight the types of sociological changes in patterns of religiosity and the importance of everyday religious citizens animating those patterns, which makes such projects imaginable. At the same time, debates over postsecularism and post-Islamism, and reflected in wider scholarship on the Axial Age, virtue ethics, and the multiple-modernities literature, have also questioned whether the very same forces which made these projects possible also deteriorate the capacity of religious forces to sustain those projects over the long run.

In many ways, interreligious dialogue has been made possible by the religious transformations, both ideational and sociological, which post-Islamism and postsecularism highlight, and responds to the tensions that those transformations have created, especially with respect to religious pluralism. In this perspective, and as the Catholic Church sought to do in the Second Vatican Council, recent interreligious dialogue efforts in the region can be interpreted as new attempts at religious synthesis with the dynamics of citizenship, pluralism, and modernity. Echoing Moyn's (2015) assessment of Christian democracy, dialogue initiatives in the Middle East and elsewhere can be read in this framework as part of a broader attempt to develop an alternative project of modernity which combines the ideals of pluralism and individual political rights within a religious, spiritual, and communitarian framework, one which does not re-sacralize closed authoritarian projects or empty religious communities of their specificity and existential self-understanding. The reflections of this chapter have also outlined the challenges that confront such projects, focusing particular attention on the possibility of these alternative religious models to simultaneously embrace epistemic humility/openness as well as to generate social solidarity/mobilization over time. Guided by these theories and debates, the next two parts of the book measure and evaluate the attempts of dialogue efforts to craft this synthesis in both theological and practical terms. Part II studies the development of theologies of interreligious dialogue in the Middle East and their connection to evolving understandings of religious authority, citizenship, and pluralism in the region. Part III explores the evolution of religious and social practices among participants in two interreligious dialogue initiatives in the Middle East and their relationship to the political development of two state-sponsored interreligious dialogue initiatives in the region.

PART II
THEOLOGIES

3
A Brief History of Interreligious Dialogue

Introduction

The first chapter of this book considered the geopolitical and regional dynamics shaping recent state investments in interreligious dialogue in the Middle East. The second chapter then introduced a theoretical framework to conceptualize the social and intellectual developments which have made interreligious dialogue possible in the region and to understand its content as a religious and political project. Theories of postsecularism and post-Islamism, it was argued, can help us make sense of the political and religious meaning of interreligious dialogue, clarify the ways in which it reflects a longer arc of social and intellectual change linked to processes of modernization and democratization, and evaluate the capacity of interreligious dialogue as a project to support society-wide mobilization in favor of political and religious reform.

The three chapters in this second part explore the evolution of theological perspectives on interreligious dialogue in light of these claims. They consider the extent to which the growth of interreligious dialogue initiatives in the region reflects postsecular and post-Islamist accounts of religious and social change. In doing so the chapters highlight how the development of new readings of freedom and religious diversity by religious authorities, particularly in mainstream Sunni Islam and Roman Catholicism, has been closely linked to religious crises provoked by encounters with liberal modernity. The chapters argue that the identification of interreligious dialogue as a positive religious idea and practice was critically shaped by religiously oriented processes of political reform in both traditions which responded to these crises through strategies of adaptation while simultaneously rejecting the framework of secular liberalism. Interreligious dialogue efforts in both traditions, therefore, and the development of theologies to accompany them, could be read as an integral part of either tradition's attempt to construct alternative projects of religious modernity.

This first chapter of Part II narrates a brief history of interreligious dialogue as a global practice and movement. In tracing its recent origins it introduces a key debate among theologians and scholars of religion about the religious meaning of interreligious dialogue and the extent to which its growth represents an Axial Age–like break in the history of world religions. Chapter 4 revisits the Catholic Church's theological evolution on interreligious dialogue at the Second Vatican Council and its subsequent development by several Catholic theologians and writers, including Piero Coda, Fadi Daou, and Christian de Chergé, whose work is closely linked to the interreligious dialogue initiatives highlighted in the case studies of the last part of the book.

Finally, Chapter 5 analyzes the political worldviews and religious discourses which have developed over the recent interreligious declarations initiated by Muslim religious authorities in the Middle East, which some have compared to an Islamic Vatican II. It also highlights the emerging networks of religious authorities who have supported but also redefined themselves through this project. In particular, the chapter connects the growth of interreligious dialogue initiatives in the region to the development of new religious positions on pluralism, religious freedom, and inclusive or full citizenship. It argues that these positions represent an important shift within official and influential Islam in the region and reflect the changing political and religious aspirations of their societies in ways that have parallels to developments in the Catholic world.

Interreligious Dialogue: Origins and Evolutions

A number of leading theologians and religious studies scholars have explicitly argued that the shift toward pluralism and interreligious dialogue in contemporary religious mentalities, doctrines, and practices represents a new Axial Age breakthrough, a veritable seismic revolution in the history of world religions (Swidler 2013; Knitter 2005; Coda 2003). While there are many historical instances of multireligious societies living together peacefully, scholars have offered few historical examples of active theologies of religious pluralism, especially within the traditions of Islam and Christianity. Even in those held up as important proto-examples of interreligious dialogue—Nicolas di Cusa, Rumi, Menachem Hameiri, St. Francis, Malik al-Kamil, the Emir Abdelkadr, and others—the relations of dialogue they advanced remained structured in a pre-Copernican, geocentric religious worldview: all other religions are seen to revolve around the one, true religion, whose core, revealed truth, represents the ordering center of the universe. For many scholars, the shift in mentality toward dialogue across the past century is truly Copernican in this sense, by shifting truth, the center of the universe, to a larger sun outside one's own religion and recognizing that that sun gives light to multiple religions which orbit around it (Schmidt-Leukel 2017).

Some have argued that the newness of pluralism varies by religious tradition in both quality and quantity. In this respect, some have noted how much newer or recently new the experience of religious diversity is for Western Christianity as opposed to Islam and other religious traditions (Bhargava 2012; Kayaoğlu 2010). Both theologically and historically, Islam has been argued to possess more resources and experience dealing with religious diversity than Western Christianity (Kayaoğlu 2010). From the perspective of political history, one might argue, on the one hand, that there is a mutual affinity between the development of exclusivist religious doctrines in the Christian tradition and successive iterations of conflict which led to the construction of relatively homogeneous nation-states in the West (Bhargava 2012). On the other hand, one might link the magnification of doctrinal threads in the Qur'an which recognize the religious legitimacy of Christians and Jews with the construction and maintenance of multireligious empires based on formally recognized communities in the Islamic tradition (Kayaoğlu 2010). Other scholars have urged caution about such interpretations and argued instead that most religious traditions have marshaled religious arguments and scriptures for apologetic and religiously exclusivist ends for most of history, and that tolerance of religious others, as in the Ottoman millet system or during periods of the Roman Empire, did not indicate a position of mutual recognition of the equal legitimacy of each others' truth claims (Michel 2013).

Most scholars of interreligious dialogue locate the real breakthrough, the beginnings of what could be defined as a global movement toward interreligious dialogue, as evolving out of the late nineteenth century and the development of a modern, scientific, and academic discipline of world religions (Brodeur 2005; Banchoff 2012; Cornille 2013; Swidler 2013; Marshall 2017). The 1893 World Parliament of Religions in Chicago is traditionally listed as the origin moment of the movement which then developed further through the Ecumenical movement in the early 1900s and in the postwar period (Brodeur 2005). A combination of growing scientific epistemology, democratic (and largely Protestant) host countries, as well as the urgency of civilization-wide violence marks this early period of dialogue development. Similar contexts of rationalization, democratization, and regional conflict might also be associated with interreligious dialogue's subsequent global waves, including the serious engagement of the Catholic world in interreligious dialogue in the 1960s, and then of the Muslim-majority world over the 2000–2020 period. In this history, the *Nostra Aetate* declaration at the Second Vatican Council in 1965 marks the full entry of the Catholic Church into a global dialogue of religions. This entry was further developed throughout the papacy of John Paul II and especially highlighted in the 1986 interreligious prayer for peace in Assisi that he organized, which brought together the heads of major world religious traditions for several days of prayer and fasting for world peace and unity, an unprecedented event at the time. Finally, as Chapter 1 began to chart out, the past two decades have seen the construction of a series of major interreligious dialogue declarations and initiatives in the Muslim-majority world, especially evidenced by the Amman Message (2004) and A Common Word (2007) initiatives as well as the 2016 Marrakesh Declaration, a bundle of declarations which some scholars have described as approaching an Islamic Vatican II (Swidler 2013).

From the broad perspective of political history, therefore, there is an apparent association between waves of democratic reformulations across several major religious traditions and the development of projects of interreligious dialogue in those same traditions.[1] In this reading, the adoption of interreligious dialogue by these traditions appears to be linked to their efforts to come to terms with encounters with liberal and secular projects of modernity and the major crises of religious authority that such encounters provoked. This combination of a crisis of religious authority and a democratic-religious reformulation can also be associated with important shifts in what we might label the missionary politics of religion and its relationship to the decolonization of the Global South. In particular, the decolonization of Africa, Asia, and Latin America, and the relative secularization of foreign policymaking goals among the great powers, made possible new and less threatening kinds of religious encounters between the great religions. In Algeria, for example, the development of a new theology of nonproselytizing presence and fraternal witness by the remnant Catholic Church in Algeria (Teissier 1984, 1998, 2002; Claverie 1996), largely organized by a cadre of French clergy and religious who had renounced their French passports to remain in Algeria, reversed the relation of power between the Catholic Church and the Algerian people. This reversal created the possibility for new kinds of experiences of religious friendship which would prove decisive in the development of a string of Catholic-Muslim dialogue initiatives in the region, as the last part of the book will highlight. Coming to terms with the violence of colonialism, it could be argued, led to a higher degree of self-criticism, awareness, and sensibility on the part of the Catholic Church and, in parallel ways, Protestant churches, of Christian complicity in the construction of repressive political regimes in the Global South. This self-awareness, in turn, fed into the search for new solutions to structure encounters with religious others and to amplify their humanitarian character. The shame of Christian inaction during the Holocaust and the destruction of the world wars also greatly affected this dynamic and, critically, led to major Christian-Jewish dialogue efforts. While it is officially a document on dialogue with religions in general, for example, the *Nostra Aetate* declaration devotes much, if not most, of its attention to the specific relationship of the Catholic Church to Judaism.

A parallel provocation of heightened religious awareness and sensitivity to the religious logics of violence can also be read into the recent development of interreligious dialogue initiatives in the Muslim-majority world, especially in their response to the growth of violent and religiously identified groups like Al Qaeda and ISIS. As Mekia Nedjar, an Algerian scholar of religion and politics put it in 2008,[2] "It is said that Christian theology is not the same since the Holocaust, and indeed, Muslim theology is not the same since 9/11" (quoted in Premawardhana 2008). Several of the most important recent interreligious declarations in the Muslim world, including the Marrakesh Declaration and the Declaration on Humanitarian Islam, in fact, begin with an observation that the Islamic civilization has reached a critical turning point and must seek a way forward to restore the credibility of religious authority in the region and overcome the logic of violence which has been linked to Islam.

Scholars of religion thus have described the growth of interreligious dialogue movements and activity as a contemporary religious development, one which is closely connected to crises of religious authority in modernity and associated with a growth in religious self-reflexivity, especially as regards the relationship of religious individuals and traditions with other religious individuals and traditions. Here, the increase in self-reflexivity is expressed not only in the political sense, as in the realization of religious complicity or inaction in the face of injustice, but in the metaphysical sense as well, as in the realization that other religious experiences may offer an enriching role in the specific religious search to understand the truth. In this sense, practices of interreligious dialogue which seek mutual learning and deeper knowledge of the other have been gradually understood by some theologians and practitioners as offering a means to a fuller understanding of the divine and its relationship to humanity.

Exclusivism, Inclusivism, Pluralism, and Beyond

This historical analysis of interreligious dialogue as an increase of religious self-reflexivity has clear echoes with the Axial Age discourses highlighted in Chapter 2 and the consensus among various theologians that the global practice of interreligious dialogue represents an authentically new phase in the development of world religions. One of the common schema religious scholars have used to categorize religious positions vis-à-vis dialogue and religious plurality in order to make sense of this new phase has been the exclusivism-inclusivism-pluralism typology. In this typology, exclusivists do not recognize the legitimacy of truth claims outside their particular religion. Inclusivists recognize that other religions may hold some legitimate truth claims which they might learn from, but they ultimately insist that their particular religion holds the fullness of truth. Pluralists believe that no religion holds an exclusive claim to the fullness of truth and that it is only by abandoning claims to absolute truth that religions can take each other seriously. Thus, Eck (2006) writes that pluralism describes a fundamentally positive attitude toward diversity rather than an empirical state of religious plurality. In this perspective, for various scholars, the axial breakthrough of interreligious dialogue is represented in the dramatic, if incomplete shift in thinking about religious truth from exclusivism to pluralism (Schmidt-Leukel 2017; Eck 2006; Hick and Knitter 2005; Swidler 2015). Various theologians of dialogue have mined the traditions of mysticism present in most religions which emphasize the fundamental unknowableness of God, as in the tradition of the unknown names of God in Islam, to posit the seeds of pluralism already ordered within existing religious traditions. These seeds redefine relations between religions, in recognition that their diverse existences reflect a broader, mysterious plan of God beyond the specific responses to incompletely understood revelations that have been developed by any one religious tradition.

Scholars have also noted a democratic and secular logic to this shift to pluralism, which also reflects the debates and criticism of postsecularism in the preceding chapter. In constructing the Parliament of the World's Religions[3] and the United Nations of Religions,[4] interreligious dialogue initiatives adapt themselves to the institutional logic of democratic decision-making and move toward encountering one another on a level playing field marked by mutual recognition, freedom, and equality. In order for those relations to be legitimately reciprocal, in a democratic sense, some scholars have argued that religions must recognize the full and equal religious legitimacy of other religious traditions. In this perspective, exclusivist religious claims which distinguish between "true religion" and "false religion" would seem to carry forward implied inequalities and render genuine partnership between religions difficult, if not impossible. Thus some scholars have argued that pluralism in its full and equal sense is a prerequisite for building sustainable dialogue and international cooperation and for avoiding a clash of civilizations (Dallmayr 2010; Casanova 2011; Schmidt-Leukel 2017). If "there can be no peace among the nations without peace among the religions," as Küng (2004:76) writes, then peace among the religions depends on the adoption of pluralism as a religious position and the relinquishment by religions to claims of absolute, exclusive truth.

There have been a number of important criticisms of this version of the pluralism stance, and in ways which parallel criticisms and debates on postsecularism in the previous chapter. For, just as Habermas required that religion must undergo a "modernization of consciousness" in order to fully participate in the democratic public sphere, this pluralism position, a priori, seems to argue that religions must accept truth claims beyond their own truth claims in order to enter into real dialogue with others and in order to avoid civilizational clash. In this account, in other words, the establishment of peaceful external pluralism in the world is made to be dependent on the adoption of at least some degree of internal theological pluralism. Scholars have argued, however, with parallels to various criticisms made of strong versions of the postsecular normative project, that such a stance places unnecessarily heavy burdens on religious individuals and communities. While advocates of religious pluralism make an egalitarian appeal to affirm the truths of multiple religions, as several scholars have argued, they do so by positing the existence of a larger, fuller truth behind the particular and incomplete truths of single religious traditions (Schmidt-Leukel 2017). This claim, however, is itself a kind of exclusive metaphysical claim about the "deeper" meaning of religion in the world (Moyaert 2012; Light 2009). Scholars have argued that it is an assumption which does not seem to take religious differences and religious contradictions seriously enough (Cavadini and Wallenfang 2019). That is to say, it does not seem to allow for the ways in which diverse religious truth claims may break from one another and not point in the same direction or toward a common, deeper meaning (Clooney 2010; Moyaert 2012; Reynolds 2019). It would also seem to misrepresent how many religious traditions and religious individuals understand themselves, and the way in which they formulate the religious truths they worship and structure their life paths around (Firestone 2015). Scholars have also expressed unease with the way advocacy for pluralism seems to be at odds with a longtime commitment to a specific religious discipline that many religious traditions recognize as necessary for the path to spiritual enlightenment (Cambridge Inter-faith Programme).[5] As Moyaert (2012) writes, the ideal of occupying many different positions, as the multiple-truths affirmation of pluralism seems to do, becomes a "surrogate for the old dream of occupying no particular position at all." In articulating this critique, Moyaert expresses the fear of many religious individuals that interreligious dialogue, deep down, follows a secular logic which flattens out religious traditions and strips them of the divine commands and specific revelations which animate their existential energies. Scholars have also pointed out the reverse problem, that the insistence on keeping within the lines of tradition and orthodoxy as a precondition of some interreligious dialogue projects, particularly in the Middle East, places unfair and coercive burdens on a growing number of religious seekers who are syncretic in their approach to dialogue (Abu-Nimer, Khoury, and Welty 2007).

We can notice a close parallel between this critique and the tensions highlighted by debates on postsecularism and post-Islamism about the relationship between those religious dynamics which push forward contemporary religious transformation, on the one hand, and those religious dynamics which create society-moving forms of solidarity, on the other hand. In particular, the critique recalls the debate presented in the previous chapter over whether the "secular age of immanence" represents a new Axial Age breakthrough which, as Casanova (2012) put it, achieves the teleological and humanistic fulfillment of axial forces introduced through the dynamic of idealism/subjectivity. In both a strong account of religious pluralism, as highlighted above, and a strong account of secular immanence, human beings begin to see and experience the world beyond specific narratives of transcendence and justify courses of right political and social action without necessarily making appeals to any particular religious logic (Armstrong 2006). In some strong theological accounts of religious pluralism (Schmidt-Leukel 2017), the end of interreligious dialogue is to verify a common knowledge of transcendence which surpasses any particular revelation of truth. It is possible to see echoes of this pluralism project in several of the major global interreligious dialogue projects originating in the West over the past several decades, including the Global Ethic produced by the Parliament of the World's Religions in 1993 and the Charter for Compassion launched by Karen Armstrong in 2009. Both projects sought to synthesize and propose a set of universally shared ethics which all religions contain in their core, and notably did so largely by not talking about particular religious traditions, employing specific religious language, or referencing transcendent truth claims.[6]

There is another way of thinking about the growth of interreligious dialogue as an axial moment in the history of religions which is closer in keeping to the positions adopted by most interreligious dialogue initiatives in the Middle East today, which, by and large, cannot be categorized as having adopted pluralism worldviews in the way described above. In fact, if pluralism somehow moves religious individuals beyond their particular truth claims, this second Axial Age interpretation of the discovery of dialogue is formulated within a rearticulation and expansion of particular truth claims, precisely through the discovery of a vast spiritual universe beyond it. In this second account, closer to the inclusivist position, interreligious dialogue, or what Swidler (2015) has named the Age of Global Dialogue, remains a breakthrough, something that is, indeed, new in the history of world religions. It would agree, therefore, with Schmidt-Leukel's (2017:234) observation that, in an unprecedented way over the past decades, "Muhammad, Jesus and Gautama" are in the process of acquiring positive religious significance in traditions other than their own. However, this newness does not cancel out the particular claims of transcendence and revelation which animate specific religious traditions.

Within this second perspective on religious plurality, the discovery of interreligious dialogue can be closely linked to the ongoing project of these religious traditions to come to terms with liberal modernity in largely positive as opposed to largely defensive terms and in ways which preserve an integral religious vision of society and politics. In this light, the crisis which encounters with modernity provoke have been reinterpreted as processes which lead to religious growth, self-awareness, and maturity. As Hatzopoulus and Petito (2003) have evocatively written, drawing on the biblical language of Exodus, the religious experience of exile—in this sense, the time of liberal-secular "captivity"—is experienced as a prelude to deeper liberation, one which is marked by religious change and growth over decades of wandering. In this perspective, interreligious dialogue has been viewed by some theologians as a means to purification and as a way to establish new religious syntheses in modernity which simultaneously reflect and appeal to the changed sociological conditions of religious belief and practice.

The following chapter examines these claims in light of the development of the Catholic Church's position on interreligious dialogue at the Second Vatican Council and then traces its further evolution through the work of several Catholic theologians and figures who have been important for the projects of dialogue explored in Part III of the book. Chapter 5 considers the development of positions on interreligious dialogue in the Muslim-majority world over the past twenty years and its implications for support of religious freedom and citizenship in the region.

4
Catholicism and Interreligious Dialogue

This chapter begins by returning to the foundational documents of the Second Vatican Council and the reformulated positions they stake out on interreligious dialogue. It then explores how those positions have been subsequently developed in the work of Piero Coda, former rector of Sophia University Institute and a major theologian of the Focolare community whose experience of Muslim-Catholic dialogue and communion in Algeria is examined in Chapter 7. Coda's theology, especially in relation to the positions of the Church taken at Vatican II, and his interpretation of them in light of the Axial Age debates, offers a useful entry point into understanding the further development of Catholic thinking and experience of interreligious dialogue, especially with respect to Islam. His theological framework can also help make sense of some of the recurring debates and positions taken by other Catholic theologians and actors in the region, including Fadi Daou, whose work in Lebanon Chapter 8 examines, as well as Christian de Chergé, Henri Teissier, Michael Fitzgerald, Francis Clooney, and others, positions which could be read as intrinsically linking questions of human dignity, religious freedom, and interreligious dialogue in their understanding of the relation of the Church to the historical shifts introduced by liberal modernity.

Nostra Aetate and Vatican II

As Chapter 2 argued, one useful way of approaching the documents of Vatican II is to trace out the case they make for linking a strong concept of universal, God-given human dignity—in that all human beings share in the same and equal dignity as being created in the image and likeness of God (as in the *Imago Dei* of Genesis)—to a strong concept of religious freedom (as declared in *Dignitatis Humanae*). In past centuries, the Catholic Church did not closely couple human dignity with political freedom. Rather, the Church understood its defense of dignity as inseparable from the defense of its own truth claims, which, it argued, defined and offered such dignity. This included not simply an intellectual defense of the Church's truth claims but also the adoption of political coercion against the autonomous will of individuals who publicly deviated from them. As Augustine, among others, would argue (Gillespie 2008; Rist 2016), under certain circumstances it could be better (and more merciful) to physically stop an individual from actions which might put both their and their community's souls in danger than abandon them to a freedom that drives them away from the truth and the possibility of eternal salvation. *Dignitatis Humane* shifts this paradigm by more forcefully declaring the necessity of freedom for the acquisition of true belief and by positing freedom as a fundamental reflection of human beings' image in the likeness of God, as especially expressed in the self-giving (free) love of the divine trinity. This shift, as Chapter 2 argued, accepts religious freedom and political democracy as a framework within which human dignity and, critically, a more meaningful religious life might be generated.

The emphasis on both religious and political freedoms as necessary conditions for realizing human dignity and for preserving the real presence of God in all human beings, religious or not, created new ways of thinking about and relating to religious (and nonreligious) others. It meant that religious freedom could be seen as an intrinsic good which reflects the liberatory logic of the Godhead, as opposed to a purely instrumentalist means, for example, to better recruit Christians or to preserve political power. By emphasizing the presence of God in religious others both now and across history, furthermore, this new understanding of religious freedom actively encourages interreligious dialogue. Coda (2015:215) goes so far as to argue that interreligious dialogue is "nothing other than the exercise of religious freedom in the relationships between peoples, communities of faith, cultures and their symbolic forms."

The Second Vatican Council therefore recognized the spiritual and religious significance of other religions, especially with respect to Judaism but also Islam. *Nostra Aetate* (§2) declares, "Likewise, other religions found everywhere try to counter the restlessness of the human heart, each in its own manner, by proposing 'ways,' comprising teachings, rules of life, and sacred rites. The Catholic Church rejects nothing that is true and holy in these religions. She regards with sincere reverence those ways of conduct and of life, those precepts and teachings which, though differing in many aspects from the ones she holds and sets forth, nonetheless often reflect a ray of that

Truth which enlightens all men." Or, in the words of Pope John Paul II in his December 1986 remarks to the Roman Curia, in which he outlined the historical importance and meaning of the interreligious prayer for peace he hosted at Assisi just a few months before, "Every authentic prayer is called forth by the Holy Spirit, who pleads with God on behalf of his people because "we do not know how we ought to pray," but he prays in us with "groans that words cannot express" and "God, who sees into our hearts, knows what the thought of the Spirit is," cf. (*Rm* 8, 26–27). We can say, in fact, that every authentic prayer is called forth by the Holy Spirit who is mysteriously present in the heart of every person" (§11).

These documents recognize the presence of God in the religious other and name the religious significance of actions undertaken by them which reflect the truth. This understanding of salvation reformulates in an expansive way the doctrine *Ex Ecclesiam Nulla Salus* (There is no salvation outside the Church), which had shaped the Church's relations with other religions for centuries. Significantly, *Nostra Aetate* opens the doors to new possibilities of mutual learning by recognizing that the diverse cultural forms and ways of thinking found in other religious traditions reflect rays of "that Truth which enlighten[s] all men." This recognition creates new impetus for Christians to study these rays in other religious traditions and seek to understand and value their religious meaning. If there are rays of the truth present in other religions, in fact, forms of interreligious dialogue which seek to learn from religious others might even be framed as a religious responsibility for the Church and its believers, as in Paul VI's (1964:78) exhortation in *Ecclesiam Suam* that interreligious dialogue is "demanded nowadays."

In Piero Coda's interpretation of these declarations, the powerful forward movement created by the dignity-freedom-dialogue relationship formulated at the Second Vatican Council represents a real religious transformation of the Catholic Church. Coda (2003:41–42) understands this transformation in an explicitly axial sense, as a dramatic growth in the self-awareness and reflexivity of the Church in relation to itself in history: after a long, difficult period of crisis provoked by liberalism and modernity, the Catholic Church finds itself liberated to pursue positive relationships with religious others. Religious freedom makes this new experience of dialogue possible, and then, in a self-reinforcing fashion, the further positive experience of dialogue opens up an expanded understanding of the religious significance of the religious other in the salvific plan of God.

Beyond Vatican II: New Readings of Dialogue in the Middle East

The historically new experience of interreligious dialogue which was made possible by this practice of religious freedom has engendered a "dialogue and unity" reading of the gospels and salvation history among some theologians (Coda 2003; Cornille 2013; Daou 2017).[1] Such a reading has emphasized the relational and dialogical nature of the trinity toward itself and humankind, the universal presence of God in all acts of self-giving love, and an idea of religious faith that is beyond confessionalism. These authors have noted, for example, that in the gospel narratives Jesus recognized the faith of non-Jews (who were also non-Christians) in addition to other-believing individuals. This can be read in Jesus's encounter with the Roman centurion and the Cannanite (or Syro-Phonencian) woman, and particularly in the parable of the Good Samaritan.[2] In none of these cases does the gospel story reveal whether the protagonist of the encounter or the parable believes in Jesus specifically as the Messiah; nevertheless, Jesus holds up their faith as saving them or their children. Daou (2017) suggests that it is through these interreligious encounters that Jesus realizes his universal mission and invites his disciples to do the same. Here Daou emphasizes the relational and journeying nature of Jesus in which the truth of his presence is discovered and made more fully known through encounters with diverse religious others.

In an explicit way, this insight is reflected in the particular experience of Louis Massignon, who was a friend of Maritain and an early French scholar of Islam whose work and thought influenced the writing of *Nostra Aetate* (Petito 2011; Krokus 2012, 2017). Massignon converted or, better, "returned" to a Christian faith after a mystical near-death experience in which his life was saved by the hospitality and affection of a Muslim family in Baghdad. The experiential roots of Massignon's theological reformulation have been central to recent developments in interreligious dialogue in both Catholicism and Islam. These roots can be seen in a similar way, for example, in the life and reflection of Christian de Chergé, the prior of the Cistercian community in Tibhirine, Algeria, who was beatified by the Catholic Church in December 2018. De Chergé's spirituality was also profoundly influenced by an interreligious experience while he was stationed as a young solider during the waning years of colonial France in Algeria. In de Chergé's case, a local Muslim friend saved his life from an attack only to have his own life taken the next morning in retaliation. De Chergé understood that his friend, whose name was Mohammad, had acted as a Christ figure to him, and this understanding fed de Chergé's desire to pour out his life in and for Algeria (Salenson 2012). De Chergé's writings and homilies search to articulate, through the gospel readings, the meaning of spiritual truth and life which he hears Muslims witnessing to him and the "greater faith" that his experience of "praying among others who pray" produced (Salenson 2012:177ff.).

It is in this way that many practitioners and theologians of interreligious dialogue, including Massignon, Coda, de Chergé, and Daou, can speak about the "mutual witnessing" that dialogue can produce in the recognition that the faith and acts of religious others, in which God is mysteriously present, calls forth the faith of the Christian believer, as in "deep calls to deep" (Psalm 42:7). In this reading, the Christian believer can also bear witness to other religious believers (Daou 2014a).

For Coda, and for the Focolare community, this intuition of mutual spiritual nourishment finds its foundation in their understanding of *unity*, the original charism that the community adopted as its vocation in the world. Chiara Lubich, who founded the Focolare community, embraced this charism following a mystical experience in which she read the Unity prayer in the gospel of John while praying for guidance on the future of her community. In the prayer, Jesus, on the night before he dies, prays to God, "I ask ... that they may all be one. As you, Father, are in me and I am in you."[3]

Originally, in the postwar setting in which the community found itself in Europe, this vocation of unity was understood to concretely signify that they should work for a world of peace, for reconciliation between peoples and nations in Europe, and against divisions among Christians and in the Church. The community did not originally understand its mission as promoting and practicing interreligious dialogue; it was only later, in the 1970s, after a series of unexpected interreligious encounters, that Lubich, Coda, and others began to reformulate an interreligious reading of unity. In a particular way, Lubich developed a friendship with the Buddhist lay leader Nikkyo Niwano, who himself had established a lay Buddhist renewal movement (Rissho Kosei Kai) and who helped found the Religions for Peace organization. It was their relationship, and the unanticipated spiritual friendship and communion they established, that gradually led to an extension of Lubich's understanding of unity, in which working for unity meant working for the greater unity of all humankind. For Lubich and many other scholars and practitioners of dialogue, there is a striking reversal of a more classic understanding of unity found in various religious traditions, in which unity is no longer understood to signify uniformity but rather harmony within religious plurality, or "unity in diversity," as Abu-Nimer, Khoury, and Welty (2007) have described it.

In a passage that she often recounts as strongly impacting her new understanding of interreligious dialogue, Lubich relates the story of a talk she gave to a group of Buddhist monks in Thailand in the late 1970s. Lubich found herself struggling to say something meaningful to the monks by translating her specific Christian experience into a language that they would understand. So she asked them what they wanted to hear from her, and the community of monks replied by inviting her to speak directly about her Christian faith and her love for Christ. She obliged and spoke about the "one, true God" and the message of salvation of Christ found in the gospels (Gabijan 2009; Catalano 2017). When she finished, she was struck with amazement by how happy the monks were to hear of her faith story and that they expressed that they had "felt as if they were enveloped by God's love" as she was speaking (Catalano 2017:61).

In this story, Lubich does not adopt a theology of religious pluralism or translate her experience into a universal language of rationality. Rather, she discovers that her particular religious experience of truth holds "concrete existential appeal," as Dallmayr (2012:969) writes, for people of other religious faiths. This appeal, as Dallmayr notes in a direct critique of Habermas, is rooted in an experience of "fullness" or "holiness" which can spur spiritual and social solidarity in a setting of religious diversity without any necessary translation, as similarly seen in the cases of de Chergé and Massignon (see also Barbato 2010). What has changed, in a dramatic way, is the social and political context: Lubich, an Italian woman with no colonial ambitions in Thailand, who preaches a gospel of unity and service which is not attached to proselytism, is invited to share her Catholic faith at the instigation of a Buddhist community. It is in this relative context of freedom and equality that Lubich becomes aware that unity, religious dialogue, and spiritual nourishment can entail different religious traditions speaking to one another in their specific religious languages.

The reversal that this new understanding of unity represents can be understood as drawing on the work of the Second Vatican Council and, in a particular way, as various theologians have pointed out (Daou 2017; Coda 2015; Salenson 2012), the Council's emphasis on inculturation. In the Catholic Church, "inculturation" means striving to speak the language of the gospels in a way that calls on that which is already present in the diverse cultures and languages and values of the world. It also means letting that diversity deepen the Christian's understanding of the mysteries of God.[4] As *Nostra Aetate* (§2) put it, "The Church, therefore, exhorts her sons, that through dialogue and collaboration with the followers of other religions, carried out with prudence and love and in witness to the Christian faith and life, they recognize, preserve and promote the good things, spiritual and moral, as well as the socio-cultural values found among these men." And as the 1991 *Dialogue and Proclamation* document authored by the Pontifical Council for Interreligious Dialogue, then directed by Michael Fitzgerald, wrote in this respect, "Concretely it will be in the sincere practice of what is good in their own religious traditions and by following the dictates of their conscience that the members of other religions respond positively to God's invitation and receive salvation in Jesus Christ even while they do not recognize or acknowledge him as their savior . . . [i]nsofar as they live evangelical values and are open to the action of the spirit" (*Dialogue and Proclamation*, §29).

In this perspective, various theologians of dialogue have seen in the story of Pentecost, and the way it reverses the Old Testament story of the tower of Babel, a foundational text for dialogue in Christianity (Pollefeyt 2011; Fitzgerald 2000). One can interpret the story of Babel as representing a false or undesirable understanding of unity, in which humankind, speaking in one language, attempts to reach God. In the Genesis account of Babel, God rejects this kind of human unity/uniformity, which reduces "the infinite to a common ground at the cost of otherness" (Pollefeyt 2011:252). From a place of contemporary democratic reflection one might express this danger in a theory of hegemony or of the dangers of authoritarianism or totalitarianism, in which human-made unity leads humans to think that they can dominate the heavens and the earth. The Pentecost event, on the other hand, introduces a new ideal of unity. One of the central features of the Pentecost story, as described in the Acts of the Apostles, is that there were people present from every nation of the world (2:5) and that the apostles spoke to them "in their own languages" about the "wonders of God" (2:5–6). From an inculturation perspective, and echoing the quote above from the *Dialogue and Proclamation* document, in the Pentecost event the Holy Spirit may be interpreted as illuminating deeper meanings already present within the language developed by diverse (non-Christian) cultures and systems of thought.

The expansive notion of unity and salvation has been criticized as opening the theological doors to syncretism, relativism, and strong versions of the religious pluralism position. And yet, present in all of these theologians, and rooted in the documents of the Church presented above, is a carefully articulated defense that such a reading of interreligious dialogue represents an orthodox reading in continuity with the Magisterium of the Church.

For Coda, whose entire theology of interreligious dialogue is itself built on a Christian understanding of God as Trinity, the Church's reordering of its relationships with religious others does not relativize the centrality of Christ to his theology nor lead to an endorsement of pluralism as an ideology. Rather, Coda understands the new experience of dialogue as a maturation, again, after a long period of crisis, of the Church in its relationship with liberal modernity, one which renews and strengthens the faith of the Catholic Church. There remains for Coda (2015:261) the *Qaestio de veritate*, which he recognizes the authority of the Church legitimately calls forward, placing the hermeneutical key of understanding within that which has been revealed and recognized by the Church as truth. That center remains the incarnational event of Christ for Coda and other Catholic theologians, as the Church documents *Redemptoris Missio* (John Paul II 1990) and *Dominus Iesus* (Congregation for the Doctrine of the Faith 2000) exhorted. *Dominus Iesus*, in particular, which was co-written by Cardinal Ratzinger and was harshly received by many working on interreligious dialogue,[5] stated, "*Equality*, which is a presupposition of inter-religious dialogue, refers to the equal personal dignity of the parties in dialogue, not to doctrinal content, nor even less to the position of Jesus Christ—who is God himself made man—in relation to the founders of the other religions" (*Dominus Iesus*, §23).[6]

In this perspective, Coda argues that the real axial breakthrough that Jaspers originally intended to describe is not represented in the dawn of pluralism as a theological position, nor the mutual recognition of equal paths of salvation, nor a rational, immanent, universal secular humanism which surpasses transcendent accounts of reality. Rather, it is simply the dramatically new, positive, and mutually witnessing way in which major religious traditions are able to be in relation with one another today. Coda (2015:258) argues that this reorientation "is in harmony with the labor pains which are working from within" multiple religious traditions. Directly referencing Jaspers, he describes how the forces of reflexivity and self-awareness push forward from within the foundational identities and beliefs of these same religions in which "the centripetal forces which mark out the identities of diverse civilizations, starting from their religious forms and matrix, are balanced and re-directed by the centrifugal forces of their inedited relationship" (258).

It is for this reason that the significance of interreligious dialogue can be understood as going beyond both classical Christian thought *and* modernity by reproposing transcendence rather than surpassing it. Here, and in a dialectical fashion, Coda employs an idea of intersubjectivity. If liberal modernity provokes an awakening of religious traditions to ideas and practices of subjectivity, authenticity, and agency, realized through an enhanced practice and awareness of individual freedom, that same process risks exhausting itself, as Chapter 2 described, in an individualism that is incapable of regenerating the solidarity necessary to sustain those same individual rights and freedoms. Hence Coda (2003:48) warns against "the eternal gnostic temptation to project one's immanent pulsations onto the Transcendent, thereby blocking the path to its real, gratuitous, never-before-heard revelation. That is why, presenting itself as the vanguard of an encounter between religions, in reality, it makes authentic dialogue between religions impossible to practice, by promoting a syncretism in which their distinct identities, in tension towards reciprocal understanding, are swallowed up in the black hole of a presumed common end and hidden so as to definitively reduce them to provisional and illusionary epiphenomenas of an indistinct and supra-historical fusional essence."

The way forward that Coda and others outline is the renewal and purification of religious thinking through the establishment of fecund relationships between religious and nonreligious others. For Coda (2015), self-flourishing is found, and exigently demanded by the gospels themselves, through a practice of "kenotic intersubjectivity," that is to say, in a gratuitous, abandoned service of the individual self toward the other. In this way, he argues, Christianity is able to establish a positive relationship with modernity and point beyond it by generating and transforming modernity from within, through a dynamic understanding of dialogical truth claims which demand and generate new patterns of social solidarity and intersubjective social cohesion (171). There is a close resonance here between this understanding of interreligious dialogue and the idea of integral human development embraced by the past several papacies, a project which grounds political and economic development in a religious vision of human solidarity.[7] Recalling the words of Turner (2011) from Chapter 2, interreligious dialogue and integral human development both attempt to sustain the division between the sacred and the profane—and the socially transformative dynamics such a division produces—in a way that does not "necessarily expel every universal and normative reference in order to guarantee pluralism" (Coda 2003:42). In other words, in this theological reading, interreligious dialogue is proposed as a way to build constructive interactions with religious and nonreligious others and remain committed to a transcendent horizon which generates out-of-oneself solidarity and service toward others.

5
Islam and Interreligious Dialogue

Chapter 4 considered how debates about religious freedom, democracy, religious authority, and social solidarity were linked to the development of a theology of interreligious dialogue in the Catholic Church. This chapter outlines a parallel but distinct process of development in the Muslim majority world. As Chapter 2 examined, theories of post-Islamism have brought attention to what have been described as democratizing sociological and intellectual tendencies in the religious field across Muslim-majority societies. In particular, post-Islamist theories have articulated the ways in which new ideas about religious choice and freedom have developed alongside more individualized practices of Islam which seek authentic, personalized, and uncoerced religious experiences. At the same time, these theories have questioned the extent to which such tendencies are able to produce social mobilization in favor of sustainable political reforms. Thus, scholars have asked whether these same tendencies end up strengthening authoritarian regimes in the region by increasing their ability to co-opt religious forces (Tezcür 2010a) while simultaneously facilitating more exclusivist understandings of Islam because of the breakdown of inculturated religious authority which could effectively delegitimize such worldviews (Roy 2004). The exploration of contemporary Islamic thinking on dialogue in this chapter complicates this narrative by highlighting the extent to which interfaith initiatives have sought to strengthen religious authority in the region and build broad, intra-Islamic consensus for political projects in favor of religious freedom and citizenship.

As various scholars have noted (Daou 2014a; Swidler 2013), interreligious dialogue activity has experienced a concentrated period of growth in the Middle East over the past twenty years. Table 1.1 illustrated, that period could be said to have begun with the 2001 United Nations Year of Dialogue among Civilizations, proposed by Iranian president Mohammad Khatami; the development of the Amman Message and A Common Word projects by Jordan in 2004 and 2007; the Turkish-promoted establishment of the United Nations Alliance of Civilizations project in 2005; and the initiation of the Doha and Saudi Arabia centers for dialogue in 2003 and 2008, respectively. This development was further reflected in the al Azhar declarations "Future of Egypt" in 2011, "Fundamental Freedoms" in 2012, and "Freedom, Citizenship, Diversity and Inclusion" in 2017, as well as the 2017 Beirut Declaration on Faith for Rights. It was especially publicized through the 2016 Marrakesh Declaration on the rights of religious minorities in Muslim-majority societies. It has parallel developments in several Southeast Asian initiatives in favor of dialogue and religious freedom, including the 2017 *Declaration on Humanitarian Islam* and the 2018 Nusantara Manifesto. It has been further consolidated in the 2018 Vienna Declaration, the 2019 Human Fraternity document, and the 2019 Makkah Declaration, as well as other forward-moving projects associated with the Marrakesh Declaration, including the 2019 Chater of the New Alliance of Virtue and the 2021 Charter for Inclusive Citizenship process.

Viewed as a collective project, these initiatives reflect a progressive shift in intra- and interreligious relations and positions within official and influential Islam on questions of religious pluralism in the region. They also reflect religious positions that a number of official figures of authority within Islam broadly share with a range of reformist religious and political movements. The development of new theological perspectives on dialogue in the region could be understood to be closely linked to the evolution of mainstream theological reflection on the relationship between Islamic values and ideas of citizenship and religious freedom. That development was accelerated following the Arab Spring as religious leaders, particularly in the Middle East, came to grips with the reality of a dramatic crisis of religious authority in the region. This crisis was evidenced in both the electoral results of the Arab Spring, in which Arab populations elected Islamist-inspired, democratically oriented political parties across the region, as well as the implosion of the Syrian conflict and the rise of the Islamic State. In this context, religious authorities across the Middle East sought a way forward to reclaim their religious and social credibility, to delegitimize the image and use of Islam for violence, and to respond to the democratic and spiritual aspirations of their societies.

As a religious project, the emerging ideas about pluralism and citizenship which have been championed in the documents produced by these initiatives do not adopt "postdogmatic" modes of reasoning nor subscribe to the position that all religions offer equal paths to salvation. Thus, while these initiatives often address themselves to the West and make the case that international cooperation on human rights, religious pluralism, and citizenship are both possible and strengthened through dialogue activity, these same initiatives do not propose to do so on the basis of a shared understanding of liberal democracy or modernity. In fact, this emerging, global Muslim dialogue project explicitly seeks to reformulate interreligious dialogue, religious freedom, and citizenship as orthodox Islamic positions that are consistent with traditions of religious authority in Islam and the long-running understanding of "correct" Islam over the centuries. It is in this perspective that we can understand the expressed self-understanding of dialogue in the Muslim-majority world as a force for "civilizational renewal" (Esposito and Voll 2003:232), one which is capable of rebuilding social cohesion and political stability in the region. This chapter highlights the evolution of these dynamics across three major inter- and intrareligious dialogue statements produced during this period in the Middle East, namely the Amman Message, the A Common Word document, and the Marrakesh Declaration.

The Amman Message

The early Iranian and Turkish initiatives in favor of "dialogue among civilizations" marked important milestones for interreligious dialogue in the Middle East, and in ways which were explicitly linked to religious reform movements in each country. Both initiatives attempted to turn the global narrative on Islam and politics in the immediate post-9/11 environment and reflected the ambitions of each country's leaders at the time (Khatami and Erdoğan) to do the same. In doing so, they helped to set the stage for the Amman Message and A Common Word projects promoted by the Kingdom of Jordan in the early 2000s.

One of the central concerns of these early efforts at dialogue in the Middle East was the question of religious authority in Islam and its relationship to religious violence in the region. In this sense, the Amman Message, first declared by King Abdullah II of Jordan in 2004, can be viewed as an ambitious attempt to establish some baseline, intra-Islamic authority on issues of belief and belonging as a prior step to further dialogue with the West. To that end, the Amman Message's stated goal was to conjure a "universal and binding consensus" among a wide range of religious authorities within the Muslim world on a basic definition of "Orthodox Islam."[1] By formalizing a statement of mutual recognition among the major schools of Islam, including among the four major schools of Sunni Islam and Shia Islam, the

Amman Message sought to delegitimize the efforts of self-declared religious authorities to denounce other Muslims as apostates and to justify political violence on such a basis. Thus, the Amman Message declared that religious authorities could not legitimately excommunicate followers of these diverse religious schools on the basis of any correct reading of Islam.

The document garnered a remarkable number of signatures from a broad range of Muslim leaders with diverse claims to religious authority in the Muslim world. This included heads of state (e.g., the kings of Jordan and Morocco), official ministries of religious affairs (e.g., the grand mufti of Egypt and the Diyanet in Turkey), heads of international unions of Muslim scholars (e.g., Yusuf al Qaradawi), important ayatollahs from Iran and Iraq (including Grand Ayatollahs Ali Sistani and Ali Khamenei), the leaders of large Muslim movements (e.g., Nahdlatul Ulama and Muhammadiyah in Indonesia) and political parties (e.g., Rachid Ghannouchi and Anwar Ibrahim),[2] important religious scholars and public intellectuals (e.g., Tariq Ramadan, Timothy Winter, Seyyed Hossein Nasr, and Hamza Yusuf), and famous Muslim singers and telepreachers (e.g., Sami Yusuf and Amr Khaled). In important ways, this striking level of participation marshaled together both new and old transnational networks of influential religious authorities that had been slowly building in prior decades within the Muslim-majority world, through associations of religious scholars like the International Union of Muslim Scholars (IUMS), the European Council for Fatwa and Research (ECFR), al Azhar networks, and Islamic *fiqh* councils based in Saudi Arabia and elsewhere (Caeiro 2011). An overlapping network of members of these international unions formed a core group of central participants and signatories on several of these interreligious dialogue declarations and initiatives: Abdallah bin Bayyah,[3] Ahmed al Tayeb,[4] Yusuf al Qaradawi,[5] Mustafa Ceric,[6] Ali Qaradaghi,[7] and Rachid Ghannouchi,[8] among others.[9] The religious worldviews of this group, in turn, had been significantly shaped by their work to issue orthodox religious rulings for Muslims seeking to live in modernizing political and social contexts in Europe and the Middle East. By consolidating and legitimizing this global network, the Amman Message marked an important mobilization of religious authority within the Muslim-majority world. Prince Ghazi of Jordan, who helped orchestrate and write both the Amman Message and A Common Word, went so far as to claim that the Amman Message, "amounts to a historical, universal and unanimous religious and political consensus (*ijma'*) of the *Ummah* (nation) of Islam in our day, and a consolidation of traditional, orthodox Islam. The significance of this is: (1) that it is the first time in over a thousand years that the *Ummah* has formally and specifically come to such a pluralistic mutual inter-recognition; and (2) that such a recognition is religiously legally binding on Muslims since the Prophet (may peace and blessings be upon him) said: *My Ummah will not agree upon an error* (Ibn Majah, *Sunan, Kitab al-Fitan*, Hadith no. 4085)."[10]

Critically, this network of religious authorities across the Muslim world would subsequently develop the A Common Word document, addressed to Christian and Jewish communities, and many of them would work together on the Marrakesh Declaration. The mutual legitimization of mainstream schools of Islam which was formalized in the Amman Message was understood by many to represent a necessary step toward the generation of a credible body of religious authority which could offer a counterreligious narrative within the Middle East and, at the same time, act as a religious interlocuter with the West. In this sense, the Amman Message, the A Common Word document, the Marrakesh Declaration, and other projects linked to them can be understood as part of a broader, self-conscious effort from within the Muslim-majority world to construct a global "dialogue among civilizations" (as the documents repeat multiple times) which would be conducted by recognized religious authorities in order to avoid a "clash of civilizations" between Islam and the West.

The emphasis within the Amman Message on the higher goals and objectives of Islam (*maqasid al sharia*), which it defines as "realizing mercy and good for all people," begins to speak to the relationship of what it defines as "orthodox Islam" with religious others. Anticipating a similar method and focus of future initiatives, the Amman Message emphasizes the intrinsic orientation of Islam toward building the public interest (*maslaha*) for all humanity, across diverse and politically evolved historical settings. The Amman Message states in this regard, "[T]he way of this great religion that we are honoured to belong to calls us to affiliate with and participate in modern society and to contribute to its elevation and progress, helping one another with every faculty [to achieve] good and to comprehend, desiring justice for all peoples, while faithfully proclaiming the truth of our religion."

The A Common Word Initiative

In this light, the form and substance of the Amman Message also served as a prelude to the A Common Word initiative. The project formally began as an open letter to Pope Benedict XVI, following his 2006 Regensburg address, in which he seemed to challenge or even accuse the violent tendencies in certain strands of Islamic thought.[11] The final document, which collected many of the same signatories as that of the Amman Message and which relied on a similar core group for its drafting,[12] could be read as an extension of the Amman Message project. In particular, the A Common Word document sought to legitimize a broad theological basis for constructing dialogue between Christianity, Judaism, and Orthodox Islam. Several points are important in this regard. First, the A Common Word document proposes that there exists a basic unity underlying the Christian, Islamic, and Jewish faiths in that (1) all three faiths deepen a call to worship the one true God of Abraham (and to hold no idols before him) and that (2) all three faiths recognize an inseparable link between worship of the one true God and love of neighbor, a love which demands religious individuals and communities to do good works, perform justice, and construct the common good. The A Common Word document, in addressing itself to the Christian community and drawing on the language of Jesus in the gospels, refers to these two points of unity as the two Great Commandants of Love that both religions share.[13]

In an Axial Age framework, the document poses recognition of a transcendent good outside the self (love of God) as both a precondition for the construction of justice (as an expression of love of neighbor) and as being fulfilled by it. In making these claims, the A Common Word document explicitly recognizes the religious worth of Christians (and Jews) and the lengths to which they worship God in truth and in good works. At the same time, the document could also be seen to propose Muhammad as a prophet who witnesses to Christians about the fundamentals of the two Great Commandments which Jesus calls them toward. Hence, the title reference throughout the document is to God's invitation in the Qur'an to Christians and Jews to come to unity, as God instructs the Prophet Muhammad in the Qur'an, "Say: O People of the Scripture! Come to A Common Word between us and you: that we shall worship none but God, and that we shall ascribe no partner unto Him, and that none of us shall take others for lords beside God. And if they turn away, then say: Bear witness that we are they who have surrendered (unto Him)" (Aal 'Imran 3:64).

The presentation of this divine invitation as a call to interreligious unity, which frames the entire document, could be interpreted as an invitation to religious reciprocity: it declares the religious legitimacy of Christianity as recognized in the Qur'an and asks for Christians to do the same. In this respect, one of the important results of the A Common Word document was to advance and synthesize, in a direct public forum, an emerging religious lexicon within Qur'anic exegeses for an expansive reading of the religious legitimacy of religious others, one which enjoyed the support of a diverse block of religious authorities across the Muslim-majority world. The religious syntax of the text, therefore, is important. It holds up and repeats a litany of Qur'anic verses that contemporary Islamic scholars and authorities have relied on to approach religious pluralism and proposes them as a hermeneutical key for understanding the higher objectives of the Qur'an (*maqasid al sharia*). Thus, the A Common Word document gives central importance to the verse "There is no compulsion in religion" (Al-Baqara 2:256), which has been set by a number of declarations and scholars as the fundamental Qur'anic verse in favor of religious freedom in Islam. The document also highlights Qur'anic injunctions to deal kindly and justly with religious others, for example, "God forbiddeth you not those who warred not against you on account of religion and drove you not out from your homes, that ye should show them kindness and deal justly with them. Lo! God loveth the just dealers" (Al-Mumtahinah, 60:8).

The A Common Word text also brings attention to the Prophet Muhammad's oft-remembered respect for a community of Christian monks, about whom the Qur'an says, "They are not all alike. Of the People of the Scripture there is a staunch community who recite the revelations of God in the night season, falling prostrate (before Him)./They believe in God and the Last Day, and enjoin right conduct and forbid indecency, and vie one with another in good works. These are of the righteous./And whatever good they do, nothing will be rejected of them. God is Aware of those who ward off (evil)" (Aal-'Imran, 3:113–115). Finally, the document emphasizes the place of diversity in God's will and his command that humans outdo each other in the performance of good works and the construction of the common good: "For each We have appointed a law and a way. Had God willed He could have made you one community. But that He may try you by that which He hath given you (He hath made you as ye are). So vie one with another in good works. Unto God ye will all return, and He will then inform you of that wherein ye differ" (Al-Ma'idah, 5:48).

Some theologians have criticized the A Common Word document for putting Islam, Christianity. and Judaism on the same religious plane and assuming a theological unity among them, which many theologians would argue does not exist. There are multiple ways of interpreting the text's positions on religious pluralism.[14] That said, it is important to note that while the A Common Word document appeals to unity and spiritual solidarity, it does not make any claims to religious equality or equal paths of salvation. In fact, the appeals made in the text could be understood to be consistent with mainstream reformist Islamic thinking in the region on religious pluralism, which is not of the equal-paths-to-salvation variety. This becomes especially clear when read in light of the network of consultants and signatories of the document, as well as the further development of the document's ideas in the Marrakesh Declaration and the Human Fraternity document, among other recent initiatives in the region.

The Marrakesh Declaration

These forward-developing logics are clearly articulated in the Marrakesh Declaration. The declaration advances the ideas of human dignity, interreligious cooperation, and mutual religious recognition which were highlighted in the Amman Message and the A Common Word document. Significantly, the declaration directly ties these ideas to a concept of active or inclusive citizenship, which it advocates as a political response to the dynamics of religious violence in the region. In his "Legal Framework" paper which outlined the Marrakesh conference's stance on the rights of religious minorities,[15] bin Bayyah (2016) formulates this case. The paper begins with a review of Islamic legal methodology meant to establish the religious authority of the text, its continuity within the tradition of Islam, and its proper application to contemporary problems and changes. The text then turns to the Constitution or Charter of Medina, which the Prophet Muhammad established in 622 CE to form a peaceful alliance with various Jewish tribes of the area following his flight from religious persecution in the city of Mecca. Similar to other contemporary Islamic scholars, including al Qaradawi, Bulaç, Ghannouchi, Gomma,[16] Esack (1997), and Sachedina (2001), the Marrakesh Declaration proposes the Charter of Medina as a foundational exemplar for building a multireligious, citizenship-based political compact in the region. In the paper, bin Bayyah specifically interprets the Medina Charter as an example of contractual and voluntary citizenship which was welcomed by the Jewish tribes of the area[17] and which established equal rights and responsibilities for Muslims and Jews in the city of Medina. In this "contractual citizenship" reading of the Charter of Medina, bin Bayyah has repeatedly referenced Habermas. Speaking at the Council on Foreign Relations in 2015, for example, bin Bayyah remarked, "And also, the question about citizenship, I argued many years ago that the citizenship based on Jürgen Habermas's understanding is actually very, very close to the traditional Islamic view because it's based on a contract. A people, residents of a society have rights and responsibilities as members of that society. In Islam, it does not go back to any tribal affiliation, it doesn't go to color. Even religion, it doesn't go to religion."[18]

The Charter of Medina is presented in the Marrakesh Declaration as formally recognizing and protecting the religious freedom of various religious tribes in the region and for establishing Muhammad as a guarantor of peace among them.[19] Critically, the Charter is also seen to propose a fair and equal distribution of taxes and military duties which enjoined all to work, as one community, in partnership for the peace and welfare of the city.

The Charter of Medina thus is held up in the Marrakesh Declaration as an orienting device for understanding the higher objectives of the Qur'anic message (*maqasid al sharia*), namely, to establish peace, welfare, and dignity between all human beings. It also enables bin Bayyah to address apparent contradictions in the Qur'an on religious freedom, including the "sword verse" (9:29) which contemporary and medieval religious actors have relied on to abrogate other Qur'anic sources calling for peace and mutual recognition among, especially, the peoples of the book. As other contemporary theologians have argued (Tabbara 2017; Sachedina 2001; Esack 1997), bin Bayyah proposes that the sword verse, in addition to other Qur'anic injunctions against peace with Jews or Christians, must be understood within the early historical context of conflict between warring tribes in which the early Muslim community sought to establish its survival. The sword verse is thus interpreted as directed against those specific Jewish and Christian tribes which had broken contracts and taken up arms against the early Muslim community, but not as an abrogating verse directing Muslims to fight against non-Muslims in all places at all times. Bin Bayyah (2016:35) argues that such a scriptural deduction is in contradiction with the underlying and persistent aims of the Qur'an toward human welfare and peace, which he holds up as the "ultimate objective and goals" of all the social values of Islam. Hence, bin Bayyah, drawing on and expanding the exegetical reading of the A Common Word letter and other contemporary Muslim theologians, proposes the verse "There is no compulsion in religion" (al Baqara 2:256) as the better hermeneutical key to understanding the Qur'an. As he writes, agreeing with Tahir bin Ashur.[20] "There is more evidence to suggest that the verse, 'There is no compulsion in faith' is the one that abrogates all rulings pertaining to religious fighting because of its strong language and the ubiquitous presence of its meaning in the Qur'an" (bin Bayyah 2016:23).

Noncompulsion, as expressed in the religious freedom guaranteed to Jewish tribes by the Prophet Muhammad in the Charter of Medina, is held up as the key to establishing and maintaining peace in multireligious societies. In ways which recall the Treaty of Westphalia or debates about tolerance in the early American colonies, the Marrakesh Declaration proposes an agreement on rights and liberties as the political antidote to religious violence.[21] Thus, the first thing the Prophet Muhammad is interpreted as doing after arriving in Medina following a period of religious violence and discrimination in Mecca is to sign a collective and contractually binding security arrangement which declares political rights, religious freedom, and fair taxes for all parties involved.

In formalizing this "peace" reading of the *sharia* with a focus on contractual rights to citizenship, the Marrakesh Declaration, as in the A Common Word document, does not advocate equality-of-salvation-pluralism. Nevertheless, the declaration continues to strengthen the exegetical keys formulated across this period of interreligious dialogue in the Middle East for understanding and approaching the religious other in a positive light from within the tradition itself. The Marrakesh Declaration thus elevates and expands many of the core Qur'anic references of the A Common Word document which have structured international work on interreligious dialogue in the Middle East over the past decade, emphasizing, for example, the Prophet Muhammad and his followers' kindness and respect for some Christians and Jews of the time, and their authentic religious worship as recognized within the Qur'an.

This expanded sense of spiritual solidarity anchors the Marrakesh Declaration's defense of the rights of religious minorities, a term the declaration suggests is itself problematic (2016:63) in Muslim-majority lands. It also anchors the declaration's commitment to interreligious cooperation, which "must go beyond mutual tolerance and respect, to providing full protection for the rights and liberties to all religious groups in a civilized manner that eschews coercion, bias and arrogance."[22] In the unabridged Marrakesh Declaration, the document grounds its idea of citizenship in the God-gifted human dignity and unity which all human beings share as sons or daughters of Adam. Thus, section 1 of the unabridged version of the declaration, titled "Invoking the Universal Principles and Comprehensive Values of

Islam," begins by observing, "God bestowed dignity on all human beings regardless of their race, color, language, or belief, for God breathed His spirit into their forefather, Adam, peace be upon him. The Qur'an says, 'We have dignified the children of Adam'" (17:70). Immediately afterward, the declaration argues that religious freedom represents the logical consequence of such dignity. Thus, the second point of section 1 reads, "This dignity requires that human beings must be granted freedom of choice. The Qur'an says, 'There is no compulsion in religion' (2:256), and 'Had your Lord willed, all the people on earth would have believed. So can you [Prophet] compel them to believe?'" (10:99). The declaration closes by calling upon Muslim scholars and intellectuals to "develop a jurisprudence of the concept of 'citizenship,' which is inclusive of diverse groups. Such jurisprudence shall be both rooted in Islamic tradition and its principles, as well as be mindful of global changes and dynamics today."

In the Marrakesh Declaration, therefore, it is possible to see the consolidation of an interreligious dialogue-informed argument linking God-gifted human dignity, religious freedom, and citizenship. Al Azhar's 2017 declaration includes a similar formulation on citizenship and religious freedom,[23] as does the Charter of the New Alliance of Virtue, signed in 2019 at the Forum for Peace in Muslim Societies' annual conference in Abu Dhabi. The Alliance of Virtue charter also connects its statement on religious freedom to its formulation of human dignity and explicitly recalls *Dignitatis Humanae* in doing so.[24] In making this argument, the Marrakesh Declaration places the concept of citizenship at the center of a theologically justified political project in which religious renewal is connected to the establishment of political rights and freedoms and mutually constructive relations among religious communities. It is in this perspective that bin Bayyah (2016), Hamza Yusuf (2016), and others have characterized the Marrakesh Declaration as a project of religious revival which stands in a positive relationship with modernity and in which Islamic values ground religious and social diversity. As Yusuf (2016:5) writes in his foreword to the publication of the Marrakesh Declaration, "I believe that if Shaykh Abdallah bin Bayyah's methodology—which is nothing other than the revival of normative Islam's methodology for over a thousand years applied creatively and intelligently to the current context—is understood properly by modern Muslim scholars and the educated among the Muslim masses, it will act as a catalyst for not only the revival of a sound Islam but for the preservation and promotion of coexistence among the various colors, creeds, and classes in the long history of Islam."

In formulating these arguments, the Marrakesh Declaration, together with the 2012 and 2017 Al Azhar declarations, have advanced the interreligious dialogue activities and goals of the past decade in the Middle East by linking the promotion of religious belief and belonging to the promotion of religious freedom and citizenship. Like the Catholic Church's formulation in *Dignitatis Humanae* or its embrace of integral human development, this faith-rooted understanding of citizenship sets religious freedom, human solidarity, societal development, spiritual renewal, and religious authority in a positive and necessary relationship. Major religious institutions and authorities across the Middle East have begun to adopt this understanding of citizenship, religious freedom, and dialogue, including the Muslim World League,[25] KAICIID,[26] and new initiatives supported by the Forum for Promoting Peace in Muslim Societies, including the 2019 Alliance of Virtue Charter and the 2021 Charter for Inclusive Citizenship.[27]

The articulation of this reading across multiple declarations marks an important development in official positions among religious authorities in the region on citizenship, pluralism, and religious freedom. They also mark important religious responses to conflicts and violence associated with Islam in the region and make appeals for renewed forms of international cooperation and multireligious solidarity on the basis of these principles. At the same time, as the analysis above indicates, these declarations clearly do not embrace a secular liberal understanding of religious freedom, citizenship, or pluralism. The next section considers how these positions are simultaneously new and distinct by reflecting on the extent to which they represent a genuine development within contemporary Islamic thinking as well as one that purposefully differentiates itself from liberal understandings of democracy, freedom, and the public sphere.

Calibrating Citizenship, Pluralism, and Religious Freedom in Recent Dialogue Declarations

Despite the historical experience of multireligious tolerance across Islamic empires,[28] scholars of Islam have argued that classical medieval Islamic thought, a corpus many contemporary religious authorities in the Middle East draw upon, is in inherent conflict with an understanding of religious pluralism that views various religious traditions as offering equally legitimate paths to salvation or as equally pointing toward the same idea of salvation in the monotheistic God of Abraham (Winter 2013; Khalil 2012; Fadel 2013; Reynolds 2019). While classical Islamic thought did not exclude all non-Muslims from salvation (especially those non-Muslims who had not received the message of Islam and in light of God's divine mercy), and while various contemporary scholars have highlighted the Prophet Muhammad's positive relations with some groups of Christians and Jews, classical Islamic thought adhered to a firm understanding of Islamic supersessionism (Fadel 2013). That understanding made clear that salvation was offered to those believers who responded to the call of the Prophet Muhammad and engaged in good works. This made it difficult and unlikely for non-Muslims to receive certain salvation, to the point that Fadel describes the dominant position as "No salvation outside Islam," in an explicit parallel to the doctrine of *Ex Ecclesiam Nulla Salus*. The A Common Word and Marrakesh documents, which recognize a more positive religious valence of Christian believers within the logic of Islam, reflect an important reformulation of that doctrine by mainstream religious authorities in the Middle East, one which has been further developed over other iterations of interreligious compacts originating in the Muslim-majority world.

The roots of this theological reformulation of religious diversity have been traced to nineteenth- and twentieth-century reformist Islamic thinkers, including the work of Muhammad Abduh and Rashid Rida (Esack 1997; Lynch 2005; Fadel 2013; Warren and Gilmore 2014). These reformists have been characterized as adopting a more expansive understanding of "excuse" for the salvation of non-Muslims which began to recalibrate the integral importance of doing good works in relation to right theological belief and practice, and thereby reframing those the Qur'an designates as "true believers" in the eyes of God. This recalibration was closely knitted into the boader reformist project of reconstructing a rational, critical, and reasoned—that is to say, modernist—understanding of the Qur'an and *hadith*. The reformists believed that the pursuit of a reasoned understanding of the higher aims or objectives of the Qur'anic text, as opposed to the literal emulation of singular, decontextualized bits of scripture, was fully consistent with the Qur'anic tradition and would lead to a more dynamic interpretation and application of Qur'anic objectives to contemporary problems of society and politics. This approach, sometimes reformulated today as a *maqasid al sharia* approach (or *maqasid cum maslaha* approach), has been a major engine driving reformist Islamic thinking of various strands up to the present day (Rane 2012-2013; Duderija 2014; Bano 2018).

A number of contemporary scholars have embraced this critical mode of Islamic reasoning for the way it demands sustained reflection on foundational Islamic principles by individual believers in order to apply them to their decision-making (Auda 2008; Nassery, Ahmed, and Tatari 2018). As Duderija argues (2018), the *maqasid* approach requires substantive engagement on the part of religious believers in order for them to cogently define the higher purposes behind the *sharia* and the Qur'an and to read contemporary problems in light of them.

Although it is not a perfect fit, there is a closeness here to MacIntyre's theory of virtue ethics, with the *maqasid* providing the *telos*—the higher objectives—to which virtues strive and the basis on which reason judges the best interest (*maslaha*) of the common good, and which provides the motivation and the religious moral responsibility to struggle against the self for its achievement. In his work reflecting on the role of natural law in classic Islamic jurisprudence, Emon (2010, 2014) makes this case by describing what he defines as a soft natural law position in medieval Islamic thought, which appealed to Aristotle in ways that recall Maritain or MacIntyre's work. Emon argues that this philosophical tradition continues to inform global Islamic political reflection, including in its attempt to delimit the extent to which human reason in relation to revelation should serve as an independent source of law and politics in modernity.[29] What emerges, Emon argues, is a middle position on the legitimacy of moral human agency which is more restricted than that elevated by liberalism and which is limited by the higher objectives of Islam (*maqasid al-sharia*) as derived from the Qur'an. Emon traces this logic through the work of al Ghazali and his oft-used five higher objectives of the *sharia* to make his point.[30]

Critically, the influence of this approach can be read in the work of a number of contemporary scholars who have helped shape the development of recent dialogue declarations in the region, including Yusuf al Qaradawi and Abdallah bin Bayyah. Al Qaradawi is especially important in this context given his status as a global religious authority in Islam throughout the 1990s and 2000s (Gräf and Skovgaard-Petersen 2009), his involvement as a key signatory of the Amman Message,[31] his role in Qatar's Centre for Moderation and the Doha International Center for Interfaith Dialogue, his ties to the Muslim Brotherhood, and his links to bin Bayyah, who was al Qaradawi's vice president in both the IUMS and the ECFR (Gräf and Skovgaard-Petersen 2009; Caeiro 2011; Warren 2021). It has been argued that the work of both al Qaradawi and bin Bayyah in the ECFR on the minority status of Muslims in Europe (*fiqh al aqalliyyat*) became a key catalyst for the reformulation of the organization's ideas on citizenship, religious freedom, and pluralism (Caeiro 2011; March 2009; Warren and Gilmore 2014). Warren and Gilmore, for example, have described al Qaradawi's evolution on issues of pluralism and citizenship as following a *maqasid* approach which emphasized the comprehensive reasonableness of Islam as a religion and which successively defined human dignity, justice, and peace as the primary guiding objectives of the Qur'an and *sharia*. They argue that such a dynamic led al Qaradawi and others to a hermeneutical reading of the Qur'an which increasingly emphasized the universal salvation of Islam, the human dignity which all humans share assons and daughters of Adam, and the political freedom required of individuals to fairly consider and decide—as into freely choose for themselves—to become Muslim believers. By recontextualizing them according to the higher purpose of Islam, such a reading shifts the emphasis on certain Islamic practices, including *ijaza* taxes on Christians, their status as *dhimmi*, and certain interpretations of *jihad*, all of which had served as sources of inequality in previous Islamic empires (Scott 2010). Thus, various scholars have argued that this reformist approach has led to more forceful support by religious authorities in the region for the concepts of citizenship, religious freedom, a civil state (with an Islamic reference), and cooperation with non-Muslims (both internationally and domestically) as aims that are coherent with the higher purposes of the *sharia* (Eyadat 2012, 2013; Baroudi 2014; Ramadan 2012). This account is clearly reflected in the text of the Marrakesh Declaration analyzed above.

Significantly, al Saify and Caeiro (2009) have observed an evolution in al Qaradawi's and bin Bayyah's language from defending Muslim "religious minorities" in Europe to defending "equal citizenship" for all, especially in their work in the ECFR. Such an approach has connected the problems of Islamophobia in Europe and North America to the increase in violence against religious minorities in the Middle East and endorses religious freedom and equal citizenship as a solution to both. The Forum for Promoting Peace in Muslim Societies' (2019) Alliance for Virtue project could be read as evidence in favor of al Saify and Caero (2009) observation. In many ways, the project has been pitched on an idea of reciprocity in which diverse religious communities pledge to stand up for the religious freedom, safety, and rights of each other in different religious contexts. Thus, the Muslim leaders and communities involved in the project commit themselves to work more actively against violence aimed at Christians and other minorities in the

Middle East, and their Christian and Jewish partners in the United States similarly commit themselves to stand up against Islamophobia.[32]

This internal religious logic is in keeping with Islamic reformist projects[33] which emphasize religious freedom, dialogue, and citizenship as means to living with religious plurality and which frame that project as consistent with the normative foundations of Islam. Some contemporary Muslim scholars have argued that religious freedom allows believers to deepen their faith and at the same time become better citizens through the pursuit of what Soroush (2000:140) has described as an "examined" as opposed to an "emulated" faith in a free Islamic society: "[A] religious society becomes more religious as it grows more free and freedom loving, as it trades diehard dogma with examined faith, as it favors inner plurality over outer mechanical and nominal unity, and as it favors voluntary submission to involuntary subservience."

In Soroush's (2000) reading,[34] this imperative to "examine" is extended to mean not just an examined life of one's own faith in a context of freedom but an examination of the religious other as well, whom God commanded the faithful to *know*, here understood as actively seeking to know the other, whose presence is a sign of God-willed diversity. Echoing the A Common Word and Marrakesh documents, this reading emphasizes the dynamic social, religious, and political energies demanded of individuals by God and implies that surrendering to God's will requires an active construction of God's mercy, peace, and justice for and with all humanity.[35] On this point, Sachedina (2001:43) has similarly highlighted the link between God-willed diversity and God's command to "compete with one another in good works" (Qur'an 5:48) as an imperative for constructing dialogue. Such an imperative, he suggests, requires an earnest engagement with the religious other and can serve as a faith-rooted basis for constructing a plural, democratic society (Sachedina 2001:35). Other contemporary Muslim thinkers have made similar arguments (Auda 2008; Sirry 2009; Ramadan 2012).

Some scholars have seen this understanding of religious plurality in the dialogue efforts and associational life of large Islamic movements like Muhammadiyah and Nahdlatul Ulama in Indonesia and the Gülen movement in Turkey. All three movements have been closely identified with the development of new, national religious-political syntheses in favor of religious and democratic reform in the early 2000s (Hefner 2000; Menchik 2016; Kuru 2007; Yilmaz 2011; Luissier and Fish 2012) and have made interreligious dialogue central to their activities (Barton 2014; Burhani 2011; Catalano 2015; Arifianto 2013). Barton (2014) has identified all three movements as connecting civic engagement and concrete associational life to a strong Qur'anic understanding of *maslaha* and as part of the earnest habits of action assumed by individuals seeking to live a purified life of faith. Competing with one another in good works, especially through the practice of interreligious dialogue by these movements, can create new possibilities for spiritual solidarity and mutual witnessing in a direct, public, untranslated religious language that recalls the experiences of Lubich, Massignon, and de Chergé in the previous chapter. Fethullah Gülen (2004), for example, in an essay describing his vision of interreligious dialogue, recalls a mystical dream experience of Seyyed Nursi, whom Gülen looked to for inspiration, in which Nursi has a vision of various circles of worshipers singing praise to God in the center of all of them. The praise of Christians in this dream unifies and strengthens the praise of Muslims. Burhani (2011) has observed a similar development in the Muhammadiyah, especially among some of its leadership, toward the type of interreligious pluralism that Sachedina (2001:35) describes, in which religious believers view each other as possessing spiritual equality here and in the next world. NU's recent campaign in favor of "humanitarian Islam" (*al islam lil insaniyah*) might also be read in this light. Through a series of multireligious manifestos, declarations, and events,[36] NU has attempted to promote the concept of humanitarian Islam as a source of ongoing religious, social, and political renewal in favor of universal rights, and in response to what it diagnoses as a civilizational crisis within the Islamic world.[37] In 2019, leaders of the Humanitarian Islam movement worked together with the Centrist Democrat International (the global network of Christian democratic parties)[38] to adopt a resolution in Rome[39] which bears witness to the centrality of religious humanism[40] in both of their ongoing efforts to support a faith-inspired human rights agenda:

> We believe that Humanitarian Islam and the diverse strands of humanist philosophy that historically emerged in the West are kindred traditions, whose spiritual and philosophical values are consonant with—and, in the case of Western humanism, helped to shape and secure the adoption of—the Universal Declaration of Human Rights (UDHR).... It is our belief that the spirit of universal human fraternity that animates UDHR, Christian humanism and the global Humanitarian Islam movement represents a compelling moral, ethical, religious and, indeed, political basis for close cooperation between CDI member parties, and between people of goodwill of every faith and nation.[41]

For the Muhammadiyah, however, and in ways that could be extended to NU and the Gülen movement, Burhani (2011:340) has also argued that to "compete with one another in Good works" (which is, in reality, the Muhammadiyah movement's official motto) is understood primarily in its competitive as opposed to religiously egalitarian sense, as in to "outdo each other in good works."[42] This second understanding emphasizes less the spiritual legitimacy of the other and more the command to win the world for Islam and to please God by exceeding the other in the performance of goodness, mercy, and justice.[43] In a parallel way, March (2009) has described the emphasis by some contemporary Islamic scholars on the importance of affection or innate love[44] for religious others (with whom one does not share a higher creedal love), as providing a foundation for civic solidarity between citizens but also calling them to Islam. In this regard, March (2009:222) quotes Faysal Mawlawi, also a member of both the ECFR and IUMS, as saying, "How can a Muslim be a caller of humanity to Islam when he is reluctant even to initiate a greeting, or speak to him a kind word, to the point that non-Muslims suspect that in the Muslim's heart there is no affection ['āt-ifa] for them. . . . If there does not exist a form of affection or respect or good will between you and non-Muslims, then you will never succeed in calling to Islam."

These various understandings of religious humanism, "affection," or "compete-with-the-other" can serve as a basis for interreligious dialogue and multireligious cooperation even as they reject a strong version of internal religious pluralism or equality. On this score, various scholars have highlighted Muhammadiyah's, NU's, and Gülen's promotion of civic and associational life in the region, including through their investment in education, welfare services, and interreligious dialogue peacemaking activities (Barton 2014; Luissier and Fish 2012), such as Muhammadiyah's collaboration with the Catholic community of Sant'Egidio to mediate an end to the Mindanao conflict (Hutchcroft 2018; Community of Sant'Egidio 2014) in addition to NU's Humanitarian Islam campaign.

And yet the religious logic of this understanding of pluralism also denotes its difference from a more liberal understanding of religious pluralism. As Menchik (2016) has argued, Muhammadiyah's and NU's conception of pluralism and tolerance is understood within a framework of what he terms "Godly Nationalism," which extends only to legitimate, Qur'an-defined peoples of the book and which does not, notably, extend to Islamic movements considered heretical—the Baha'is, in particular—nor to atheistic movements like communism. It is, therefore, what Menchik describes as a form of "illiberal tolerance." Similar tensions and ambiguities between liberal and Islamic pluralism can be seen within many of these interreligious declarations and movements and the statements of religious personalities featured in this chapter. The Amman Message, for example, is silent on the status of Baha'is; the A Common Word document does not make a case for interreligious legitimacy or unity with religions outside the people of the book; notions of religious freedom in the Marrakesh Declaration and Alliance of Virtue texts do not challenge blasphemy or apostasy laws;[45] and ambiguities remain in the religious discourses of the authors of these texts on the guarantee of the salvation of Christians and other non-Muslims in the afterlife.[46]

To a certain extent, these "limits" serve to identify the distinct and integral religious worldviews of these initiatives as well as to emphasize that they have not adopted a political framing which separates the transcendent order from the public order and which continues to reject the primacy of a neutral public sphere governed by secular reason between autonomous individuals alone. These interreligious declarations, therefore, consistent with the *maqasid* approach, seek to justify their vision of pluralism in the values and commands revealed in the Qur'an, not in liberalism or a fully independent process of human reasoning. The defense of blasphemy laws, in particular, which essentially preserve the "rights of God" in public,[47] highlight the ways in which these projects ground their meaning and logic in a religiously identified public sphere or state (Ramadan 2012). The formulation of religious freedom in many of these declarations is not understood to be incompatible with a public and legislative defense of God's rights in society. Nor is it incompatible with an understanding that such a defense may help guarantee the social values and norms which make political cooperation and social cohesion viable in these societies.

This alternative reading has led to important disagreements with Western policymakers over the meaning of religious freedom and the forms of religion-state arrangements which might guarantee it. Debates over the final text of both the 2019 New Alliance of Virtue and 2021 Inclusive Citizenship charters, for example, included spirited discussion about the definition of religious freedom. The final text of the New Alliance of Virtue charter rejected a more expansive definition of religious freedom proposed by American participants.[48] Instead, the charter opted for a more general formulation of religious freedom which restated the Qur'anic injunction that "there is no compulsion in religion" and asserted the principle that states are required to protect the religious freedom of individuals without defining in detail what that religious freedom entails.[49]

Regardless of these disagreements, the religious logic of recent dialogue declarations in the region, including language on religious freedom, has not been proposed as an exclusionary religious logic. When the A Common Word document or Marrakesh Declaration evokes the "universal principles and comprehensive values of Islam," it is not to justify openly excluding categories of religious others from political rights or to explicitly delegitimize ideas of democracy, citizenship, and religious freedom, as various Islamists, especially in the 1970s and 1980s, did with similar phrasings. Rather, this language is used to articulate the religious authority and continuity of these principles in order to support citizenship and to promote the active contribution of multireligious societies to the common public interest.[50]

The distinctiveness of this vision of religious freedom and citizenship can be seen in the way that these documents emphasize Article 29 of the Universal Declaration of Human Rights. In particular, part 2 of Article 29 is often recalled: "In the exercise of his rights and freedoms, everyone shall be subject only to such limitations as are determined by law solely for the purpose of securing due recognition and respect for the rights and freedoms of others and of meeting the just requirements of morality, public order and the general welfare in a democratic society." Article 29 is referenced twice in both the 2019 Alliance of Virtue Charter and 2021 Charter for Inclusive Citizenship, implicitly acknowledged in the 2016 Marrakesh Declaration,[51] and is a prominent feature of bin Bayyah's recent writings. In a 2018 keynote address launching their co-sponsored initiative on inclusive citizenship, for example, bin Bayyah argued that two of the primary objectives of inclusive citizenship were to maintain public order and social peace. Referencing Article 29, he stated, "The rights that comprise citizenship must take into account the context of time and place, so as to ensure the balance between the collective rights and the individual rights and thereby preserve public order.... The correct understanding of religious freedom must be connected to social peace, and the principle of freedom of expression, which has become a sacred principle in the prevailing culture, should be linked to the principle of responsibility for the results of expression."

Later in the same text, bin Bayyah approvingly acknowledges the United Arab Emirates' 2015 Law on Combating Discrimination and Hatred, which criminalizes blasphemy *and* discrimination against individuals on the basis of "religion, creed, doctrine, sect, caste, race, colour or ethnic origin."[52]

Once again, in a way that recalls Axial Age debates and recent virtue ethics formulations, the law legally holds up the protection and preservation of the sacred as a political foundation for religious tolerance, social peace, and human rights.[53] Various scholars have expressed concern that this law, and the position it is based on, gives too much latitude to states to abuse their power against dissenting religious individuals in the name of public order and morality (Mumisa 2016; Hayward 2016; Quisay and Parker 2019).

In a striking similarity, Kristina Stoeckl (2014, 2016) has also described this "discovery of Article 29" as a key catalyst in the recent evolution of the Russian Orthodox Church on human rights discourses and, in particular, their shift to embracing the role of an active "norm entrepreneur" in international debates on the theme. As she writes, in a way which captures the dynamic described above, the discovery of Article 29 "allowed the church to position itself no longer simply in opposition to a western progressive understanding of human rights, but instead to actively present itself as the vanguard of a more *original* understanding of human rights according to article 29, an understanding which emphasizes the importance of morality, duties and community. . . . It was the precondition for the ROC to become a norm entrepreneur in the field of international morality politics" (Stoeckl 2016:135).

This originalist embrace of Article 29 and the (re)discovery of what Moyn (2015) has referred to as the profoundly spiritual and communitarian nature of the Universal Declaration of Human Rights has thus found common cause among various religious actors and policymakers across the globe. The Alliance of Virtue project, for example, helped solidify high-level collaboration between US and UAE policymakers on the international religious freedom agenda, despite their disagreements over the definition of religious freedom. Sam Brownback, who was the US ambassador for religious freedom abroad during the Trump administration, participated in an earlier iteration of the Alliance of Virtue pact in 2018 and then again at its 2019 launch. Hamza Yusuf, who helped lead the Alliance of Virtue efforts and who is a close associate of bin Bayyah on the Forum for Promoting Peace in Muslim Societies, was also an important presence at the US-sponsored ministerials on Religious Freedom in 2018 and 2019. US Secretary of State Mike Pompeo appointed Yusuf to the Commission on Unalienable Rights, which was charged with reviewing the role of human rights in US public policy and which was interpreted by many as a conversative effort to resist the expansion of rights language on an array of social issues, including sex

120 THEOLOGIES

and gender. The commission was chaired by the prominent Catholic scholar Mary Ann Glendon (1997, 2002), whose work on the history of the Universal Declaration of Human Rights has also emphasized its roots in the concept of human dignity and cautioned against overly individualist readings of the document.[54]

From a virtue ethics perspective, the recuperation of a "more original" understanding of human rights through the principle of human dignity can serve to reaffirm the task of religious traditions to construct and maintain the kinds of strong moral community which makes the exercise of rights and freedom possible and motivates citizens to work together for the common good. In this sense, and as the name suggests, the Alliance of Virtue project is also intellectually linked to a virtue ethics approach to political life and could be seen to exemplify this approach. William Vendley, emeritus secretary general of the Religious for Peace organization and a member of the Alliance of Virtue steering committee, recently summarized the Alliance of Virtue project and its relationship to human rights:[55]

> Our Alliance of Virtue is an utterly essential compliment [sic] to one of the great achievements of the modern era. We are [in] a period that is dominated by human rights which is a common language for us. We prospered because of it. But rights alone are not enough. Rights protect, but virtues perfect. Virtue is the domain where we raise the question how can we become a good society. Virtues link becoming a good person with becoming a good society. They are the two legs upon which inclusive citizenship can stand firmly. In modernity we are trying to stand on only one leg, the rights leg. It is not enough.[56]

With respect to bin Bayyah (and, by extension, the various dialogue projects he has promoted in the region), al Azami (2019) and Warren (2020) have argued that his essential quietism and his emphasis on loyalty to the nation-state, both of which extoll obedience and reject rebellion (*khuruj*) (Quisay and Parker 2019),[57] have made him a post–Arab Spring counterrevolutionary actor.[58] Warren's (2021) analysis of bin Bayyah's post–Arab Spring writing and activity highlight how his neotraditionalist influences, fears of social chaos, and emphasis on a "jurisprudence of peace" have led him to take a skeptical view of democracy. Above all, Warren argues, bin Bayyah prizes the moral and political authority of the state and the need for social cohesion and stability before democracy. Following the victories of the Islamic

State in 2014, for example, bin Bayyah forcefully asserted the legitimacy of the nation-state within Islamic jurisprudence, rebutting claims by the Islamic State and others about the religious necessity of a caliphate in Islam.[59] In doing so bin Bayyah can also be interpreted as bolstering the political legitimacy of ruling authorities throughout the region, in particular his current host country, the UAE, and embodying the dynamics of authoritarian state-Ulema alliances which Kuru (2019) and others argue have stunted political development in the Muslim-majority world over the long run.

At the same time, bin Bayyah (2016) has crafted his defense of the nation-state and loyalty to its rulers in a way that is consistent with the modernist Islamic logic described above, defining the nation-state as a rational, modern, human innovation which is capable of promoting citizenship and fulfilling political responsibilities to the common good (*maslaha*) and shared international objectives. The realization of these ideals, he argues, requires a gradualist approach guided by careful religious reasoning, moral virtue, and conviction by citizens and scholars: "The solution to our situation does not lie in making a clean break with our history, nor does it lie in becoming imprisoned by the past and launching an all-out war against innovation and modernity. It is by using the set of deductive tools provided for by the religion with expert hands, open minds, and firm religious conviction, without doubt or hesitation, that we can strive for what is in the best interests of humanity" (36).

Notably, as Warren (2021) and others have emphasized, bin Bayyah's support for citizenship, religious freedom, and pluralism has not been coupled with either explicit support or condemnation of democracy as a preferred regime type. On the one hand, therefore, bin Bayyah strongly endorses a contractional understanding of citizens' rights and duties within a modern nation-state and the political necessity of religious freedom and human dignity. On the other hand, however, the Marrakesh Declaration, like the Amman Message, the A Common Word document, or the Makkah Declaration, does not openly advocate for democracy. In fact none of these interreligious documents mentions the word "democracy" at all.[60] All are clearly ambivalent about declaring a preferred regime type or constitutional form for the state, leaving considerable ambiguity about the avenues for participation and decision-making which the state should guarantee to its citizens as well as the extent to which religious authorities might autonomously critique the state when needed. Bin Bayyah's explicit approval of UAE political projects, including its condemnation of the Muslim

Brotherhood as a terrorist organization and its blockade of Qatar, have fed into this perception.[61] Such a forceful insistence on citizenship rights and religious freedom without asserting the political necessity of democracy as a regime type holds out the promise of partnership with the state and ruling authorities to pursue a gradual reform agenda on these ideals together. The ambiguity that results from this silence on the relationship between citizenship and democracy, however, as a regime designed to uphold citizenship, raises important questions about the capacity and the intent of the state to strengthen the former without enacting the latter. It also raises questions about the relative independence of religious authorities envisioned by these declarations and their capacity to challenge state authority when rights are not granted.[62] The book's case studies and conclusion revisit this ambiguity in further detail.

The Human Fraternity Document

A number of the arguments, goals, and dynamics outlined above, which have influenced the development of interreligious dialogue in the Middle East, were on full display in the signing of the Human Fraternity document between Pope Francis and the grand imam of Al Azhar, Sheikh Ahmed al Tayeb, in Abu Dhabi in 2019. The Human Fraternity document represented a landmark moment in the region for a number of reasons. It was the first time a pope had visited and celebrated a public mass in the Arabian peninsula. It was also the first time such a public charter involving al Azhar and the Vatican had been signed and presented to such a wide audience. The immense symbolic weight of the images of Francis embracing al Tayeb, in this sense, was widely noted and greater than the actual representation either garners: although it has been sometimes framed as the meeting of the two highest authorities in Islam and Christianity, neither Sheikh al Tayeb nor Pope Francis can claim to represent those titles in either religious tradition. That the document's conference and signing were held in the UAE was also noteworthy and reflected the strategic vision and diplomatic power of the country's ruling family, who had to negotiate with Egypt's President Fattah al Sisi to allow al Tayeb to make the trip[63] and to convince Vatican diplomats to do the same for Francis.

The language of the document reflects many of the developments highlighted throughout the second part of this book. The Human Fraternity document, like the Marrakesh Declaration, links dialogue to religious freedom, which it defines as the "right to freedom of belief and the freedom to be different." It also adopts a concept of "full citizenship" as a way to overcome what it describes as destructive majority-minority dynamics which inhibit the full, affective bonds of equality and brotherhood. The Human Fraternity document proposes full citizenship as the means to protect the rights of all members of society, but especially the weak, poor, and powerless, whose welfare and being, the document notes, is the central concern of these religions. Critically, the document also proposes the importance of religious renewal as a response to the crises of modernity. The document therefore affirms the "importance of awakening religious awareness and the need to revive this awareness in the hearts of new generations" in order to "confront tendencies that are individualistic, selfish, conflicting, and also address radicalism and blind extremism." The document further locates the causes of "the crises of the modern world" in "a desensitized human conscience, a distancing from religious values and a prevailing individualism accompanied by materialistic philosophies that deify the human person and introduce worldly and materialist values in place of supreme and transcendental principles" (Human Fraternity document 2019).[64]

The document's theme of fraternity[65] is at once innovative but also consistent in the way it builds on prior developments in the region, and in both religious traditions, which have increasingly emphasized mutually enriching spiritual witness and multireligious solidarity.[66] The proposed role of religion in fostering fraternity and social cohesion can be read as presenting a classic public role of religion in society and that hoped for from religion by a wide range contemporary political theorists, namely, regenerating social solidarity, as argued in Chapter 2. With its dual emphasis on citizenship and solidarity—and its insistence that one requires the other and that both require a social-religious reawakening—the document continues in the vein of the Marrakesh Declaration in its construction of an increasingly positive political proposition for development in the region. In this sense, the document is less dominated by any defensive discourse which marked earlier interreligious declarations in the post-9/11 era, which had sought to disassociate religion from violence and conflict or discrimination against minorities. Instead, the document outlines a positive political vision for how to live together well in society, urging its religious members and communities to take care of the poor and the elderly and the environment and drawing on religious language and theology to do so.

In his *Fratelli Tutti* encyclical, published on October 3, 2020, which was presented as a further development of the themes addressed in the Human Fraternity document,[67] Pope Francis (2020) continues in this vein. Thus, the encyclical advances an idea of "religions at the service of fraternity in our world" (§271). It lifts the Human Fraternity document's insistence on citizenship and argues that transcendent religious horizons are necessary for the construction of a political foundation that can protect and sustain human dignity and religious pluralism. Like the Human Fraternity document, *Fratelli Tutti* lauds the virtues of multilateralism and the responsibility of religious actors to work in partnership with their governing authorities for the common good. Directly quoting from the Human Fraternity document, *Fratelli Tutti* also condemns individualism, materialistic philosophies, and the closing of the public sphere to religion, emphasizing instead the responsibility and necessity of religion to generate social solidarity. Francis writes, "As believers, we are convinced that, without an openness to the Father of all, there will be no solid and stable reasons for an appeal to fraternity. We are certain that only with the awareness that we are not orphans but children, can we live in peace with one another" (§272). Quoting Benedict XVI's 2009 encyclical *Caritas in Veritate*, he continues, "[R]eason, by itself, is capable of grasping the equality between men and of giving stability to their civic coexistence, but it cannot establish fraternity" (§272).

The Human Fraternity document, therefore, reflects the analysis of the arc of documents in both Catholicism and Islam presented in the chapters of this second part of the book, and the political theology either tradition has formulated to synthesize ideas on freedom, multireligious solidarity, citizenship, and religious growth or renewal. As these chapters have argued, the development of theological perspectives in each tradition to support this vision has involved intellectual reformulations about the meaning and desirability of religious pluralism and the spiritual worth and political rights of religious others vis-à-vis core revealed truth claims. In many ways, the text also reflects the insights of postsecularism and post-Islamism, especially in its interreligious advocacy for religious authorities, communities, and individuals to publicly contribute to the construction of viable projects of citizenship and political solidarity. The Human Fraternity document, like its recent predecessors, is also squarely postsecular and post-Islamist in its approach to global politics. According to the document, international cooperation requires a strengthening of citizenship rights and freedoms at the domestic level, but also social renewal through religious and spiritual awakening: "[T]here exists both a moral deterioration that influences international action and a weakening of spiritual values and responsibility." Therefore, responding to current international crises will require religious-cultural renewal and the development of a "culture of dialogue" which prizes and orients international cooperation. This perspective can also be understood as responding to the tensions and limits raised by debates on the Axial Age and postliberal virtue politics presented in Chapter 2. By combining acceptance of religious pluralism with promotion of public and inculturated religious authority, these interreligious dialogue initiatives seek to keep the division between sacred and profane for society and use it to mobilize for social cohesion.

At the same time, despite their insistence on full citizenship, religious freedom, and the religious desirability of diversity,[68] the Human Fraternity document, too, remains silent on the question of democracy. In part, this silence certainly represents the political context of the host country, the UAE, but it is also consistent with the 2016 Marrakesh Declaration and the 2017 al Azhar declaration, among others.[69] This silence reflects the ambivalence about democracy in the aftermath of the Arab Spring assumed by a number of senior religious leaders and their conviction that, at the moment, strengthening social cohesion and stability is more important than democracy. In these declarations, and reflected in the Human Fraternity document, these religious leaders can be seen to make a religious appeal for a more inclusive society that is guaranteed by political rights, religious freedom, and affective social cooperation. In doing so, they have increasingly emphasized an ideal of full, inclusive, or comprehensive citizenship, which includes active citizen participation in society and politics. They have simultaneously avoided any detailed discussion of the constitutional form or limits on state power that such politics might require.

While this chapter has attempted to establish how these new theological perspectives reflect mainstream religious reflection, including its endorsement by a growing network of influential religious authorities in the Middle East, one of the recurrent questions about interreligious dialogue is whether these authorities have lost their relevance and credibility. Many citizens across the Middle East, especially youth, do not recognize the religious authority of official and mainstream Islam, which is viewed as a co-opted, spent force, nor are they attracted to its theological positions. As a result, many everyday youths have turned to more dynamic religious proposals outside the realm of Official Islam or have simply lost interest in religious matters altogether. The social and political aspirations of Middle East youth, in other words, which these new theologies are in part designed to respond to, may bar their very viability. The sustainability of these interreligious dialogue ideas and their capacity to inspire social change therefore remain important questions. In order to address these questions, the next part of the book explores the experiences of two communities of youth participants in interreligious dialogue activities in Lebanon and Algeria as well as the evolution over time of two state-based institutions of dialogue promoted by Qatar and Saudi Arabia.

PART III
PRACTICES

6
Comparative Contexts

Introduction

A central claim of postsecular and post-Islamist scholarship is that contemporary political change has been conditioned by society-wide shifts in patterns of religiosity which were made possible by long-running processes of modernization and democratization. As a result, the capability of the state (as analyzed in Part I) or religious authorities and ideas (as analyzed in Part II) to regulate, direct, and guide their local religious fields has become increasingly dependent on the new religious practices and beliefs assumed by individuals in the current global and religiously plural environment. Within this framework, therefore, support for interreligious dialogue initiatives by the state or by religious authorities could be seen to reflect contemporary transformations of religiosity but also to be beholden to them.

The chapters in this last part of the book consider these dynamics through four case studies of interreligious dialogue activity in the Middle East today. These case studies serve to examine the sociological context of interreligious dialogue initiatives in the Middle East in light of the theoretical expectations developed in the book so far. Together, the case studies measure the insights of postsecularism and post-Islamism and, in doing so, resituate both the state-centered and ideational-centered accounts of interreligious dialogue analyzed in Parts I and II. The first two case studies, on the Focolare community in Algeria and the Adyan Foundation in Lebanon, focus on the religious experience of participants, especially youth participants, and the relationship of their experiences to the development of particular attitudes and practices of political and civic life. Both chapters ask to what extent participants in interreligious dialogue are likely to become more active agents in their religious and political activity and to assume more democratic religious attitudes and practices. To what extent, in other words, can these religious experiences be described as favoring "individualized" or "authenticated" religious choices and practices? And how do such processes of authentication or individualization impact the social desires and actions of these same participants? The second two case studies examine the extent to which these dynamics are also reflected in the experience of two state-supported interreligious initiatives in the Gulf, namely the Doha International Center for Interreligious Dialogue (DICID), sponsored by Qatar, and the King Abdulaziz International Center for Interreligious Dialogue (KAICIID), sponsored by Saudi Arabia. Following the expectations raised by the theoretical framework of Chapter 2, these chapters employ the case studies to analyze whether these initiatives reflect dynamics of religious change, citizenship development, and solidarity production.

This first chapter begins with a brief introduction to the four case studies in order to place them in their comparative political and religious contexts as well as present the research methodology and data assembled for each one.

Case Selection and Comparative Contexts

The four case studies presented in the following chapters capture a range of religious characteristics, organizational structures, and relationships with state institutions that reflect the dynamic variety of interreligious dialogue initiatives in the region today. Chapter 7 begins with an examination of the Focolare community in Algeria, which belongs to what might be described as an international, grassroots, Catholic-inspired religious movement whose Algerian members are predominantly Muslim. Chapter 8 examines the experience of the Adyan Foundation in Lebanon, which could be described as a nongovernmental, civil society organization that draws on the support of a grassroots network of participants. The Adyan Foundation was founded by five individuals from different religious backgrounds in Lebanon and is currently directed by two of them, Nayla Tabbara, a Sunni theologian, and Fadi Daou,[1] a Maronite priest. Finally, Chapter 9 examines two international centers promoting interfaith dialogue originating in the Gulf, namely DICID and KAICIID. While the initiatives differ in their structure—KAICIID, notably, was created as a transgovernmental organization—both are state-sponsored institutions, initiated within the Muslim world, and have close ties to their respective foreign ministries.

This range of initiatives, communities, and organizations, from the grassroots to the state-based, helps to maximize variation on two key parameters of interest for this study: the religious nature of the initiative and its relationship to the state. As such, these four case studies better allow us to

COMPARATIVE CONTEXTS 131

register the sociological and religious dynamics produced and reflected in contemporary interreligious dialogue activity in the Middle East as well as the links between those dynamics and the questions of state interests, religious authority, and political theologies raised throughout the book.

These initiatives differ not only in their organizational form, origins, and activities but also in the political and religious context in which they operate. Table 6.1 charts several baseline religious and political characteristics of the countries hosting or sponsoring these initiatives, namely Algeria, Lebanon, Qatar, and Saudi Arabia, using the most recent Arab Barometer and World Values Survey data available for them. The table confirms the outlying position that many scholars of the Middle East assign to Lebanon, in terms of both its religious makeup and religious and political attitudes within the Arab world. Thus, Lebanese respondents are significantly less likely than their counterparts elsewhere to describe themselves as a religious person, regularly attend religious services, or pray daily. Lebanese respondents are also more likely to hold what might be termed inclusivist or pluralist attitudes toward individuals of other religions: they are the most likely to believe that "people who belong to different religions are probably just as moral as people who belong to mine" and the least likely to agree that "the only acceptable religion is my religion." Lebanese respondents also score higher on a number of issues which we might categorize as registering support for political secularism, that is to say, a public and political sphere highly distinct from the religious sphere: Lebanese respondents are the least likely to support legislation based on *sharia* law and the least likely to be in favor of religious influence on elections or lawmaking.[2] Some of these differences in attitudes likely reflect the religious diversity already present in Lebanon, which has a sizable population of Christian and other non-Muslim religious communities, like the Druze community.

While different, however, Lebanon's attitudes on democracy, religious pluralism, and religiosity are not unique or fully disjoint from its neighbors' in the region. The survey results, for example, indicate significant support for democracy in all four of these countries, including in Saudi Arabia and Qatar (where 73% of respondents ranked the importance of democracy as 8 or higher on a scale of 1–10), in addition to similarly high levels of religious identification, even in Lebanon (where 63% of respondents reported praying on a daily basis). Likewise, while Lebanon's levels of religious diversity are distinct, all four countries have been shaped by important dynamics of pluralism. This includes the relatively high levels of intra-Islamic diversity

Table 6.1 Religious Characteristics of Algeria, Lebanon, Qatar, and Saudi Arabia

		Algeria	Lebanon	Qatar	Saudi Arabia	Survey and Wave
Religiosity	Religion is very important in life	90.7%	52.9%	98.9%	88.7%	WVS6 (2010–2014)
	Religion is very important in life (youth age 18–29)	88.5%	49.2%	100%	88.5%	WVS6 (2010–2014)
	Pray daily (always)	79.6%	63.2%	–	87.8%	AB2 (2011)
Religion in Public Life	Religious practices are private and should be separated from social and political life (agree)	62.6%	87.8%	–	37.9%	AB2 (2011)
	Support for Islamic law (agree)	68.7%	23.2%	92.3%	–	AB2 (2011)
	Support for democracy (agree)	67.4%	81.3%	73.4%	55.9%	AB2 (2011)
Religious Pluralism	Only my religion is the right religion (agree)	91.6%	45.8%	97.6%	–	WVS6 (2010–2014)
	People who belong to different religions just as moral (agree)	33.2%	71.3%	55.9%	–	WVS6 (2010–2014)
	Would not want to have religious others as neighbors (agree)	28.7%	4.8%	11%	45.1%	AB2 (2011)
	Religious minorities have the right to practice their religious ceremonies (agree)	59.6%	91.9%	–	56%	AB2 (2011)
Religious Demographics	Total Muslim population	**98.3%**	**60.8%**	**72.8%**	**91.7%**	RCS (2015)
	Sunni	97.4%	28.1%	63.4%	81.9%	RCS (2015)
	Shia	0.4%	27.7%	8.7%	9.3%	RCS (2015)
	Total Christian population	**0.1%**	**32.5%**	**10.5%**	**4.4%**	RCS (2015)

Political Characteristics						
GDP/capita (current US$)		$4,115	$8,270	$68,794	$23,340	World Bank (2018)
Human Development Index (rank)		82nd	93rd	41st	36th	UN Development Program (2018)
Democracy Index		NF (35)	PF (43)	NF (24)	NF (7)	Freedom House 2018 (status and aggregate score on scale of 1–100)

All survey data use most recent available data from World Values Survey (WVS) Wave 6 (2010–2014) and Arab Barometer (AB) Wave 2 (2011). Saudi Arabia data on the World Values Survey come from Wave 4 of the data (2003), the most recent available year. Qatar data for support for democracy and desirability of religious neighbors are from WVS Wave 6 (2010). Cells report respondents who strongly agreed or agreed to each statements. Full wording of the questions can be found in the Appendix.

Data on religious neighbors from WVS Survey from Wave 6 (2010) were used for Qatar. Respondents were asked to choose as many categories from a list of various groups of people they would *not* like to have as neighbors. In contrast, for the Arab Barometer Survey data (reported in the table), respondents were asked to specifically choose whether or not they objected to having "followers of other religions" as neighbors. For the WVS Survey, 42.7% of Algerian and 33.8% of Lebanese respondents mentioned not wanting to have "people of a different religion" as neighbors, notably higher than in the Arab Barometer data.

Religious demographics taken from Religious Characteristics of States Dataset Project year 2015. GDP/capita from World Bank Data and Human Development Index from the UN Development Program, all for year 2018.

in Qatar and Saudi Arabia (both of which have sizable minorities of Shia adherents), as well as their growing populations of Christians. And while Algeria would appear to be the most religiously homogeneous of these four countries, its contemporary history has been strongly marked by other forms of ethnic and linguistic diversity, as expressed, for example, in the political and linguistic claims of its Amazigh movements. The table also indicates important distinctions which scramble the way states in the Middle East are often lumped into more open/secular categories as opposed to more closed/conservative ones. Despite sharing a longer history of constitutional reform and support for secularism with Lebanon, for example, Algerian respondents were the least likely of the group to agree that people who belong to different religions were "just as moral." And on other measures of religious pluralism Algerian respondents were closer to the more traditionally identified Gulf states than to Lebanon.[3] These variations, as each case study will explore, have also developed upon diverse experiences of authoritarian rule, economic development, and political conflict, which have shaped the religious and political landscape in which individuals participate in interreligious dialogue activities.

Data Collection

For each of the four cases, visits were made to the initiative's principal institutions and centers; interviews were conducted with the initiatives' founders, directors, and employees (where applicable); and primary data materials were gathered on each initiatives' activities. In the case of the two nongovernmental initiatives, the Focolare Community and the Adyan Foundation, semi-structured interviews were conducted with participants in their youth programs drawing on a ten-question survey instrument. The survey, which was translated into English, Arabic, and French, was also offered to participants who were unable to join in a physical interview, either through email or social media. Over a five-year period (2014–2019), with longer summer stays in Algeria and Lebanon in 2017 and 2018 and shorter trips to Egypt, Jordan, UAE, Austria, and Qatar throughout, a total of 153 face-to-face interviews were conducted, including a little more than 50 interviews each with the Focolare community and the Adyan Foundation (with at least 25 interviews with youth participants in each initiative), and 10 interviews each with KAICIID and DICID. As points of reference, another

35 interviews were conducted with a variety of other interreligious dialogue initiatives in the region, including the Gülen movement in Turkey and the community of Sant'Egidio in Rome, both of which can be categorized as religious movements; the Royal Institute for Interfaith Studies in Jordan and the Coptic Evangelical Organization for Social Services in Cairo, both civil society organizations operating with more and less state support, respectively; and the Forum for Promoting Peace in Muslim Societies, which enjoys close ties to the Ministry of Foreign Affairs in the UAE. Another 30 participants in Algeria, Egypt, Lebanon, and Jordan responded in writing to the survey.

The survey questions are included in the Appendix . As the questionnaire illustrates, the survey was designed to capture narrative arcs in the individual's religious and political trajectories. It was therefore intended to serve as a qualitative instrument to gauge the religious, political, and social meaning of interreligious dialogue for each participant; the changes in attitudes and practices these individuals have experienced following participation in interreligious dialogue activities; and the reception to and interaction with their political, social, and familial environments that they perceived this activity created. In general, the survey attempted to measure whether the religious activity of participants in interreligious dialogue increased, was simultaneously marked by greater openness to religious pluralism, and was linked to higher levels of associational life and civic activism.

With regard to religious dynamics, the questions asked participants about the relationship of their interreligious dialogue activity to the development of their personal religiosity and attitudes about religious institutions and authorities. They also solicited views about individuals from other religions, the relationship of religion to the state, and the legitimacy of interreligious dialogue as a religious endeavor. With regard to social dynamics, the survey asked participants about their social and civic activities and whether they perceived a relationship between their participation in interreligious dialogue activities and the development of their communities and countries. It also asked participants to gauge the social reception and legitimacy of interreligious dialogue in their countries and, in particular, whether their participation was supported and viewed positively by their immediate families and home communities. With regard to politics, the survey asked participants about the political dimensions of their participation in interreligious dialogue activities and whether they understood their activity as a force for democratization and peace in their countries, as well as whether they believed it played a part in counteracting religiously expressed violence and exclusionary politics. Finally, the surveys asked participants about their views on the relationship between religious and political authority and the role of states in promoting interreligious dialogue and religious pluralism.

The interviews, drawing on the survey questions, provide an account of how participants in interreligious dialogue activities in the Middle East understand and communicate about themselves; how they position themselves vis-à-vis official religious authorities and theology; and what social, religious, and political future they hope their interreligious dialogue activities might foster.

7
The Focolare Community (Algeria)

Introduction

The origins of the Focolare community in Algeria date to 1966, when the community was gifted a Benedictine monastery in the town of Tlemcen, in the west of Algeria, following the end of the Algerian war and the flight of most Europeans from the country (Dutru 2018). As Chapter 4 began to describe, a number of Catholic priests, nuns, and religious communities remained in Algeria following independence, led by Cardinal Léon-Étienne Duval, who was then the archbishop of Algiers and who had been opposed to the war and in favor of independence. These questions had bitterly split the Catholic Church in France, especially among French *pieds-noirs* living at the time in Algeria, most of whom would leave for France in the years following the end of the war in 1962. Following independence, the Algerian government took control over much of the Catholic Church's land, buildings, and properties, converting churches into a variety of public buildings and projects. Many Catholic clergy who remained in Algeria after the war renounced their French citizenship in order to do so, often in response to what they felt was a vocation to work for reconciliation with Muslim Algerians after the brutality of the war.

It is in this context that the Focolare community arrived in Algeria, at a time when the community had not yet developed a clear vision or theology of interreligious dialogue and was not looking to expand into Muslim North Africa. Nevertheless, somehow the invitation fit into the community's desire to foster "friendship, peace and unity" in the world. The Benedictine monastery had been constructed during the Second World War by Dom Raphael Walzer, who had been a spiritual director of Edith Stein and had to flee Nazi Germany. Walzer had built the monastery with the intention of creating a school and being a place of service to the poor in Algeria (Cocchiaro 2006). The community sent three members to take up residence in the monastery and establish a *focolare*, a home of celibate laymen (or women) which forms the central core of the Focolare community. The three men renamed the monastery Dar-Es-Salam and dedicated it as a center intended to create friendship for and with the local community. The small group knew very little about Islam or Algeria. Archbishop Henri Teissier (1984, 1998), who became bishop of nearby Oran in 1972, worked closely with the community to help them articulate their presence in Tlemcen and, later, in Oran and Algiers, in harmony with the Algerian Church's developing vision of its non-proselytising presence in Algeria, a vision which the Focolare members eagerly embraced.

Ulisse Caglioni, an Italian from Bergamo who lived for thirty years in Algeria, became a point of reference for the small community, his personality and actions giving their history in the country form and substance. Ulisse was a handyman with mechanical experience and had worked in a number of industrial jobs in Europe before coming to Algeria. He sought the friendship of his neighbors by building, repairing, and constructing homes and cars in anticipation of what he understood to be their needs. For many years, the small group of Focolare worked without a formalized program or goal, other than to seek to live in "unity" and "love" with their neighbors. European members of the community from that period recall a time of "hidden work," a slow, long, discrete period of building trust, of convincing their neighbors that their only agenda was to live in solidarity with them, that they did not harbor designs to proselytize or judge them. They also recall it as a time of learning to recognize and love their new setting. One of Ulisse's companions described that time thus: "We were not used to confronting ourselves with such a different culture from our own. So we had to undergo a deep conversion. Ulisse was a master in this and he helped us, through his example, to accept the other as they were, without asking anything in return. We began to perceive this world not through our own schema but with their eyes, without judgement, looking only to the positive and to that which united us" (quoted in Cocchiaro 2006:55). Early Muslim friends, neighbors, and members of the community recall a similar period and describe how they did not quite know at first what to make of these rather ordinary, simple European men who were mechanically adeptthey, and that they did not understand what the men's desire to live "in unity" with them meant. In interviews, many of the early Muslim members of the community described being intrigued and eventually drawn toward Ulisse's kindness; his honest, spiritual presence, the transparency of his work, and his steadfast attention to the needs of his neighbors.

Over time, the community grew. Two women established a Focolare home in Algiers in 1967, and a growing cadre of Algerians, including young persons and families from Tlemcen, Oran, and Algiers, began to join the group for meals, reflection, and spiritual sharing. More Focolare members visited them from Europe. Critically, the group formed a friendship with a local imam in Tlemcen, Hadj Ahmed Barkat, whose son had begun to frequent the group of youth forming under Ulisse's guidance. These Muslim Algerian friends began to participate in Focolare activities, including group reflections on the community's "word of life," a monthly gospel phrase often with a meditation by Chiara Lubich, the founder of the Focolare community, and annual *mariapoli*, retreats in which the entire community, Algerians and Europeans, would spend several days together in the Dar-Es-Salam center for prayer, songs, and celebration.

In the early 1990s, the community experienced what came to be a defining moment in their history. Following the victory and then invalidation of the Front Islamique du Salut's electoral results in 1992, Algeria entered a period of violence between armed Islamist groups and government and paramilitary groups (sometimes with shadowy ties to the armed Islamist groups). Although most of the violence was suffered by Muslim Algerians, European Christians, and those who defended them, became high profile-targets during this period. After a time of reflection, many of the religious communities decided to continue to live in their homes in order to remain faithful, as they saw it, to their mission of friendship with their Algerian neighbors. Between 1994 and 1996, nineteen religious brothers and sisters were killed in the violence,[1] including seven Trappist monks at the Notre Dame d'Atlas monastery in Tibhirine. One of them, Christian de Chergé, the prior of the Tibhirine monastery, had been an important figure promoting interfaith solidarity and spirituality in Algeria and knew the Focolare's Dar-Es-Salam center in Tlemcen well. More than one hundred imams were also killed, including Islamist leaders, for refusing to sign a fatwa justifying the killing of Christians in the country. In 2018, as the Catholic Church beatified the nineteen martyred religious, it also sought ways to remember these imams and their act of solidarity with the Christians of Algeria.[2]

During this time, a core group of Algerian Muslims found themselves being drawn closer to the Focolare home in Tlemcen, whose members had also decided to remain in Algeria. Focolare friends from Oran and Tlemcen would travel in the evening to spend the night in the community home, especially during periods when the violence worsened in the West of Algeria. In interviews, older members of the community in Oran and Tlemcen recalled hearing the sound of bullets whizzing overhead as they drove up the hill behind Tlemcen, where the Focolare home is located. Their friendship with the community intensified. At the time, there was no precedent for Muslims to formally join the Focolare community, and yet, during this period, the Algerians began to fully identify themselves as such. A group of them eventually wrote to Lubich and requested that they no longer be considered "Muslim friends of the community," as they were frequently referred to, that such a designation was not coherent with the charisma they had received from the community and which they were faithfully living out. The Christian leaders of the community recognized that the Algerians were actively participating in the construction of the community's religious self-understanding, helping the community to redefine or, as they would say, view their own charisma better. In interviews, various Algerian members said they had grown to understand that the spirituality of the Focolare did not belong to Christianity alone and that they had begun to live out the Focolare ideals of love and unity within their own Islamic spirituality. Lubich responded to their desire in the affirmative, and the Algerians of Tlemcen became the first Muslim members and families of the community.

While numbers are difficult to judge, community leaders estimated that there are now between six hundred and a thousand Algerians who might count themselves members of the community or who regularly participate in community events, spread out principally among the cities of Algiers, Oran, and Tlemcen, but with families in more remote cities, like Béni Abbès, also participating in the community. The community continues to host a *mariapoli* every year at their Dar-Es-Salam center in Tlemcen; the demand has grown so great that the community can no longer host everyone on its grounds. The center also holds conferences on Muslim-Christian dialogue and hosted a large, international Muslim Focolare conference in 2016. The center also helps animate the formation of new generations of Focolare members, a growing number of youth of various ages, who participate in international Focolare events during the summer and meet regularly throughout the year to prepare for the events, as well as for times of sharing and reflection. It is to the reflections of these Muslim youth that this chapter now turns. In nearly every interview, with both the youth and elder members of the community, the theme of spirituality emerged as a central term which participants used to explain their initial attraction to the Focolare community in Algeria and to describe the type of religious growth and change they experienced after joining. The chapter considers how participants characterized the spirituality they developed during their time in the Focolare community and how their spirituality related to their social and political attitudes, hopes, and actions.

Interreligious Dialogue, Spirituality, and Religious Life

Many participants used the term "spirituality" to describe how and why they were originally attracted to the Focolare community. They described experiencing an initial curiosity about the community, sometimes after hearing about friends participating in the group. The ideals they expressed (and, especially *how* they expressed them) intrigued them enough to visit the Focolare center or participate in a Focolare event. In many of the interviews, participants said it was the unexpected atmosphere of warmth, happiness, love, and fraternity they encountered during these initial events and visits that drew them further in. Oftentimes, these feelings were associated with the presence of one specific member of the Focolare, such as Ulisse, but also often with the place of the Focolare home itself, particularly the Dar-Es-Salam center in Tlemcen. Various participants said they did not want to leave "that place" and wanted to spend more time with "these people." As one young man described spending time with the Focolare home, "When I come here, it is happiness, it is God, we do things, we serve others."[3] Another said, "When I first came, I felt an enormity of peace and I saw people with strength and coherence and that is what I wanted."[4] Yet another explained, "When I first came to the Focolare I wanted to stay, I wanted to spend all my time there, with Gesim, I don't know why, but that place, I wanted to be there. And it gave me peace."[5]

Here, "spirituality" becomes a way to describe what was most attractive about the Focolare community for the Muslim participants, not the specific Christian identity, history, or practices of the group but its spiritual way of living, which Muslims felt they could also live, including its emphasis on practicing the "art of love," cultivating a "listening presence" with others, and the centrality of "reciprocal love" and "service" as guiding principles. Critically, as various Algerian members pointed out, the community emphasized the gratuitous nature of these ideals, as a love which is "freely poured out," which "expects nothing in return." This understanding of love as gratuitous was a key for both Muslim and Christian members in their approach to dialogue and anchored their mutual conviction that the love they witnessed to did not seek anyone's religious change. Rather, in ways which recall the Pontifical Council for Interreligious Dialogue's remarks on inculturation, diversely religious members simply tried to see and encourage what was already deeply good in each other's lives.

Often, members described these spiritual values and practices as a form of religious humanism and as having a "humanizing" effect on them. Muslim participants expressed how they had learned to become "more human" through the Focolare community, that is, more alive to their surroundings, their neighbors, their faith, and the meaning of their own existence. In this sense, the term "spirituality" was also a way for the Algerian members to speak about their experience with Christians in the Focolare community in shared religious terms. To that end, several of the "elder" Algerian members of the community who counted themselves members for twenty or thirty years were deliberate in their characterization of their membership as a form of "dialogue of life," one of the Pontifical Council for Interreligious Dialogue's categorizations, as opposed to, especially, a "dialogue of theology." Although theology is important for many of them, by referring to "dialogue of life," these members emphasized the prevailing dimension of "community" that characterizes their shared lives together with Muslim members in Algeria and Christian Focolare members further away, in Europe and elsewhere. In other words, the Algerian community sought to prioritize the intimacy and intentionality with which they have structured their lives around each other's needs and joys and sorrows.

In this sense, various members expressed unease at describing their activity in the Focolare community as a form of interreligious dialogue, as if that implied their primary action and sense was to be in dialogue, to increase their knowledge about Christianity, or to explain Islam to others. The theological framework of the Algerian community, in this sense, is quite loose and unimposing. The lived experience is primarily one of building community, of sharing with and serving one another. As one longtime Muslim member in Oran said, "This is not dialogue. This is living religiously together. We are not trying to figure Christians out. We are within the community. We are already in the family, sharing everything, and that is not a problem. Dialogue is surpassed."[6] A Christian member of the community in Algeria put it this way: "We forget that they are Muslims and vice versa. We are walking together on a path towards the truth, in confidence, trusting in the experience of love, of the Muslims themselves, that God is there, that we are all one, that God is bigger than all that."[7]

Here the central practice and experience of community, not a strategy of dialogue, orients the interactions between Muslims and Christians and the development of their understanding and practice of religious pluralism. As various members remarked, shared moments of faith and spirituality developed out of their friendships in an organic, spontaneous, natural way, not structured by a predetermined theological program or explicit formation. "We sing Christian songs, and vice versa, without any complex,"[8] one young man put it. In this, as Roberto Catalano (2010:47), co-director of the Focolare Community's Center for Interreligious Dialogue, notes, the Focolare community did not have a thought-out plan when it came to interreligious dialogue but followed the spiritual intuitions of the moment, letting the experience of interreligious friendship, and their spiritual testimony, to guide the development of their interreligious encounters.

"Spirituality" therefore offers a way for community members to describe the nature of their interfaith friendships and community that goes beyond a specifically Muslim or Christian framework. At the same time, "spirituality" is also a way to describe the religious growth that members experience, and the relationship of that growth to their specific religious traditions. In nearly all of the interviews, participants described a deepening of their lives of faith, as Muslims (or Christians), following their time with the Focolare community. Oftentimes, this spiritual growth was described as a "transformation" of faith. In these cases, Muslim participants would often describe a discovery of "Muslim spirituality" or a "spiritual reading" of Islam or the Qur'an through an encounter with the spiritual life of the Focolare community. Christian participants, too, would describe how the discovery and encounter of Muslim spirituality led to an expanse and deepening of their Christian spirituality. In describing their "discovery of Muslim spirituality," Algerian members of the community emphasized the personal "awakening" of their faith from that of an unconscious Muslim identity. "I was a non-practicing Muslim, well, a Muslim by default," one young Algerian described his faith before coming to the Focolare;[9] another young Algerian described her experience within the Focolare as the discovery of a "spiritual Islam, Islam as a religion of peace, humanness, love, tolerance."[10] Thus, participants described the discovery of an Islam of the heart, an "interior Islam," as one member put it.[11] Another young Algerian said of his time with the Focolare, "[It] liberated me, to live, to rediscover my faith as a Muslim, to practice Islam, to understand Islam."[12] "I began to see the Qur'an with new eyes of love," said another Algerian member.[13] Farouk Mesli, one of the Muslim leaders of the Algerian community, related, "We had not understood anything in the Qur'an until then."[14]

There is a clear way, therefore, in which spiritual Islam describes the discovery of a living, conscious Islam, and the development of a religiosity that would fit Deeb's (2006:113) description of "authenticated Islam" or "purposeful and knowledgeable Islam." Adnane Mokrani, a Muslim theologian with close links to the Algerian Focolare community,[15] described how it had provided "interreligious pastoral work" for Algerian Muslims.[16] The presence and approach of the Focolare community encouraged the cultivation of the interior spiritual life of Muslim Algerians, a cultivation which had been submerged in recent years in Algeria by the domination of both politicized religious discourse and an ossified state Islam. Cheikh Sari-Ali Hikmet, an Algerian scholar and leader of a zawiya sufi order in Tlemcen, summed up this sentiment:

> Paradoxically we have re-found our spirituality thanks to the Focolare community. We did not educate our young, we did not know, were not capable of modernizing our spirituality. We are still living in the ninth century here, insisting on the law, and our youth do not understand themselves in modernity. Modernity creates a rupture with religion, so either our youth leave their religion or they remain stuck in the ninth century. . . . The Focolare community discovered a modern spirituality, they understand better the meaning of *zakat* and *ramadan*. . . . This has helped me to reread the Qur'anic texts, to see the spirituality within. . . . I can say that I am in the process of entering into modernity thanks to the Focolare.[17]

Religious Practices and Religious Pluralism

The history of the Focolare community in Algeria is one of religious plurality lived as a mutually enriching religious experience. How has that experience informed the members' understanding of their own truth claims, theology, and specific structures of religious authority? There is confidence among the members of the Algerian community that their experience with the Focolare community strengthens their specific faith as Muslims, even if it does so in unexpected ways. In this sense, the stories of the Focolare members in Algeria reinforce the observations of Dallmayr (2012) and Barbato (2010) from Chapter 4 of the existential power and appeal of untranslated religious experience. The recognition of "fullness" and "holiness" in a religious other can call forth the same in one's own specific tradition. Several of the longtime members of the Algerian community recounted an earlier effort of the Focolare community to translate the community's monthly "word of life" meditations into more neutral or Muslim terms with the help of a Muslim theologian.[18] The Algerian members rejected these translations as a fabrication and as blocking them from fully participating in the Focolare spirituality. As Adnane Mokrani put it, "The Focolare community has not adopted a neutral language that hides their Christianity because they know that the Algerians understand their spirituality—they can interpret it without the need for translation."[19] For Mokrani (2017: 169), "Reading that book [the *Word of Life* by Lubich] the Muslims understand the Bible as the Word that communicates Life, which deals with our existence, our way of living and acting. Though there are differences and in spite of the fact that the language is typically Christian they do not feel as strangers. . . . It has helped some Muslims to rediscover their faith and their Qur'an, to re-read it and live it in a better way. This is deeply Qur'anic and reminds us of the verse that invites Jews and Christians to live fully their Scriptures."

In a new development within the Algerian community, and representing the extent of spiritual solidarity some of the Algerian members feel, a young Algerian Muslim has joined the consecrated community of Focolare men following several years of reflection and discernment. This development is unusual not only for its interreligious dimension but also because historically the practice of consecrated celibacy has not been favored in the Islamic tradition, and the decision became a central point of reflection for many of the Muslim youth of the community. The young man joins the Focolare every morning for mass, although he does not pray with them at the mass but says his prayers in a common prayer room in the home. He meditates together with the Focolare on the words of Chiara Lubich and is still searching with the others to find their spiritual way together. He says, "Certainly this is what we believe—we are working towards peace in the world. To love, that is above religion—it is in all religion. But it is not the patrimony of any."[20]

In a similar way, the Christian members of the Algerian community have recognized the extent to which their encounter with Muslim spirituality has strengthened their Christian faith. One consecrated Christian Focolare woman in Tlemcen recounted how she had first met the Focolare community in Turkey and how that experience had provoked in her a mystical sensation of love and joy.[21] At her first Focolare event, she listened to a member speaking about how one can fully love Jesus in self-abandoned hidden acts every day of the week, and, upon hearing this, she realized she had found what she had been searching for her whole life. That night, she went home and made up her brother's bed, without his knowing it, and she did it for Jesus, and she could not sleep that night because of the joy she felt burning within her. Later, she became a consecrated Focolare member and was unexpectedly sent to Algeria. She was nervous and harbored conflicting thoughts about Islam as a Christian from a small minority living in Muslim Turkey. She had joined the Focolare to dedicate herself to Christ and was unsure what to think about how being a Focolare member in Algeria would impact her desire to become a better Christian. When she moved to Algeria, she attended her first *mariapoli* in Tlemcen and, following the sharing, songs, and fellowship of the day, experienced the same mystical sensation she had when she first met the Focolare community in Turkey. She could not sleep that night because of how much joy she felt. Although she was unprepared to do so, she felt the presence of God in the faith of her new Muslim friends, and she realized that this experience was encouraging her to become a better Christian. Bishop Paul Desfarges, who is the current archbishop of Algiers and considers himself close to the community of the Focolare, explains, "There is a spiritual proximity between us. There is a Muslim spiritual life. It is a form of mysticism. But there is something more there, if we recognize that there is a true Muslim spirituality, that it is a fact that they believe in God, and that they can feel in us the same."[22]

Various members of the community, both Muslim and Christian, were quick to emphasize in interviews that their positive and spiritually enriching experience of religious pluralism, even within the intimacy of shared community life, did not represent a form of syncretism, nor would it lead to syncretism. Said Farouk Mesli, "We understood then that we were living, between us as Muslims, that we were living this experience in unity with ourselves and in unity also with Christians, far from any form of syncretism."[23]

Henri Teissier described the work of the Focolare community in Algeria by saying, "This is the summit of inculturation."[24] The conviction of the Algerian members is that their commitment with the Focolare community is good for their personal faith as Muslims and good for Islam in general. By "good for Islam," they mean that their experience of interreligious community and interreligious spirituality has a role to play in stimulating religious renewal, here especially interpreted as healing, reconciling, or humanizing the Islamic faith in Algeria. By "renewing Islam," they often mean making

Islam more relevant in the lives of Algerians, particularly the youth, as a spiritual force for peace and service to others in Algeria and the world. The rediscovery or renewal of faith that members of the community speak about, therefore, is tied to a specific understanding of Muslim spirituality and is not, as such, necessarily linked to a common or shared increase in Muslim religious practices. This has consequences for the attitudes of various members toward other Muslims and Islamic religious authorities in the country. As a result, while all respondents spoke about their spiritual growth as Muslims, that growth was connected to a very wide range of specific Islamic practices.

Thus some young members connected their experience with the Focolare community to an enriched religious experience in their local mosques. One young man, for example, described how, after meeting with the Focolare community, he began to experience a warmth in the mosque that he had not experienced before.[25] Another youth recounted how he had felt encouraged to study the Qur'an and the *hadith* through the Focolare community, and how he had also discovered the beauty of going to the mosque.[26] Yet another youth felt similarly encouraged by the Focolare community to be more steadfast in his daily prayers and said that he had come to experience a deeper goodness when reading the Qur'an during Ramadan: "There is a syntony between what I experience with the Focolare, living with Christians, and the peace of going through the full actions of Ramadan—praying, eating, fasting, praying, eating."[27] He felt that this experience was further encouraged by his imam and the brothers with whom he prayed at the mosque.

Various members recognized a growing desire within themselves for a deeper Islamic theological reflection on their interreligious experience. Several members expressed the need for guidance and reassurance by Muslim religious authorities who could help them understand and interpret what they were living and confirm that it was coherent with their Islamic faith. In their early days in Algeria, the community enjoyed a close and comforting relationship with Imam Barkat, who helped them to reflect on the religious meaning of their time with the Focolare community. Since the imam's death, the community has turned to a number of other Muslim theologians, including Adnane Mokrani of the Pontifical Institute for the Study of Islam and Arabic, Amer al-Hafi of the Royal Institute of Interfaith Studies in Jordan, and Sherazad Houshmand of the Gregorian University in Rome, to help guide them in their theological reflections and decisions (Lemarié 2017). Some members shared how important it was for them to have conversations with these theologians and to share with them their struggles and doubts about what they were living and whether they were living their faith in harmony with the Islamic tradition. This was particularly the case for responding to religious questions raised by their neighbors and family about their actions—if they were not wearing a veil, for example, or if they spent time with Christians in a church. Mokrani, al-Hafi, and Houshmand helped them to develop their faith experience in the Focolare community within the context of the Islamic tradition and through the lens of Islamic scriptures.

And yet some youth in the community explicitly defined themselves as nonpracticing Muslims, in the sense that they did not regularly go to the mosque or say their daily prayers, and they felt distant from institutional Islam. Others, while not explicitly defining themselves as such, made clear that nonbelievers were also welcome in the Focolare community and that they were aware of nonbelieving members whom they admired. Many of the young Algerian women in the community had chosen not to wear a veil, although many of their friends who sometimes participated in Focolare events did. Similarly, some of the young Algerians were comfortable drinking alcohol, although some of their Muslim friends in the Focolare would take them to task for doing so. For the most part, participants who expressed these views did not see a necessary connection between the Muslim spirituality that they were discovering and living in the Focolare community, on the one hand, and the religious practices expected of them by what they perceived to be tradition or social pressure, on the other. In fact, often the distance from "official Islam" expressed by members was directly linked to the perception of what they described as a hardening or closing of mainstream Islamic discourse and practices in Algeria and the region. As one Algerian mother put it, describing her dilemma in raising her children in the current religious context, "I don't go to mosque regularly, but I would like to, and I can't come to send my kids there either. It's as if we belong to a different Islam."[28]

In terms of the theoretical language employed by postsecularism and post-Islamism, these spiritual transformations could be aptly described as marked by an increase in religious reflection, awareness, and religious subjectivity. To some degree, they would also seem to prize religiosity over institutional religion, and the personalization or individualization of the religious experience, especially in the case of the Algerian members of the community. It is interesting to note that this religious authentication process, however, is not associated with what Mahmood would describe as the external politics of piety, namely, the drive to construct a deeper personal Islamic faith by outwardly marking one's activities as Islamic. The awakening of faith here is primarily an interior and spiritual experience, not necessarily linked to a greater, lived orthopraxis. At the same time, however, the Algerian members' emphasis on increased spirituality, and the greater agency they have assumed in the construction of their religious lives, is not captured by categories employed to describe liberal or consumerist religiosity. Thus, Algerian Focolare members could not be described as being "spiritual but not religious" nor as "moral therapeutic deists" or "expressive individualists." The practice of community remains too central, the experience of transcendent faith too strong, the abandonment of self too emphasized, and the formal spiritual formation too constant and regular to fit these categories. Some young Algerian members may describe themselves as nonpracticing Muslims and emphasize the spiritual dimension of their growth, but they would also consider their experience to be a deeply religious one, which requires regular practice, the constant support of a faith-inspired community, and actionable service to others to grow.

This understanding of what Coda (2015) referred to as "inter-subjective" spirituality orients the relationships of the Algerian Focolare members with religious others in Algeria and, in particular, their attitudes and openness to those whom they would describe as "Islamists," "salafis," or "integralists" in the country. In this sense, various young Algerian members held the firm conviction that interreligious dialogue furthered the construction of peace in the world and in their country, and that dialogue worked in a specific way to counteract the attraction and hold of what they would describe as the religious extremism of some of their fellow Algerian youth. For many, the experience of spiritual Islam, or "real Islam," as they would define it, could open Islamists' minds to see the true nature of Islam as a religion of peace. The earnest desire to work for a world of unity and peace and their training to see the good in others led various members to hold out hope for dialogue with Muslim Algerians who believed that salvation could be found only through an exclusivist interpretation of Islam. Two Christian women Focolare members, for example, expressed gratitude that they had been invited to live in a neighborhood in Tlemcen that was considered more closed and conservative as opposed to a more open, secular neighborhood in Oran. They felt that the common search for God they shared with "the veiled women and bearded men" created an opening for them and had made for a richer experience of spiritual friendship.[29]

While many held open the possibility for dialogue with exclusivists, they also recognized the difficulty or even impossibility of doing so. They were very aware of their fragility as a small community, especially in the face of stronger, exclusivist-oriented religious forces in the country. Members would often formulate their experience as a "sign" for the country, as a witness to the possibility of an enriching religious pluralism. That said, they would also emphatically recognize that they constituted a very small sign. In explaining how the aliveness and warmth of the Focolare community's faith life represented a sign of hope for what she described as Algeria's social and political crisis, one young woman shared a story about a man who had come to the educational institute she was working at, which was run by the Algerian Catholic Church, in order to take an Arabic-language course. The man was very worried about taking the course inside a church space, and she assured him that the institute was not a church but a center and that there was no proselytization involved in the course. The man eventually agreed to take the course; later, however, he emailed her, "Sister, if you believe in God you must leave this place—if you have converted, come back, but flee, for if you do not, your soul will be in danger and you will suffer the blazing fires." The young woman replied, "First of all, this is the month of Ramadan, which means a month of charity and mercy, and second, Islam is about mercy and love for others, so why do you judge me because my hair is not covered?" For her, the story served as an example of dialogue. It created an opening to live out what she had learned with the Focolare community about reciprocal love, seeing the good in others, and forgiveness, and it led her to respond to the man with love and faith and without anger in her heart. She felt that, in general, in such a way it was possible to "reach them" and to make a difference.[30]

Spirituality and Social Solidarity

The spiritual awakening articulated by many members of the community, and as embodied in this last story, was also associated with a greater social activism and the alert desire to help others. The spiritual discovery of many young members unleashed springs of energy within them, often in positive response to a feeling of the same active, disinterested service among Focolare members which had originally attracted them to the community. For many, this was embodied in the figure of Ulisse and his prodigious capacity to lose time to meet the needs of others (Cocchiaro 2006:64). Taking on the task of self-giving, self-abandoned, gratuitous love, in the language favored by many in the Focolare community, led members to help elderly family and neighbors and friends not doing well. Most of the youth events include a community project in which young members spend structured time reflecting on how to serve their neighborhood. Recently, a group of young Focolare initiated a community-based ecological project to clean up their towns and forests, and bicycled along the entire Algerian coast to mobilize for their project. In interviews, various members explicitly equated their spiritual values to citizenship values[31] and expressed their belief that their activity played an important part in the social and political development of the country. Although these were not the terms they used to describe themselves, their increased desires and actions to serve others might be categorized as increases in social or civic capital, and their practice of community and reciprocal love might be formulated as a form of social solidarity and cohesion. In other words, their religious experience has led them to participate in the creation of a thicker associational life and energies actively spent on building the common good.

8
The Adyan Foundation (Lebanon)

Introduction

The Adyan Foundation, from the plural form of religion in Arabic, was founded in 2006 by a group of five young Lebanese professionals belonging to a range of different Muslim and Christian denominations. All of the founders had grown up surrounded by the violence and interreligious tension which marked the Lebanese Civil War. And yet, drawing on their religious experiences, study, and interreligious friendships, they had developed a conviction that their faith traditions provided the resources necessary for reconciliation, and in the context of the country's postconflict reconstruction, they sought ways to channel that conviction into professional civil society action. In 2008 the Adyan Foundation was formally incorporated as a nonprofit, nongovernmental organization, and two of its founders, Fadi Daou and Nayla Tabbara, continue to direct the foundation today. Both Daou, a Maronite priest, and Tabbara, a Muslim theologian, were teaching and writing on interreligious issues in the early 2000s at the University of St. Joseph in Beirut. At the time of writing, Daou was acting CEO and chair of Adyan's board and Tabbara was the vice chair and director of the foundation's Institute of Citizenship and Diversity Management.[1] The Adyan Foundation grew rapidly over its first ten years—it currently employs a professional staff of nearly twenty—and quickly expanded its interreligious work into multiple domains. Its work has been positively recognized by regional and international audiences, winning, most recently, the 2018 Niwano Peace Prize.

The original inspiration of the Foundation combined various elements which reflected the diverse professional skills and experience of its five founders. According to Daou,[2] these include (1) a deep attraction to the spiritual richness of interfaith communion; (2) a dedication to youth education and community service; (3) a conviction that peace and reconciliation in Lebanon and the region depends on a substantive evolution of religious discourse and interreligious relations; and (4) a confidence that religious traditions can play a positive public role in the political development of the region.

In its first years of existence, Adyan organized interreligious encounters and spiritual experiences throughout Lebanon, brought together young Lebanese for times of religious and interreligious formation, visited interreligiously significant pilgrimage sites, and sought to engage religious leaders on their project. Even as it worked to build its status as a professional, nonprofit organization in Lebanon, the theological, spiritual, and community dimensions of the Foundation were particularly strong in this first phase of growth. Daou and Tabbara developed a series of theological reflections inspired by their friendship which they would eventually publish as a book in 2013, *Divine Hospitality: A Christian-Muslim Conversation*,[3] which has now been translated into five languages. They helped produce several films on Muslim and Christian religious leaders, including Emir Abdelkader of Algeria, Imam Muhammad Ashafa and Pastor James Wuye of Nigeria, and Bishop Salim Ghazal of Lebanon, all of whom worked in favor of interreligious reconciliation and peace in conflict settings. In 2007, they organized their first annual Spiritual Solidarity Day, which brought together religious leaders from across Lebanon's sects, traditions, and denominations around a common intention of prayer for the country. Each year they also give a Spiritual Solidarity award to often unsung interfaith leaders in the region, like Sheikh Abdul Rahim Hasyan of Syria and Sayyida Rabab El Sadr and Sister Mariam Nour of Lebanon.

Reflecting these interests, the original proposal for the name of the foundation was the Adyan Foundation for Interreligious Studies and Spiritual Solidarity. (The website now describes itself as a "foundation for diversity, solidarity and human dignity.") Tabbara explained, "In the beginning we wanted to be a community, then we realized we can't be. But we wanted to keep these two sources which were feeding each other.... Early on we were using the idea of community, but ... we became an NGO. Maybe God wanted it this way, not to become a monastery, but a village."[4]

The Foundation quickly reached out to local mosques, parishes, and schools and formed its first youth network, the Alwan clubs, in 2008, in partnership with Lebanese high schools. In doing so, the Foundation also began to elaborate its public presence in a more formal way. In 2012, for example, Adyan initiated an important policy-oriented project to reform the way the

National Lebanese Curriculum taught religious education in public schools, a project which would entail managing a delicate set of negotiations with a range of religious and political stakeholders across Lebanon, as described in more detail below.

The Foundation's combination of spiritual roots and professional organization and its ability to simultaneously construct grassroots interfaith networks and high-level religious and political networks injected a new dynamic into the Lebanese interfaith landscape. Although Lebanon has a long history of interreligious dialogue activity, especially relative to the rest of the region, much of it had remained elite-focused or scholarly in orientation (Haddad and Fischbach 2015; Driessen et al. 2020). Adyan's civil society focus and its emphasis on spirituality and youth marked the beginning of a new phase of growth for dialogue in the Middle East, one which would resonate with a number of the political dynamics which erupted across the region in 2011. The beginning of the Arab Spring, in fact, and the growth of ISIS in Syria and Iraq intensified the interest of international and regional actors in Adyan's activities, especially those seeking to support alternative narratives and models in the region. Daou believes that the heightened interest in Adyan, which happened very quickly beginning around 2010, coincided with a marked shift in Western policymakers' approach to religion in the public sphere and a new willingness, particularly within the European Union, of governmental and development agencies to support a stronger public role for religious actors in their response to religiously expressed patterns of violence and conflict.[5] As a result Adyan was able to establish new partnerships with European actors for its projects, and they began to collaborate with aid agencies and research institutes based in Europe, such as Danmission, the Konrad Adenauer Institute, and Wilton Park, with more or less explicit ties to their home governments. At the same time, Adyan also sought, and received, increased support from local governmental and nongovernmental agencies. They began collaborating on a number of projects with the Middle East Council for Churches, the Hariri Foundation for Sustainable Human Development, Arab Reporters for Investigative Journalism, the Forum for Promoting Peace in Muslim Societies, and other regional organizations.

As it took on an increasing public role, Adyan worked to develop its political and religious vision. From its earliest stage of growth, Adyan had connected the idea and practice of interreligious dialogue to an idea and practice of citizenship. In reality, the Foundation rarely uses the term "dialogue" to describe what it does. Reflecting the widespread presence of interreligious dialogue in the postwar Lebanese context and the feeling that such a presence was not working, Tabbara comments:

> From the beginning, we were fed up with dialogue, everyone was talking about it. . . . Here I would talk more about "encounter" than "dialogue" on both the level of spirituality and citizenship. "Dialogue" is still remaining external, but "encounter" is about a human being being moved internally by another human being, in which I open a small window on myself to be moved. "Encounter" is fundamental for both spiritual solidarity and citizenship. It is fundamental for spiritual solidarity because you are really leaving a place for the other within you. It is fundamental for citizenship because it allows a place for empathy, not just one-on-one empathy between two individuals, but empathy for the whole group.[6]

In the Adyan Foundation, therefore, there is a close link between a lived interreligious spirituality and political development along a civic, citizen-centered trajectory. Dialogue is one instrument to be used toward their goal of interest, which is creating spiritual solidarity among different religious people. For Adyan, spiritual solidarity represents an active affective and practical state which requires the adoption of a certain religious attitude and disposition. In their conceptualization of spiritual solidarity, Adyan has drawn on the work of the Catholic Patriarchs of the East, whose 1994 Christmas message developed an idea of spiritual solidarity: "Spiritual solidarity signifies that every person, both Muslim and Christian, brings before God the troubles of their brother, their sufferings, their hopes and their desires. . . . Spiritual solidarity purifies our day-to-day relationships and strengthens them. Everyone puts themselves in the place of the other; with them; in the presence of God, in an attitude of submission and conversion, they live together the same difficulties, the same challenges and the same hopes or desires that they wish to achieve."

In this formulation, spiritual solidarity represents more than just the technical ability to manage religious diversity (which Adyan is also interested in achieving). It also signifies something different from "religious tolerance" (another term they do not use very often) or simply "coexistence." For Adyan, the goal is to live together as diverse religious individuals and communities in a positively felt way, in which they mutually sustain one another as well as their wider national and political community.

Inclusive Citizenship Embracing Diversity

Adyan has developed the concept of "inclusive citizenship embracing religious diversity" to define their approach to spiritual solidarity and public religious presence. This concept orients the approach of multiple branches of the Foundation and helps it stake out how their approach is different from a typical interreligious dialogue initiative. Critically, the idea of inclusive citizenship allows Adyan to synthetically express several of its core underlying beliefs and, at the same time, promote them in an appealing fashion within the emerging religious and political landscape of the region. Several components of Adyan's conceptualization of inclusive citizenship bring this expression and attraction into relief.

First, Adyan employs the idea of inclusive citizenship to connect religious responsibilities to national political responsibilities. In the particular context of Lebanon, Adyan's promotion of "inclusive citizenship embracing religious diversity" has attempted to flip the script on problems associated with religious sectarianism. Rather than diagnosing them as a hindrance to national unity, Adyan presents a range of specific religious identities and commitments as foundational sources for the construction of a multireligious common good. Thus, in the teacher-training workshops that Adyan leads in Lebanon, in the textbooks they have developed, in their Alwan clubs and other youth networks, they have sought to present "core religious values" in Islam, Christianity, and other religions present in Lebanon as "core citizenship values."

The Foundation therefore explicitly links religious education and civic education in Lebanon, and it makes the case that religious citizens and communities are charged with "religious social responsibility" toward their local and national communities. Adyan teaches that individuals can learn to become active citizens when they strengthen their commitment to divine justice, for example, or service towards others, or respect for the law. Conversely, as one Adyan educational expert explains in a video the Foundation produced about religious education on citizenship values, "[J]ust by being a good citizen and by applying the values that are asked from him, he will be fulfilling God's will."[7] Within Lebanon, Adyan's programs have sought to portray the country's multireligious nature and, in particular, its multireligious past as a cultural treasure rather than a burden which limits the ambitions of specific religious denominations. The Foundation speaks about the need to reconcile religious identities with national identities and regularly facilitates field trips with students to national cultural sites. Each Alwan club, for example, is "twinned" with another club of a predominantly different religious identity, and the two clubs organize and visit Lebanese cultural sites together. In interviews, students and teachers expressed awe at these experiences. Many had never visited the major historical sites of Lebanon, nor had they had prior opportunities to make friends from other religions.

In developing these ideas of inclusive citizenship and religious social responsibility, Adyan has articulated a model of public religion in the region which has proved attractive to various sectors of society and politics. This model can be traced in their educational materials, for example in the *National Charter for Education on Living Together in Lebanon: In the Framework of Inclusive Citizenship Embracing Religious Diversity*. Adyan originally wrote and endorsed the *Charter* in 2013 along with the Lebanese minister of education and the heads of several educational institutes associated with Lebanon's major religious denominations. In the *National Charter*, Adyan presents the model of inclusive citizenship as a constructive "third way" between two other models of citizenship which, they argue, define the relationship between religion and state in equilibrium-deteriorating ways. Thus, the *National Charter* distinguishes the inclusive citizenship model from what it refers to as the "fusion model," which it associates with certain models of secularism and nationalism in the context of the Middle East in which national unity prevails and subsumes diverse religious identities in the process. On the other hand, the *National Charter* also distinguishes inclusive citizenship from a "sectarianism model," which it associates with certain confessional models of religious rule in the Middle East in which singular religious identities prevail over national identities and religious diversity. For Adyan, therefore, inclusive citizenship is congruent with both substantive religious engagement in politics and society and the promotion of a religiously diverse public sphere. Inclusive citizenship encourages the formation of active religious citizens and promotes religious knowledge as an antidote to religious passivity and religious extremism.

Finally, Adyan's model of inclusive citizenship identifies religious authorities as essential agents of political development in the region. Adyan therefore has actively sought to partner with traditional religious leaders and communities to support the political rights and liberties of diverse religious individuals. By promoting its understanding of inclusive citizenship as a virtuous cycle for both religious communities and the state, Adyan has been able to challenge religious leaders in the region without directly challenging their religious authority in society and politics per se. At the same time, Adyan's promotion of democracy, religious pluralism, and religious freedom has also created tensions with various religious leaders in Lebanon and elsewhere whose political goals are at odds with Adyan's model. Adyan promotes a vision of a shared public sphere, for example, with more public religious diversity manifested than many preachers have found tolerable. Definitions of religious freedom have proved to be especially contentious and a central issue in Adyan's negotiations with various religious actors throughout Lebanon, as the next section explores in more detail.

Adyan's conceptualization of "inclusive citizenship embracing religious diversity," therefore, might be categorized as a "strong" (Almond, Appleby, and Sivan 2003) and inculturated (Roy 2010, 2020) understanding of religion in society and politics, one which promotes religious reform and renewal as a response to religiously expressed violence and conflict. In articulating this model, Daou notes, Adyan has been very careful not to be identified as a "liberal" religious agent in the region or as promoting a liberal secular model of religion and state: "We don't want the liberal label. We want to be a space where an extremely conservative person can feel comfortable."[8] This stance has caused a number of difficulties for the Foundation on both sides of the divide. By emphasizing the role of religion in political development, the Foundation has sometimes been at odds with more secular or laicist actors in Lebanon or Europe who advocate for a stronger model of secularism as the solution to Lebanon's difficulties with religious confessionalism. At the same time, by promoting religious pluralism and critical religious discourse, Adyan has also been accused by more conservative religious actors in the region of supporting a version of religious reform which undercuts religious authority over the long run.

Insitutionalizing Inclusive Citizenship

In order to develop inclusive citizenship and to coordinate its promotion, Adyan established an in-house Institute of Citizenship and Diversity Management, directed by Tabbara, and, more recently, the Rashad Center for Cultural Governance, directed by Daou. The Institute of Citizenship and Diversity Management has sponsored a number of international conferences over the past ten years to promote research and publications on religion, democracy, and citizenship in the region. It has also worked to promote the concept abroad. In 2016, together with Prince Hassan bin Talal of Jordan's Royal Institute for Interfaith Studies, Adyan presented the concept of inclusive citizenship to the grand sheikh of Al Azhar, Sheikh Ahmed al Tayeb. They have also promoted the concept at the Arab League and the Ministerials on Religious Freedom hosted by the White House in 2018 and 2019. And in 2018, they initiated a process along with Sheikh Abdallah bin Bayyah of the Forum for Promoting Peace in Muslim Societies and Wilton Park to draft a charter on inclusive citizenship for the Arab world.

Within Lebanon, Adyan has led several public campaigns to promote and substantiate the ideas of inclusive citizenship and religious social responsibility, particularly within the realm of education. Beginning in 2012, and with the support of the UK government, Adyan embarked on a project to reform the way in which religion was taught in the Lebanese school curriculum. As part of this project, Adyan drafted the *National Strategy for Citizenship and Coexistence Education* together with the minister of education. The Education Ministry subsequently tasked Adyan to help lead a multilateral process to develop a new curriculum on religious diversity to be taught in civic education classes in Lebanese schools. Over a five-year period, Adyan helped coordinate a series of consultations with Lebanon's major religious centers of authority, including the Islamic Dar al Fatwa (the leading Sunni religious institute in the country), the High Shiite Islamic Council, the Druze Council, and the Middle East Council of Churches. Together, they drafted a common textbook promoting values of religious pluralism and civic duties to religion, as well as a series of training manuals and other educational materials. As a result of this process, Adyan published a boxed set of two books in 2014 titled *The Role of Christianity and Islam in Fostering Citizenship and Living Together*. Critically, the books were published with the formal stamp of approval of all the major religious institutions in the country and marked the first time they all agreed on a common religious education textbook.

While this process represented a major step in the development of a new curriculum on religious pluralism in Lebanon, it also produced difficult tensions among its participants. The various institutes involved in the project were unable to agree on a common definition of religious freedom, for example, or strike a consensus on the relationship between the promotion of religious freedom and the teaching of specific religious truth claims. These disagreements led to the production of the textbook as two separate books, one for the Muslim communities and the other for the Christian communities. The books, however, are wrapped together in the same boxed set, with the formal logos of all the major religious institutions stamped on them. Although the team producing the textbooks was able to negotiate the approval of Lebanon's leading religious institutions, the Lebanese Ministry of Education has yet to adopt the textbook as part of its standard curriculum for Lebanese schools, an act which would require the support of the Lebanese Parliament. Nevertheless the textbook continues to be promoted and supported by many teachers and religious communities. Wadiaa Khoury, an education scholar at the Lebanese University who helped to develop the textbook, remarked, "We are not yet a creative minority but now we have these purple and green books on active citizenship, as Christian and Muslim books together. Before there were not these books. And now they are being taught; training is being done with them. That is a change. When they first tried to do a culture of religions book, they did not accept it. But now, they are more accepting."[9]

Adyan has distributed the book widely to Lebanese schoolteachers as a reference book for their lesson planning. The Foundation is also currently working with Lebanon's Center for Educational Research and Development to formally pilot the program in schools and to work for its eventual adoption by the Ministry of Education. Nada Oweijane, the director of the Center, which reports to the Ministry of Education, blamed the reluctance to formally adopt the textbook on Lebanese party politics as well as on the funding offered to the project by the British Embassy, which created suspicion in some quarters about the intent and political context behind the material.[10] In interviews, various participants in the process with Adyan also interpreted this reluctance as expressing unease from certain religious quarters about the religious ideals and practices represented by Adyan and the extent to which they challenged the religious status quo. The next section examines these dynamics in more detail.

Religious Attraction and Change among Adyan Youth

To a large extent, Adyan has promoted and embodied a mindset or a "way of life," as various young participants put it, that has proved attractive to a diverse set of religious individuals and communities in Lebanon. Adyan's religious approach emphasizes a positively lived religiosity, one that is in harmony with contemporary social and democratic values while remaining faithful to core religious teaching. In many ways this emphasis recalls Bayat's (2013:307) description of the post-Islamist religious sensibility, one which seeks to fuse "piety and freedom, religiosity and rights." In expressing this sensibility, there is the feeling among many working close to Adyan that it is both channeling and expressing desires that are widely present in Lebanon and other Arab societies but which have been inadequately represented by religious and political authorities. Dalia al Moktad, Adyan's media manager, described this sensibility in the following way: "We are criticizing without crossing borders. We are speaking to the unconscious thoughts for people. Adyan is giving knowledge, expressing an idea that is already there but does not have [a] voice."[11]

In 2017, al Moktad helped launch Adyan's media channel, Taddudiya (from the word for "pluralism" in Arabic) with a short film she posted about a visit she made to a mosque with another young Lebanese woman from a different religious background. Al Moktad, who is from a Shia Muslim family, had posted, on a lark, an online "challenge" during the month of Ramadan, in which she invited a Sunni Muslim to come pray with her at a local mosque. A Sunni woman responded to the challenge, and the film portrays several intimate moments between the two women praying together in a brightly lit mosque, with al Moktad gently placing her hands on the other woman to show her how to pray the *salat* following the Shia tradition. The various elements of the film, including its cheerful depiction of two young Muslim women, both veiled, from two different religious backgrounds praying together, as well as the spontaneity of the film, which was not linked to any specific religious institution or state ministry and which included no political or religious endorsements, struck a chord, and the film was quickly viewed nearly three million times. Taddudiya went on to produce half a dozen follow-up films, which generated similar numbers of hits, as part of a series which featured user-generated stories about similarly styled, affirmative interfaith experiences in Egypt, Iraq, and Syria. The website has also posted a dozen interviews of pairs of local religious leaders and scholars from different faith backgrounds talking about their respective religious traditions in a relaxed atmosphere. (Each video begins with a shot of the two personalities laughing together in an unguarded moment.) These have been regularly generating several hundred thousand hits each.

Adyan participants recognize a similar pattern of religious attraction at work in their religious outreach programs, including its Religious Public Affairs (RPA) course, which they offer each semester, and, more recently, their Political Literacy for Religious Leaders (PLR) course, which targets midlevel religious leaders from across the Levant. The PLR course offers religious leaders interfaith training on homily and sermon writing "in the service of public life."[12] It is designed to create interfaith cohorts of young religious leaders in the region who regularly meet and share their sermons with one another on online platforms. The PLR course, in particular, has had success reaching out to more conservative religious milieus and the audiences they preach to, both online and in the mosque or church. A recent iteration of the program, for example, included a man who coordinates al Qaradawi's website and other young imams close to the Muslim Brotherhood. Ahmed Nagi, a Yemeni scholar who helps lead the program, cites stories of these participants posting favorable messages online after the course in support of interreligious dialogue (and subsequently defending those messages against negative online comments) as evidence of the attraction of Adyan's model in the contemporary religious landscape of the Middle East.[13] Adyan has also built close relationships with Shia circles in Lebanon, including with some in Hezbollah (especially in its early years) and with the Fadlallah family and the various charity organizations it manages.

The diverse religious appeal of Adyan's approach can also be registered in the growth of its various community networks, in particular through its Alwan clubs. The Alwan clubs were one of the first projects that Adyan undertook, developing out of a series of religious awareness training sessions that Tabbara began teaching at one school in 2006. The Foundation then developed these sessions in collaboration with UNESCO into what they describe as a "nonformal educational program." The program lasts two years (in the tenth and eleventh grades of high school) and is taught and guided by a teacher within the school who has participated in Adyan Alwan training. There are currently forty-two schools participating in the program, from very diverse religious backgrounds, including predominantly Sunni schools, predominantly Shia schools, Latin Catholic parochial schools, Greek Orthodox and Evangelical schools, as well as predominantly Druze schools. Adyan leverages this diversity to pair schools from different religious compositions to work with one another on community service projects and cultural heritage trips. The program seeks to connect core religious values to the ideals of

Lebanese citizenship within a framework of active and inclusive citizenship. It also creates a place to talk about, study, and explore diverse religious ideas and beliefs. Hiba Ballout, a teacher who leads the Alwan program in Saint Georges School in Beirut,[14] describes the program as fostering a critical reasoning approach to faith: "We try to give them a question in their mind and then teach them how to research those questions. With a question, we should have a research. We are widening their circles—their introduction to people from around the world. At the same time, they strengthen their point of view on their own religious identity—when they are asked about their own religion, they need to have answers."[15]

As Ballout and other teachers participating in the club pointed out, this approach at first often created concerns among parents. They worried that exposure to other religions would cause their children to question and lose their own faith. As a result of these concerns, Adyan developed a training session for Alwan parents and requires them to sign a permission letter for their children to attend the programs. Ballout described the fears of parents and Alwan's response: "Parents were at first afraid of their children changing their religions in time. But it is not about changing beliefs, but to know the other. It is an intense reflective training session. . . . Alwan shapes the person not only to accept the religion but the individual as well. . . . Alwan allows us to see the beauty in the other."[16]

In a way that recalls the experience of the Focolare community in Algeria, various participants in the Alwan clubs and other Adyan networks emphasized how their participation in interfaith activities led to a strengthening of their faith lives. One young veiled Alwanist, who characterized herself as a Muslim feminist, described her enthusiasm for the program this way: "Alwan is focused on self-identity—so it got us to put our identity out there, to highlight our beliefs. . . . Many NGOS ask me to get rid of my beliefs. Alwan is different. I keep my beliefs." At the same time that she found her faith reaffirmed through the Alwan program, she also saw her faith develop: "Alwan changed a lot my beliefs. At first I thought my religion was the only right one. Alwan taught me that this was wrong—we live in a world with many different religions. Alwan taught me to live in peace with that."[17]

Another young woman active in Adyan's young adult youth network who also attended Adyan's RPA course said, "Some concepts [seemed] fake at the beginning, but then I worked to better understand them over time. It changed the way I looked at religion. I was a believer. RPA allowed me to enhance my faith, to find ways through faith to understand. It deepened my faith. People say I sold out my faith, they accused me. I used to be very defensive, so I have tried to find a way to explain it to them."[18] A young man in the network wrote on a survey following a course with Adyan, "Now I feel I am more in relation with God, I feel that I understand more my holy Qur'an, I can understand more the value of human beings."[19]

As illustrated by these quotes, various participants described how their faith was deepened through the process of self-examination which they felt Adyan had invited by provoking questions about their faith that they had to work out over time. A Greek Orthodox priest involved in Adyan's family network, for example, shared how recognizing the spiritual depth of families from other religious traditions posed difficult questions for him about the specificity of Christ's salvation, which he was forced to reckon with:

> Adyan was answering for what I needed. I needed to be as a Christian, not less, as a priest, not less. I am a Christian, I have all my faith with me. But Adyan is where I can go really deeper into my faith, it is there where you understand—go deeper into the spirituality of your faith—the more you understand the other. If God came to be crucified for the other, how could I believe that this other man is not worth my time? If God has created all humanity, how can I create these walls? And in becoming man, he did not lose any of his divinity. On the contrary. So why can't I put all my faith onto the other without losing my Christianity?[20]

At the same time that various participants and members of Adyan described a deepening of their faith lives, many of them recognized how the heightened reflection on their religious beliefs and identities also led to a more critical examination of their faith. This could prompt religious growth but could also result in further religious crises and new questions being posed. For many youth, these critical reflections raised particular questions about the role played by religious leaders and communities in the region's recent conflicts. One young Christian woman described this process and the difficulties it created in her relationship with her mother:

> My mom is worried that I am changing my beliefs. She is worried about me becoming less Christian, but also being different from the rest of the family. I am still Christian in my own way. I have the challenge to convince her, I want her to be confident about her daughter.... I believe in God, Jesus and the Prophet Muhammad. I believe in the goodness of God. We were taught

that God will be angry. I am not practicing my Christian beliefs. I feel more human. I pray every day because I want and I feel comfortable with my life with the other.[21]

Significantly, a few young women engaged in Adyan's youth networks who work with the Foundation recently stopped wearing the veil as part of a cumulative personal religious transformation process. One of the women described her change in this way:

The main turning point for my family was when I stopped praying in an Islamic way. I stopped fasting in Ramadan. ISIS was there. And I asked myself, "Am I Muslim?" I still don't know. Religious institutions weren't actively accusing ISIS and I felt, "I need you to say something right now!" They did not say something. Adyan was very helpful at that moment, very helpful to see and to know what I was going through. . . . At some point, I identified myself as agnostic. Now I feel I am in good terms with God. Last August I removed the hijab in order to be the same person on the outside as the inside. It was one of the most exciting moments for me.[22]

The religious changes of these Adyan members did not go unnoticed. A disparaging article was published in a local newspaper, and stories began to circulate about Adyan's negative religious intentions, worrying the parents of students involved in their youth programs. The Foundation defended the religious coherence of their young women's choices and were able to get the newspaper to retract its story. They also interpreted the episode as a reaction to the development of religious dynamism outside the channels of traditional centers of religious authority in Lebanon, as opposed to genuine concerns about the faith life of the two women featured in the newspaper article. By supporting their freedom to make individual choices, Adyan had been seen to challenge the influence of communal religious authority. Daou admits that the question of faith, and the way in which Adyan is influencing the spiritual lives of its youth members, is one of his central concerns as director. For Daou (2014a), even as the public dimension of Adyan has grown, as well as its role in civic education and policymaking, Adyan has sought to develop its faith-based dimension and highlight the dual, interconnected, "spiritual and political fecundity of dialogue." The questions which Adyan tries to pose to its participants, Daou says, can lead to "the possibility of a deeper experience of faith. Questioning, being critical, can lead to more spirituality and less sectarianism."[23]

Towards Interreligious Communion

In the case of both the Adyan Foundation and the Focolare community, religious and spiritual experiences were central to their interreligious identity and self-understanding. Members of the Focolare community in Algeria explicitly sought to structure their lives and design their community activities around a deeply felt sense of interreligious communion. Adyan's increasing engagement with national and regional policy work explicitly draws on its spiritual and theological understanding of religious pluralism that it developed alongside and out of the experience of many of its grassroots volunteers and members. The success of both movements offers evidence that new syntheses can be made in the region which combine a variety of contemporary religious orientations in the Middle East and the desire of many to find a new way to live together as diverse citizens. The Adyan Foundation's conceptualization of "inclusive citizenship," "spiritual solidarity," and "religious social responsibility" and the ways in which both Focolare and Adyan members embody these concepts in their activity and attitudes capture a distinct sensibility that interreligious dialogue offers an opportunity for the religious dynamism of Middle East societies to contribute to a more inclusive project of political development. While the extension of these movements remains localized and relatively new, their success recalls that of similar organizations and initiatives in the region, such as the Royal Institute for Interfaith Studies in Jordan, the Coptic Evangelical Organization for Social Services in Egypt, and the Gülen movement in Turkey. All these initiatives have combined a positive theological and spiritual approach to religious pluralism with more or less articulate visions of democratic political development.

The social resonance of the Adyan Foundation and the Focolare community, in addition to their religious appeal, goes a long way toward dismantling the claim that interreligious dialogue in the Middle East is primarily a political project that is imposed and implemented by state elites from above. At the least, interreligious dialogue activity in the Middle East also represents an organic social and political development in its own right, reflecting democratic developments across the region. The final chapter considers two key examples of state-based interreligious dialogue initiatives in the region, KAICIID and DICID, in light of this observation.

9

Interreligious Engagement in the Gulf

DICID (Qatar) and KAICIID (Saudi Arabia)

Introduction

The King Abdullah bin Abdulaziz International Center for Interfaith and Intercultural Dialogue (KAICIID) and the Doha International Center for Interfaith Dialogue (DICID) are both state-sponsored interreligious dialogue initiatives which would seem to epitomize the criticisms raised by multiple scholars, as detailed in Chapter 1, that interreligious dialogue activity in the region has largely served as a useful distraction for states to shield and extend authoritarian practices at home and abroad. In contrast to the Adyan Foundation or the Focolare community, KAICIID and DICID were created ex nihil by the heads of state of Saudi Arabia and Qatar; both have ties to their respective foreign ministries, and both are heavily invested in publicizing its activities to foreign audiences. Questions of theology or interreligious spirituality, at least on the surface, do not appear central to either KAICIID or DICID, and both institutes are wary of discussing Islam per se as a religion at their events. In addition, as Table 6.1 illustrates, the political, religious, and social contexts in which these institutes operate are vastly different across a number of key parameters. The social and democratic histories which mark Lebanon and Algeria, the legacies of social movements and political parties present in both countries, and their specific histories of religious identity and diversity, to name a few examples, could not be further apart from Saudi Arabia and Qatar. In critical ways, Saudi Arabia and Qatar, both wealthy, Wahhabi-identified kingdoms, officially ascribe to a religious and nondemocratic vision of society and politics that is not shared by either Algeria or Lebanon. As various scholars and policymakers have pointed out, the very idea of Saudi Arabia championing interreligious dialogue appears inescapably incongruous. Saudi laws currently prohibit public worship by non-Muslims within their territory,[1] and churches and other non-Islamic

The Global Politics of Interreligious Dialogue. Michael D. Driessen, Oxford University Press.
© Oxford University Press 2023. DOI: 10.1093/oso/9780197671672.003.0010

religious institutions are banned in the kingdom, one of the reasons why high-ranking Vatican diplomats and other non-Muslim religious leaders had refrained from visiting Saudi Arabia for decades and why Cardinal Jean-Louis Tauran's formal visit to Riyadh in 2018 represented such a breakthrough in relations between Saudi Arabia and the Holy See. That visit inspired the reporting by various news outlets that Saudi Arabi would finally allow churches to be built in the kingdom, although this has not been officially announced and there is no news of church construction. While Qatar has relaxed its own religious policies, notably allowing the construction of churches within the church city compound on the outskirts of Doha in 2008, its policies remain more restrictive than most of the other states in the Gulf besides Saudi Arabia.

This chapter explores these incongruities through an in-depth study of DICID and KAICIID's history, activities, and production. In general, it illustrates that there is, indeed, a disjunction between much of the rhetoric of either institute and the religious policies pursued by their home states. At the same time, however, both institutes escape categorization as mere puppets of their states' policies which are easily instrumentalizable for authoritarian purposes. Indeed, both enjoy a surprising amount of independence and confidence from their ministries and have institutionalized themselves and pursued important activities that are consonant with those of both the Adyan Foundation and the Focolare community. In important ways which neither Adyan nor the Focolare community is capable of doing, KAICIID and DICID have helped legitimize new ideas about religious pluralism and citizenship in the region and have connected multireligious collaboration to concrete policymaking efforts in the process. Although many members of these institutes, as explored below, recognize a paradox inherent in their work, they tend to see themselves as participating in a process of historic change in their own countries and in the region, one which is in tune with both the history of their nations and a more inclusive, religiously plural future.

DICID and KAICIID: Origins and Early Development

DICID officially began in 2003 as an international interreligious conference which was willed and hosted by Qatar's then emir, Sheikh Hamad bin Khalifa al-Thani. To a large degree, the conference reflected the increasing global diplomatic activity of the sheikh and his goal of constructing a Muslim state which fully and successfully participated in the globalized world economy. In part, this goal meant coming up with new ways to promote the Islamic identity of Qatar while simultaneously responding to the national religious reality which had been produced by the economic model that Qatar and its Gulf neighbors had adopted (Fahy 2018a, 2018b). That model largely relied on imported workers, many of whom were Christians or other non-Muslim adherents, producing new levels of religious diversity in the Wahhabi country. In Qatar, this need was particularly acute given the relatively small population of citizens relative to imported workers. In a country of nearly 3 million inhabitants, in fact, native Qataris make up little more than 10% of the population. In 2015, the Religious Characteristics of States Dataset Project estimated that Christians in Qatar also made up 10% of the population, among whom were more than 250,000 Catholics, many of them low-skilled (and low-paid) workers who immigrated from the Philippines, India, and Sri Lanka.[2] This means that there are roughly as many Qataris as there are Christians living in the country today. In Saudi Arabia, while the percentage of Christians is much lower relative to the overall population (4% according to the Religious Characteristics of States estimates), there are still 1.5 million Christians living in the country, many of them low-skilled workers.

In order to manage this situation, sustain open relations with the West, and retain its Islamic identity, Qatar has assiduously sought to make the case that it is in the process of constructing a successful Islamic model of global modernity. Or, as Fahy (2018b:11) has put it, "[P]reserving or protecting Qatari identity, culture or values has not come at the expense of embracing modernity. In fact, presented with the choice between tradition and modernity, Qatar has quite simply chosen both." In more specific terms, Qatar has presented itself as a wealthy Muslim-majority state which contributes to, as opposed to threatens, the core values and aspirations animating international discourse at the beginning of the twenty-first century, including on human rights, religious freedom and pluralism, good governance, and economic development. As with other state-based interreligious initiatives constructed recently in the Middle East, the impulse for such a strategy was heightened in the immediate aftermath of 9/11 and the need to more forcefully respond to the challenges the state faced in dealing with the rapid political and social changes associated with globalization.

In this light, the creation of DICID in 2003 can be closely linked to Qatar's establishment of official diplomatic ties with the Vatican in 2002 and the inauguration of the parallel US–Islamic World Forum by Sheikh Hamad with the Brookings Institute in 2004. Following the success of the first DICID conference, a second edition was held in 2004 with the participation of high-ranking Vatican officials, including Cardinals Jean-Louis Tauran and Michael Fitzgerald. Tauran was, at the time, the former secretary of state for the Holy See and then, beginning in 2007, the incoming president of the Pontifical Council of Interreligious Dialogue. Fitzgerald was then the sitting president of the Council and an important figure in Catholic interreligious dialogue circles. Yusuf al Qaradawi was also in attendance at the meeting and sat on a panel with Tauran and Sheikh Hamad.[3] The conference would continue to be hosted as an annual event until 2011 and biannually afterward. In 2007, Sheikh Hamad formally inaugurated DICID under the auspices of the Qatari Ministry of Foreign Affairs, which officially organized the annual meeting and whose minister typically offered the opening speech at the conference.

The origins of KAICIID contain a number of important parallels with those of DICID. King Abdullah bin Abdulaziz, who came to the throne in 2005 but had been acting regent of Saudi Arabia since 1995, made religious reform a central part of his public policy efforts (Mouline 2015; Kéchichian 2013). Like Sheikh Hamad of Qatar, Abdullah promoted dialogue initiatives partly in response to the negative image of Islam generally, and Saudi Arabia particularly, following the 9/11 attacks. The presence of Al Qaeda in Saudi Arabia, which made a series of attacks inside the country in 2003, had strengthened King Abdullah's views in this direction. In 2003, he created what would become the King Abdulaliz Center for National Dialogue, which was headed by Faisal bin Muaammar, who would become the director of KAICIID. The Center for National Dialogue brought together Saudi nationals from various religious and political backgrounds on issues of national identity and belonging. The Center also reflected the growing understanding by Saudi elites that they needed to construct a new model to manage its religious and social diversity (Thompson 2011). The global Muslim response to Pope Benedict's 2006 Regensburg speech, in the form of the A Common Word between Us document, pushed King Abdullah into further action on this front.[4] In 2007, a month after A Common Word was released, King Abdullah visited the Vatican on a much-publicized trip and there first proposed the idea of creating a Saudi Arabia–Holy See interreligious dialogue initiative, emphasizing the kingdom's role as a privileged interlocutor for the Muslim world as the custodian of the Two Holy Mosques.[5]

A form of high-stakes diplomacy developed over the course of 2008, with various leaders in the Arab world, including King Abdullah, Sheikh Hamad, the A Common Word network based in Jordan, and, to a lesser extent, members of the al Azhar establishment, positioning themselves with the Vatican as the principal leader of the emerging, Middle East–based dialogue efforts between Christianity and Islam (Horsfjord 2018; Markiewicz 2019). Cardinal Tauran acted as a chief negotiator for the Holy See throughout this process. In June and July 2008, King Abdullah hosted two important interfaith dialogue events. The first, held in Mecca, brought together several hundred scholars and religious authorities from across the Muslim world, including both Sunni and Shia leaders, for a conference on the theme of interreligious dialogue, the first of its kind in Saudi Arabia. The second event, held in Madrid and attended by Tauran, was a high-level Muslim-Christian-Jewish conference co-hosted by King Abdullah and King Carlos of Spain. Later, in October of the same year, Doha officially inaugurated DICID at its sixth interfaith conference, with Taraun again in prominent attendance, along with a high-level cast of other Muslim actors and organizations. Finally, in November, the Holy See hosted a major Catholic-Muslim Forum with many of the signatories of the A Common Word document; there Tauran went on the record suggesting that the A Common Word group might become the Holy See's "favored channel" for doing dialogue with Islam (Heneghan 2008).

In an institutional sense, KAICIID won this diplomatic game, at least for a time.[6] The center designed its organization to be an intergovernmental body with Saudi Arabia, Spain, and Austria as founding member states. In a way that paralleled its official status at the UN and other international organizations, and after a series of long negotiations, the Holy See was officially inscribed as a "Founding Observer" to the center. One of the practical implications of this arrangement is that the Holy See sits on KAICIID's Council of Parties, which elects the center's board of directors (which a member of the Pontifical Council of Interreligious Dialogue also sits on) and Advisory Council, and generally helps set the center's agenda.

In a more general sense, both Qatar and Saudi Arabia gained a great deal from these developments, especially in their relationship with the United States. And despite the diplomatic competition, major players from both Qatar and Saudi Arabia actively participated in each other's dialogue efforts up through the Arab Spring and beyond. Diplomatic cables in the Wikileaks database show enthusiasm by US diplomats for the creation of both centers. One cable reporting on then US senator John Kerry's meeting with King Abdullah in 2008 about the upcoming Madrid conference offered the following analysis:

> The upcoming multi-faith Madrid conference sponsored by Saudi Arabia is extremely significant. Saudi Arabia has long been known for its religious intolerance and xenophobic attitude towards outsiders. It is remarkable that King Abdullah, the Custodian of the Two Holy Mosques, is now equating Judaism and Christianity with Islam. Abdullah believes Islam has been hijacked by violent, radical extremists, who have threatened Saudi Arabia itself. A reconciliation movement such as King Abdullah's Inter-Faith Dialogue is a viable venue to counter this extremism. That Saudi Arabia is the sponsor of this Dialogue, and is actually getting traction from other Muslims, including the Saudi religious establishment, is even more telling. This Inter-Faith Dialogue could be a method to counter the threat of extremist terrorist ideology and help eliminate future generations of turning to religious violence. (Wikileaks 2008)

Similar positive feedback accompanied the 2007 and 2008 Doha conferences, along with notes about the novelty and potential of interreligious dialogue efforts within the Middle East to combat religious extremism (Fahy 2018a, 2018b). In addition, while registering the contradictions between their actual religious policies, particularly with respect to Saudi Arabia, the 2008 International Religious Freedom Reports for both Saudi Arabia and Qatar dedicated significant attention to their interreligious activities and their potential to reframe US-Islam relations (US Department of State 2008).

The enthusiasm of these reports would seem to buttress the claims of various scholars that DICID, KAICIID, and other state-based dialogue efforts in the Middle East represent baldly political attempts to curry international favor with little religious substance or credibility to them. The apparently unchanged domestic religious policies of Saudi Arabia, in particular, would seem to substantiate these claims. Moreover, as the next sections demonstrate, the tensions which arose throughout the first international conferences sponsored by both KAICIID and DICID, especially with regard to leading Middle Eastern clerics' views on interreligious dialogue, would only seem to add to this depiction.

Subsequent Development: Institutionalization of Dialogue in the Gulf

DICID: Growth and Change

Despite Sheikh Hamad's enthusiasm for interfaith dialogue in Doha, and despite Qatar's official discourse of celebrating a religiously open national environment, the organization of DICID's first several conferences proved difficult on account of a number of sensitive issues. These difficulties revealed how much distance existed between the sheikh's promotion of dialogue and the religious sentiment among many of Qatar's Wahhabi-trained clergy and scholars. Participants in these early conferences described how the first several meetings were held in an almost secret fashion, with strictly closed-door sessions and no press access for most of the conference.[7] While the regional anglophone press covered the conferences positively and celebrated their historic nature, imams in Qatar and elsewhere were critical of the project. Cardinal Fitzgerald noted in an interview at the time that the conference offered sharp contrasts in participants' understandings of religious freedom, dialogue, and the nature of human rights, even as he underscored the importance of the event (*Catholic News Agency* 2004).

These tensions came to a head in the third Doha conference, in 2005, when Yusuf al Qaradawi and Muhammad Sayyid Tantawy, who was then grand sheikh of al Azhar, boycotted the meeting because invitations were extended to Jewish speakers (e.g., *Deutsche Presse Agentur* 2005). Although Sheikh Hamad had already publicly expressed his wish to expand the conference to include Judaism in 2004, al Qaradawi stated that he would not enter into dialogue with Jewish participants until Israel ended its occupation of Palestine, a position that he would maintain for subsequent Doha conferences. Several Jewish leaders from Israel also declined to participate in the meeting, but five rabbis, four from the United States and one from France, traveled to Doha for the event.[8] Al Qaradawi's boycott was particularly significant and appeared to undercut the religious legitimacy of dialogue in Doha. At the time, he was perhaps the most authoritative and popular religious voice in the Middle East (Gräf and Skovgaard-Petersen 2009), a position he had achieved in no small part due to Qatar's sponsorship of his work and his weekly popular show, *Sharia and Life*, that aired on Qatar's Al Jazeera network. Al Qaradawi had also served as the dean of Qatar University's College of Sharia and Islamic Studies, a school he had helped build and intellectually guide through its early stages. Several prominent professors at the college, including Ali al Qaradaghi, were also high-ranking members of al Qaradawi's International Union of Muslim Scholars.

In interviews, the current directors of DICID described how managing the basic legitimacy of engaging in dialogue, of having Muslims, Christians, and Jews simply talk to one another, consumed the first years of the center. To that end, despite the high-level boycotts and the foreign policy framework of the conferences, the center also sought to keep Muslim scholars deeply engaged in the process. Notably, Qatar University's College of Sharia and Islamic Studies began to jointly organize the conference along with the Ministry of Foreign Affairs. Aisha Yousef al Mannai, the first woman to be appointed dean of the college, was also appointed vice president of DICID's board of directors. And even as al Qaradawi continued to decline attendance at the meetings, he generally did so quietly, and high-ranking members of the IUMS and the College of Sharia and Islamic Studies did attend, even the contentious 2004 conference. Qaradaghi, for example, who became the secretary general of IUMS, has regularly given keynote speeches in favor of interreligious dialogue at the DICID conference throughout its almost twenty-year history. In a similar way, despite Tantawy's boycott of the conference, Ahmed al Tayeb, who was then acting president of al Azhar, actively contributed to the conferences in 2007 and 2008. The DICID conference thus played an important role in involving key Muslim actors in an international interreligious dialogue setting who were considered to be religiously conservative, close to institutions like al Azhar or the Muslim Brotherhood, and generally skeptical or even opposed to dialogue with the West and Christianity. In the process, DICID built a network of religious scholars and actors from across a wide range of Muslim-majority countries, from Mauritania to Algeria and Brunei, who were not typically involved in dialogue meetings, and brought them into conversation with their Christian and Jewish counterparts from across the globe.

This steady network-building allowed Qatar to boost its diplomatic ties with numerous states, and the conferences typically ended with the signing of new agreements and official memoranda of understanding between the DICID or the Qatari Ministery of Foreign Affairs and religious ministries, foreign offices, and institutes across the Muslim-majority world.[9] The conferences also helped facilitate as well as legitimize important changes in Qatar's religious policies, including, most notably, its 2008 decision to allow churches to be built on Qatari soil. Doha's first Catholic church was officially opened immediately prior to DICID's 2008 conference, which simultaneously inaugurated its new center and included high-level participation by Tauran, al Tayeb, and numerous other officials. The following year, the Orthodox, Protestant, and Catholic priests and pastors leading the new Qatari churches were invited to the conference as honored participants. And in the same month of the 2008 conference, al Qaradawi issued a fatwa which justified the construction of new churches in Muslim-majority countries.

Once again, the figure and thought of al Qaradawi offers a useful gauge of the more generally growing shift toward dialogue within the wider Middle East and the intellectual and religious support that shift could draw upon. In 2008, Qatar also inaugurated the Qaradawi Center for Islamic Moderation and Renewal, which would become part of its new, signature Hamad bin Khalifa University (HBKU) College of Islamic Studies that would grow to include research centers on Islamic ethics, economics, finance, and civilizational studies. HBKU was constructed inside Qatar's Education City project, a sprawling campus site on the US model that includes satellite centers from leading US and British liberal arts universities like Georgetown, Cornell, and Vanderbilt, where Qatari and international students can earn US degrees taught by resident faculty of those same universities. HBKU drew several top names from the world of Islamic studies, including Tariq Ramadan and Emad Shahin, both of whom have had prominent careers reflecting on the distinctive Islamic contribution to modernity. Within this context, both the work of DICID and Qatar's expanding university system can be linked to the wider attempt by Qatar to attract and support Islamic intellectuals and authorities who could further its aspirations to build a successful model of a modern Islamic state.

The high-water mark of this project, as well as of DICID, was reached in the early years of the Arab Spring. For Qatar, which exercised outsized diplomatic influence on the events unfolding on the ground, the electoral triumphs of the Muslim Brotherhood in Egypt, Ennahda in Tunisia, and the Justice and Development Party in Morocco in 2012 and the continuing rise of Erdogan's stature in Turkey seemed to confirm that its political and religious goals were both attractive and triumphant. By 2011, Qatar was coming off a successful World Cup bid, had just opened the world-feted Museum of Islamic Art designed by I. M. Pei, and was receiving glowing publicity from both the West and the Muslim world. In 2012, Tariq Ramadan became the inaugural chair of the Center for the Study of Islamic Ethics and Legislation at HBKU and delivered several electric public lectures on the triumph of the Arab Spring. The 2011 and 2013 DICID conferences were among its most important, both in substance and in their breadth of participation. The Reverend Jesse Jackson gave the keynote at the 2013 conference, which was virtually a who's who of the interreligious world in the Middle East. The conference included presentations by KAICIID, the Royal Institute for Interfaith Studies, Adyan, the Wasat Party in Egypt, the Pontifical Council for Interreligious Dialogue, and Religions for Peace; important interreligious scholars like Edward Kessler of the Woolf Institute and Muhammad Abu-Nimer of American University; ministers of religious affairs from across the Muslim world; and the newly appointed high representative of the UN's Alliance of Civilizations Office, Nassir Abdulaziz Al-Nasser, himself a Qatari national.

In an interview, Dr. al Mannai described what she calls the "normalization of dialogue" among Middle East imams and intellectuals that had occurred in DICID meetings over the past decade and as highlighted by the 2013 conference.[10] Over time, participants assumed and expanded much of the interreligious grammar, explored in Part II of this book, that had been developing throughout interreligious dialogue initiatives in the Middle East. They offered more in-depth reflections on the roots of human dignity, rights, religious freedom, and solidarity within the Islamic tradition, and did so on an important international stage in a conservative Gulf state. In many ways the 2013 conference served as an illustration of the breadth of the normalization of this discourse and a confirmation that a new era of interreligious dialogue had been constructed in the region.

The events of subsequent years, particularly the devolution of violence in Syria and Iraq, the fall of the Muslim Brotherhood in Egypt, and the blockade of Qatar by Saudi Arabia, the UAE, and Egypt (all of whom had participated actively and regularly in prior DICID events), represented a sharp reversal for Qatar and its leadership in the dialogue field. The DICID conference switched to a biannual format, lost many of its participants from the blockading countries, and received more sporadic participation from the Vatican. Despite its attention to religiously expressed violence, no major declaration on the theme has been produced by DICID or garnered traction outside Qatar. When Pope Francis visited the UAE in 2019, the first papal visit to the Arabian Peninsula, and signed the landmark Human Fraternity document with Ahmed al Tayeb, Qatar was absent. Al Qaradaghi issued a bittersweet statement on the visit, noting that the IUMS "was all in favor of dialogue," but he also voiced his concern that the pope was unintentionally legitimizing the authoritarian politics of the UAE (Al-Qaradaghi 2019). Despite its relative decline in prominence, the DICID continues to hold its conferences and attract key actors from the interreligious dialogue world. Its 2018 conference, for example, included important religious figures from the United States, like Pastor Bob Roberts, who has led on recent efforts for interreligious dialogue between Muslim, Evangelical, and Jewish audiences, including the UAE-supported Alliance of Virtue project. Interviews with several scholars who have been longtime participants confirmed the sense that the Doha conferences, despite Qatar's regional isolation, have continued to grow in intellectual depth and self-criticism. Speakers at the 2018 conference, for example, were more open in presenting ideas that were critical of Qatari policies, including with regard to its blasphemy laws and policies in Syria. Even as the center of gravity of interreligious dialogue in the region has shifted to its neighbors, therefore, Qatar has continued to invest in its dialogue activities.

KAICIID: International and Regional Development

Throughout its first years of operation, in ways similar to DICID, KAICIID also struggled to convince international audiences of its credibility and, at the same time, muster religious legitimacy within its founding country. King Abdullah's back-to-back conferences in 2008 were particularly revealing of the magnitude of resistance to interreligious dialogue that existed in Saudi Arabia and elsewhere in the region. The 2008 Mecca conference was organized in conjunction with the biannual conference of the Muslim World League and tasked with building consensus among Islamic scholars on the idea of interreligious dialogue and to set guidelines for it (Kéchichian 2013). While an Islamic declaration in favor of dialogue, called the Mecca Appeal, was issued at the end of the conference, various observers noted the tensions between Abdullah's position on dialogue and the views of many participants, including the grand mufti of Saudi Arabia, Abdulaziz al ash Sheikh (Heneghan 2008; Kéchichian 2013; Thompson 2014). Riazat Butt (2008b), who covered the event as a correspondent for the *Guardian*, reported that the grand mufti told delegates to the conference that "converting people to Islam was the ultimate goal of dialogue, a point made several times. 'It is the opportunity to disseminate the principles of Islam. Islam advocates dialogue among people, especially calling them to the path of Allah.'" Al Qaradawi was also present at the meeting and made a well-received speech in which he disparaged Shiites, repeated his stance that he would not dialogue with Jews until the Israeli occupation of Palestine ended, and encouraged Muslims to dialogue with atheists, Buddhists, and Hindus instead (Butt 2008a).

Critically, at the end of the conference, Saudi Arabia's grand mufti and most of the kingdom's leading clerics refused the king's invitation to participate in the international interreligious dialogue event with Christians and Jews the next month in Madrid (Heneghan 2012), and several issued a statement against the growing anti-Sunni bias of Shiites immediately before the conference (Heneghan 2008; Kenyon 2008). The grand mufti would go on to famously declare in 2012 that "it was necessary to destroy all the churches" in the Arabian Peninsula (Abrams 2012; Broomhall 2012). Mohammad Sammak, a prominent interreligious dialogue actor from Lebanon who joined King Abdullah for his personal visit to Pope Benedict in 2007 and is one of the founding board members of KAICIID, recounted in an interview[11] how enraged King Abdullah was by this rejection of his invitation. When the king inaugurated the Madrid conference a month later, which included important Christian, Jewish, and Muslim leaders in favor of interreligious dialogue (but almost no Saudi religious leaders), he ordered the ceremony to be live-streamed on Saudi television so that the Saudi public, according to Sammak, including Saudi clerics, would personally witness the king shaking hands with these participants.[12]

The discrepancies between the king's support for the twin interreligious dialogue conferences in 2008 and the lack of religious support for dialogue in Saudi Arabia, as well as the continuing restrictions on non-Muslims within the kingdom, led to a great deal of doubt and skepticism as the king pushed to develop KAICIID into an international institution. Faisal bin Muaammar, the secretary general of KAICIID, described a period of intense and difficult diplomatic activity as he and others worked to establish an agreement with the Austrian government to host the new center in Vienna and, at the same time, to get the Vatican on board.[13] Austria nearly pulled out of the agreement several times, and political opposition to the center would continue periodically after it formally opened its doors in 2012. Then, in June 2019, following months of protests, often staged in front of the KAICIID building, against Saudi Arabia's imprisonment and flogging of the young blogger Raif Badawi, the Austrian Parliament finally voted to expel KAICIID from Vienna.[14] The Khashoggi case, Saudi Arabia's intervention in the war in

Yemen, and the news of a possible death sentence for a teenage Saudi dissident, Murtaja Qureiris, helped bring the vote to a head.

In a critical way, the vote embodied the argument that KAICIID operated as a fig leaf for Saudi Arabia's authoritarian politics, which enabled the kingdom to stall rather than facilitate substantive religious and political reform in the country. The institutional development of KAICIID, and the kinds of activities and policies it has engaged in, however, are at odds with this depiction. Despite the difficulties of its first conferences and the weakness of religious backing in Saudi Arabia, the center has developed in substantive, independent, and innovative ways since officially opening in 2012. In particular, KAICIID has constructed an institutional structure that has connected interreligious dialogue efforts in the Middle East to global policymaking organs like the United Nations in unprecedented ways. At the same time, KAICIID's activities have helped legitimize new ideas about religious pluralism and citizenship in the region that are broadly in tune with those championed by grassroots organizations and movements like Adyan and the Focolare. The rest of this chapter takes up these developments.

International Institutionalization of Interreligious Dialogue and Multifaith Collaboration

Despite its origins as a Saudi-backed project, KAICIID built its organizational structure to operationalize its wish to act as a multifaith, intergovernmental institution. Even though Saudi Arabia continues to fund the center and the secretary general of the organization is a Saudi national, the governance structure of KAICIID is genuinely both multifaith and intergovernmental. The board of directors, for example, which makes major decisions on a majority-vote basis, is composed of representatives of various faiths, with no faith making up more than half of the team. KAICIID's advisory council is similarly diverse in terms of nationality, faith, and gender,[15] as is its team of experts who oversee day-to-day operations. Thus, prominent religious authorities and interreligious leaders representing major faith traditions sit on the board and advisory council and have advocated on its behalf, including Rabbi David Rosen of the American Jewish Council, Cardinal Miguel Ayusho of the Pontifical Council for Interreligious Dialogue, Dim Syamsuddin of Muhammadiyah, Bill Vendley of Religions for Peace, Metropolitan Emmanuel of the Ecumenical Patriarch of Constantinople, and the Reverend Kosho Niwano of Rissho Kosei Kai.

This hybrid nature has allowed KAICIID to do several things. First, its multifaith structure gives it broad credibility as an interreligious organization. Second, its official support in Saudi Arabia enables it to position itself as a privileged interlocutor to and from the Middle East. And its intergovernmental structure offers KAICIID a position at policymaking tables that is typically reserved for states. As such, in various ways, KAICIID has come to operate as a new sort of institutional container which more practically allows international organizations to construct projects characterized by multifaith collaboration and connect them to policymaking goals. In doing so, KAICIID could be understood to be one response among others to the recommendations of various scholars and policymakers (Appleby, Cizik, and Wright 2010; Marshall and van Saanen 2007; Marshall 2008; Johnston and Sampson 1995) to more explicitly incorporate faith-based actors into the humanitarian goals and actions of international, state-based organizations. They are important protagonists, in other words, of interreligious engagement activity. As noted in Chapter 1, this recommendation took on new urgency in the aftermath of 9/11 and then the rise of ISIS. As Muhammad Abu-Nimer, a senior expert at KAICIID and professor at American University in Washington DC, points out, KAICIID has been repeatedly called upon by states seeking faith-based partners as part of their larger response to religiously inspired violence, particularly in the Muslim majority world.[16] For Abu-Nimer, the securitization framework that such partnerships represent, in which Islam is typically framed as a problem in need of reform, has posed a major challenge for KAICIID. Partly as a response to this challenge, KAICIID has sought to build up its independent capacity as an institution and reframe interreligious dialogue outside of a security framework. Rather than framing Islam as a problem in need of reform, KAICIID has tried to more clearly present the resources that Islam and other religious traditions already possess to enact positive social change.[17] KAICIID's work in this direction mirrors the efforts of others in the region, including the interreligious declarations surveyed in Chapter 5.

The success of KAICIID in helping to institutionalize these new forms of multifaith collaboration can be measured in a number of ways. At the United Nations, KAICIID has become an increasingly important actor on a range of new faith-based policy initiatives. In 2017, in cooperation with the UN Office on Genocide Prevention and the Responsibility to Protect (2017), KAICIID helped launch a plan of action on the Role of Religious Leaders in Preventing Incitement That Could Lead to Atrocity. The plan of action was the result of a series of regional consultations with religious leaders and policymakers dubbed the "Fez Process"; it involved the participation of high-level interreligious actors in the Middle East, including Sheikh Abdallah bin Bayyah and the Adyan Foundation. Scholars have generally regarded the process as a model for partnering multifaith-based networks and capacities with international humanitarian agencies and goals (Petito 2018). In 2019, while working with the UN Office of Development to support the Sustainable Development Goals, KAICIID also helped construct the new Faith-Based Advisory Council for the UN's Interagency Taskforce on Religion and Development, to which Faisal bin Muaammar, KAICIID's general secetrary, was elected co-chair. KAICIID has also been a principal actor in the G20 interfaith forums and has signed agreements of cooperation with the EU, the African Union Commission, World Scouting,[18] and the Organization for Security and Cooperation in Europe, as well as other UN agencies like UNESCO and the UN Alliance of Civilizations office.

Legitimizing New Ideas on Pluralism and Citizenship
Part of the institutional success of KAICIID has been rooted in its efforts to build and support national networks of interreligious leaders. Much of KAICIID's activity over the past years, in fact, has been devoted to on-the-ground capacity and organizational training for what it terms national interfaith platforms. They have been especially active in countries where conflicts between Muslims and Christians have been acute, including Myanmar, the Central African Republic, and Nigeria and in the greater Arab region. The goal of the platforms is to help construct readily identifiable interfaith leadership structures which are capable of responding to (and preventing) interfaith tensions and which can serve as a point of mediation for international actors and bodies. The interreligious platform that KAICIID sponsors in the Central African Republic has played a role in mediating tensions between Muslim and Christian communities there, and it launched an ambitious Arab regional platform in 2018 which brings together an array of religious leaders in the region for regular working meetings. KAICIID also inaugurated an international fellowship program in 2015 which, as of 2019, had offered professional training to over two hundred young leaders of multiple religious traditions from all over the world. Not surprisingly, the two leaders of the platform in the Central African Republic, Cardinal Dieudonné Nzapalainga and Imam Omar Kobine Layama, were among the first to publicly come

to KAICIID's defense after the Austrian vote, as have many of their recent colleagues and religious partners.

While KAICIID insists that it "does not do theology" nor, like DICID, seek to "touch the core of Islam," it has been effectively legitimizing new ideas about religious pluralism and citizenship that are consonant with those championed by more grassroots and state-independent groups in the region. In 2016, for example, as violence spiraled in Syria and Iraq, KAICIID (2017) coordinated an important interreligious statement, the Vienna Declaration, against the use of violence in the name of religion, signed by a wide cohort of Middle East religious leaders. As part of a follow-up action to the Declaration, the following year KAICIID (2018) launched the Network of Arab Faculties and Institutes, meant to strengthen the development of Arab intellectual discourse on pluralism. In the same year, KAICIID began a on a long-term project with UNESCO as part of UNESCO's Forum on Global Citizenship to promote the revision of educational curricula to combat negative religious stereotypes.[19] Many of these ideas and networks crystalized around KAICIID's launch of its Interreligious Platform for Dialogue and Cooperation in the Arab world in Vienna in 2018. The platform has the support of the grand muftis of Egypt and Lebanon, the grand imam of the Great Mosque of Mecca, the Maronite, Armenian, and Greek Orthodox Patriarch Churches, as well as Pope Tawadros II of the Coptic Orthodox Church. KAICIID launched the platform as part of a conference, Interreligious Dialogue for Peace: Promoting Peaceful Coexistence & Common Citizenship, which also brought in the participation of Cardinal Tauran and Muhammad al-Issa of the Muslim World League.[20] Finally, KAICIID has continued to promote a citizenship agenda through its work with bin Bayyah's Forum for Promoting Peace in Muslim Societies, along with the Adyan Foundation.

Faisal bin Muaammar is enthusiastic about these developments and the increasing pull of the ideas of both dialogue and citizenship in Saudi Arabia and the region. In interviews for this book, he described dialogue as the "voice of the silent majority" in the region. For him, the discovery of interreligious dialogue was revolutionary in a personal way. The theological coherence of dialogue with the Qur'an and the early life of the Islamic community was like an awakening, he said, the discovery "of a fourteen-hundred-year project which was never alive for us," particularly in Saudi Arabia. He believes his experience is the experience of many others, and that dialogue in the Middle East represents a movement, a project of "wakening up."[21] Patrice Brodeur, another research expert at KAICIID, describes dialogue in similar terms, as part of an international paradigm shift over the role of religion in public life in which Saudi Arabia recognizes itself.[22] The activities of KAICIID intersect with the development of new religious discourses and pushes for reform within Saudi Arabia and the region. In an interview before the Khashoggi murder case, just as Crown Prince Muhammad bin Salman was making his international debut, bin Muaammar gushed about bin Salman's reforms and how they represented a boon for KAICIID's interfaith efforts, noting, "King Salman and Prince Mohammed have a strategy to move Saudi Arabia ahead, and we are benefiting from this. . . . The support we are getting from King Salman and the crown prince is unlimited, financially and politically" (quoted in Heneghan 2018). Bin Muaammar and KAICIID have been on hand for several of the major interfaith breakthroughs in Saudi Arabia and the Gulf since the arrival of the crown prince, including Cardinal Tauran's 2018 visit to the kingdom, the first visit of a high-ranking Vatican official to Saudi Arabia, as well as at Pope Francis's visit to Abu Dhabi in 2019. In 2017, the Maronite patriarch visited Saudi Arabia for the first time, as did the Coptic pope Tawadros II, who said a mass there in 2018. Sheikh Muhammad Karim al Issa, whom bin Salman helped appoint as the current president of the Muslim World League, has also been key in orchestrating several of these Christian-Muslim meetings, including the visit of Cardinal Tauran, and has sounded tones similar to bin Muaammar's on interreligious dialogue and citizenship. Notably, al Issa has also struck a new tone on Muslim-Jewish relations, visiting the US Holocaust Museum in 2018 and writing an 2019 op-ed in the *Washington Post* on the importance for Muslims of remembering the Holocaust. In 2020, al Issa led a delegation of Islamic scholars to visit Auschwitz with prominent Jewish leaders, including Rabbi David Rosen, who also sits on the board of KAICIID.[23]

Many scholars have criticized bin Salman's reforms and argued that his much publicized arrests have more to do with the consolidation of power than any religious reforms. As Lacroix (2019) has pointed out, for example, several of the leading clerics capable of enacting liberal religious reforms have been specifically targeted by bin Salman, while more conservative clerics preaching governmental obedience have stayed in place (see also Salem and Alaoudh 2019). While many of those working for KAICIID ascribe to a transformative understanding of dialogue, they also explicitly recognize the paradox that this view holds in the current context of Saudi Arabian politics. Like bin Muaammar, however, they tend to view themselves as participating in a historic process of change, in which dialogue has gained significant legitimacy. As Sammak points out, ten years ago, no leading cleric from Saudi Arabia joined King Abdullah for his interreligious conference in Madrid. Today, many Saudi clerics participate in KAICIID and Muslim World League events on dialogue, and a growing number of religious authorities, as well as ordinary citizens, speak openly in favor of it. The recently signed Charter of Makkah (2019), which declares its support of both interreligious dialogue and "global citizenship" and which was signed during the Saudi-hosted 2019 Organization of Islamic Cooperation conference, is an example of how these concepts are being newly enshrined in the international declarations emanating from the Muslim world.

In bin Muaammar's and al Issa's speeches, and in ways that parallel those of bin Bayyah's highlighted in Chapter 5, support for ideas like religious pluralism and inclusive citizenship are not coupled with endorsements of democracy or liberalism. What is new, however, as Abu-Nimer notes, is that they are no longer speaking against these concepts.[24] Rather, citizenship and pluralism are held up as attractive ideals within an Islamic framework, in ways that echo the language of the Marrakesh Declaration and other recent interreligious declarations from within the Muslim-majority world. Whereas in the past, differences between Islamic and Western ways of thinking about or practicing human rights and equality were emphasized, these same differences are now being touted as a source of support for those same rights. Thus, in a 2018 speech at the Wilton Park Inclusive Citizenship Dialogues conference bin Muaammar argued that the values of Islam strengthen common ideals of rights and equality in ways that Western, secular ideals have been incapable of doing: "[T]he ideal of common citizenship is not something imposed on us, but something that has grown from the very same societies that struggle to find it today."

Conclusion: Interreligious Dialogue and the Future of Citizenship in the Middle East

Introduction

This book began with a number of questions raised by current debates about the place of religion in contemporary global politics, and it proposed that the growth of state-sponsored interreligious dialogue initiatives in the Middle East represented fertile ground for examining those questions. In particular, it linked the growth of interreligious dialogue initiatives to questions about the return of religion to global politics, the emergence of new models of religion-state partnership, and the apparent reconstruction of religious authority in international institutions. It noted that these processes have often been supported, adopted, and legitimized by states as responses to fears about religiously expressed conflict and problems associated with religious pluralism, and that scholars have scrambled to understand their impact on patterns of international cooperation and conflict.

The book also proposed that interreligious dialogue initiatives in the region were connected to key features of a broader, global story about religious development in late modernity. As reflected in scholarship on postsecularism and post-Islamism, the book argued that the growth of interreligious dialogue was at once a reflection of global religious changes—both sociological and theological—and also a response to them. Religious changes, including the marked shifts in the way religious traditions have come to think about religious pluralism and the marked shifts in the way religious individuals have come to combine faith and political choices, have conditioned the geopolitical investments of states and international institutions in interreligious dialogue activity. Whatever political power is transferred to religious authorities through the institutionalization of interreligious dialogue initiatives and whatever political legitimacy is afforded to states in doing so, those processes are also simultaneously drawing on, advancing, and reconfiguring these ideational, practical, and religious shifts.

As an ideational and theological development, the book linked the growth of interreligious dialogue to reformist or modernist traditions and movements in Islam and Catholicism (as well as other religious traditions), which had largely adopted positive approaches to modernity and articulated religious readings of democracy, citizenship, and pluralism. As theories of postsecularism and post-Islamism highlighted, this development reflected attempts by religiously oriented political parties, including Christian democratic parties and reformist Islamic political parties, to directly draw on religious worldviews within a democratically constructed or contested political arena. Like these reformist traditions, interreligious dialogue initiatives in the region have championed a transcendent understanding of reality as essential to political modernity. In doing so, they have adopted a view of religion which reflects insights from Axial Age and virtue ethics scholarships and which sees transcendence or strong accounts of the good as necessary for generating social mobilization and orienting the state in its struggle to establish citizen rights and manage social and religious pluralism.

At the same time, the book observed how the growth of interreligious dialogue initiatives was closely linked to the search by religious and political elites to rebuild their authority and relevance in changed political and social settings. In this sense, scholarship on post-Islamism and postsecularism also highlighted the concomitant importance of religious changes in social practices and sensibilities across the region, including the development of more individualized forms of religiosity, and observed their implications for the relationship between individual religious believers and their religious institutions, religious authorities, and traditions. These shifts in religious practice constitute the new religious terrain on which religious leaders, political parties, and state elites have worked to reconstruct religious authority and dynamism within contemporary society and politics, including through the creation of interreligious dialogue initiatives. The insights of this scholarship also point to the tensions inherent in such projects of religious renewal which attempt to adapt to these new conditions of religious practice. Ideationally and socially, the accommodations interreligious dialogue makes to pluralism might eat away at the capacity of religion to mobilize society as a whole and risks strengthening forms of religiosity which ultimately weaken religious authority, traditions, and movements, and which may end up reconsolidating the authoritarian power of the state.

The book therefore adopted a framework of power, ideas, and practices to understand the growth of state-sponsored interreligious dialogue initiatives in the contemporary Middle East and their meaning for global changes in the relationship between religion and politics in general.

The case studies featured in Part III of the book, in all the ways in which they fork and converge, capture the various parts of this story and indicate how they are interacting to reshape the role of religion in politics in the post–Arab Spring, post-ISIS context of the Middle East. The collective meaning of these various parts is revealed in a particular way through the political discourse and action on citizenship, religious change, and solidarity which many of these initiatives share but which add up together in complex ways. As a way of conclusion, this chapter briefly revisits these themes, which form the subtitle of the book, and reflects on their relationship to the interests of state power and the future of public religious engagement in the region.

Religious Change and Solidarity

In evident ways the experiences of the Focolare community in Algeria and the Adyan Foundation in Lebanon highlight the emergence of interreligious dialogue as a new religious and spiritual practice in the region endowed with important social force. Thus both groups have developed distinct, interreligious spiritualities defined by strong feelings of solidarity with religious others and communal, interreligious practices that are lived as enriching faith experiences. In either group, this discovery of living together faithfully as diverse religious peoples has also represented an existential religious experience, one which releases social dynamism to work for change in this direction. In the cases of the Adyan Foundation and the Focolare community, that dynamism funnels in an explicit way into a democratic vision of politics, into citizenship formation and participation in a common good marked by democratic rights and freedoms.

The materialization of the possibility which these groups and others like them represent—to live religious pluralism in a religiously vital way—has fed the emerging theological synthesis in the region about interreligious dialogue sketched out in Part II and increasingly adopted by religious officialdom in Islam and Christianity. One of the keys to this synthesis is the way interreligious dialogue has enabled religious actors to repropose revealed religious truth claims as a resource to sustain further openness, as a foundation for religious pluralism and equal citizenship, of modernity lived well. The book observed parallels between this synthesis and the positions taken at the Second Vatican Council on religious freedom, democracy, and human rights, including in the link that formed between those positions and the burst of political activity by Catholic actors and communities in the years which followed and preceded it. In that case, the practical synthesis fed a theological synthesis, both of which enabled the political mobilization of religious forces oriented by powerful new visions of democracy and modernity and which set ideals for international cooperation on the basis of them. Interreligious dialogue might be understood as a similar process of synthesis making (whose outcome is not yet clear), which is in the midst of developing new practical and theological orientations on pluralism and citizenship that are capable of mobilizing religious forces on its behalf.

This discovery also corresponds to a number of the expectations raised in Chapter 2 about the larger background of contemporary religious change within societies in the Middle East. As the religious experiences of participants, especially youth participants, in the Adyan Foundation and Focolare community highlight, interreligious dialogue responds to the shifting religious sensibilities of society, especially those which prize personal spiritual encounters, authentic faith choices, and introspective life paths. The book saw important echoes in these sensibilities to the enduring social and political appeal of a democratic-*cum*-religious vision of the future (Driessen 2018), as especially described in Bayat's (2013:307–308) formula of the post-Islamist religious-political worldview in the region, namely, one that fuses "religiosity and rights, faith and freedom, Islam and liberty."

The embrace of interreligious dialogue is also indicative of the types of tension that such religiosity creates with religious authority even as it enables its ongoing relevance. Thus the religious experiences of various participants highlighted in Part III depict a dynamic relationship between religious individuals and religious authorities marked by both autonomy and respect. Dialogue participants, often simultaneously, expressed the need to root their spiritual growth in their traditions and communities but also to develop their religious reasoning and life decisions on their own, often outside of traditional channels, in interreligious contexts, and not always leading to a reconfirmation of neat religious orthodoxy. In the post–Arab Spring context, the embrace of interreligious dialogue by religious authorities appears to acknowledge the reality of this religious sensibility in society and the political aspirations they are tied to. It would also seem to recognize the potential of a dialogue-oriented strategy of religious growth and renewal, even if such a strategy entails that the relationship between religious authorities and the religious life of society is apparently more tenuous as a result, beholden to the level of moral and spiritual credibility afforded to them by religious individuals, especially young religious individuals.

Many of these dynamic elements of discovery—the conviction of participating in a historical process of change, the realization of new sources of spiritual solidarity and religious growth, the sense of arriving at a new religious orientation which reconciles past tradition and revelation with what seemed to be the insurmountable challenge of the present—also characterize the state-based initiatives and examples of interreligious engagement studied throughout the book, including KAICIID, DICID, and the Forum for Promoting Peace in Muslim Societies. These initiatives elevate the new approach to religious pluralism advocated by groups like Adyan and the Focolare community by articulating it in their charters and declarations and by partnering with them on a regular basis. Many leaders of these state-based initiatives and participants in interreligious efforts personally express their work for interreligious dialogue in terms of a religious awakening of some sort. This shared sense of spirituality, the development of a new religious mentality of pluralism, is an important characteristic of contemporary dialogue initiatives in the Middle East. Among other things, it represents the development of an authoritative discourse in favor of multireligious solidarity which has altered the way in which religious pluralism has been understood in the region. As Chapter 9 highlighted, a decade ago the religious approach to dialogue was essentially rejected by many religious authorities in Saudi Arabia, Qatar, and the UAE. Today instead, it is possible to speak about the religious normalization of dialogue and the religious desirability for multireligious partnerships among religious authorities and communities.

Inclusive Citizenship

One of the key elements which binds many of the interreligious dialogue initiatives featured throughout the book, including state-based and civil-society-rooted initiatives like KAICIID, the Forum for Promoting Peace in Muslim Societies, the Adyan Foundation, and the Focolare community, as well as across a number of declarations that have emerged from their collaboration with others, is an ascendant discourse on citizenship.

This focus on "inclusive citizenship," as the Adyan Foundation and others have named it, clearly resonates with the enlarged sense of spiritual solidarity that has characterized various dialogue initiatives in the region. As Chapters 4 and 5 highlighted, it also reflects important, long-running theological developments which have accompanied these spiritual ones. In particular, the emphasis on citizenship in contemporary dialogue initiatives can be directly linked to the formal, theologically grounded, and increasingly forceful recognition of the religious legitimacy of religious others, as articulated in major interreligious declarations from *Nostra Aetate* to the A Common Word letter and the Marrakesh Declaration, and which remains a foundation for interreligious dialogue meetings in the region today.

The growing link between interreligious engagement strategies and the promotion of citizenship, therefore, also represents a specific language and understanding of religious pluralism which has developed out of a twenty-year process of high-level dialogues. In the early phases of interreligious dialogue growth in the Middle East, the practical expression of this recognition could be seen in the efforts to delegitimize religiously expressed violence and defend the rights of religious minorities (as in the Marrakesh Declaration), or to establish a basic legitimacy for dialogue among Christians, Muslims, and Jews in the region (as in the A Common Word letter and the Amman Declaration). Over time, as chronicled in Parts II and III, interreligious engagement strategies have increasingly promoted a concept of citizenship as a model of political development which embodies these goals and ideals and is required by them. Citizenship, in this model, becomes necessary for the reduction of religious violence, the establishment of religious freedom, the construction of a just political order, and the renewal of religion's place within society.

The shift in language from protecting religious minorities to promoting citizenship therefore represents an important change of narrative and the development of a new phase of dialogue activity, one which emphasizes the positive role and responsibilities of religious actors and communities to building inclusive, stable, and socially cohesive societies. In part, by employing the language of citizenship, of strengthening political rights and liberties and interreligious tolerance, "inclusive citizenship" offers a response to the dynamics of the Arab Spring which continued to animate civil society movements that upended politics in Sudan, Algeria, Lebanon, and Iraq throughout 2018–2020. As a framework, inclusive citizenship also offers a way to name a model for multireligious collaboration and political development and to propose that model as a genuine way out of the religiously expressed violence which has marked many recent conflicts in the region.

One of the important dimensions of this emerging, dialogue-developed discourse on citizenship in the region has been its explicit rooting and framing within contemporary Islamic theological reflection. As highlighted in Chapter 5, regional declarations like the Al Azhar Declarations of 2012 and 2017, the Marrakesh Declaration (2016), and the Makkah Declaration (2019), with links to declarations and movements in Southeast Asia like the Humanitarian Islam movement, have defined citizenship as restoring or renewing basic Islamic principles that were already instituted in the foundational Islamic experiences and which reflect the higher objectives (*maqasid*) of the *sharia*. In a particular way, as articulated in the Marrakesh Declaration and expressed by a variety of contemporary Muslim scholars, the Charter of Medina (622 CE) has been embraced as a strong precedence for a multireligious, contractually based political arrangement which offers political rights to citizens and which requires political responsibilities of them.

This vision of "rights and responsibilities" justifies the engagement of religious actors for a multireligious common good defined by religious freedom, equality, and inclusion. It also prescribes the necessity of a moral order, sustained by religious commitments, as the basis for securing freedom and rights lived well. In this perspective, religious tradition and faith are understood to generate essential political virtue for the state, as well as a substantive vision of justice, both of which impel individual action on behalf of others. As Chapter 5 registered, the "discovery of Article 29" (Stoeckl 2016) of the UN Universal Declaration of Human Rights has proved to be an important legitimizing device in this sense. By emphasizing citizen duties to the community and "the just requirements of morality, public order and the general welfare," Article 29 underscores the support of religious authorities in the region for a model of citizenship which is at once interreligiously set, community-focused, and traditionally conservative. The conservative nature of this model is reflected in its emphasis on religious virtue, but also in its insistence on stability, social cohesion, and the national good as necessary for the provision of rights and as the responsibility of religious authorities and individuals to cultivate. This, too, offers a way out of a defensive religious stance for religious authorities in the region, positioning them as norm entrepreneurs who are engaged in the construction of a just and durable political future, respectful of international standards of human rights. In this vision, religious authorities from different religious traditions act as indispensable mediators between politics and society and work to preserve a political ideal of human dignity and to build inclusive, rights-based political communities which might also serve as the basis for better international cooperation. The substantive embrace of religious freedom and multireligious engagement as values which reflect and protect a God-endowed human dignity marks them as orthodox positions which are consistent with long-held religious principles. Thus, rather than viewing pluralism as an expression of secularization, as some have theorized (Berger 2014), interreligious dialogue initiatives have developed an understanding of religious pluralism that is consonant with religious growth in the region.

State Power, Democracy, and the Future of Interreligious Dialogue

As Chapter 1 highlighted, by morally defending citizenship responsibilities, national stability, and multireligious collaboration, interreligious dialogue initiatives have also been attractive to state authorities in the region. Through their investments in these initiatives, states have promoted a social order that encourages loyalty to the nation-state and cultivated an international image which facilitates lucrative international collaborations. Interreligious dialogue has appealed to states as a counterweight to both the mobilization of revolutionary violence by groups like ISIS and Al Qaeda and the popular electoral appeal of Islamist-oriented political parties, most importantly the Muslim Brotherhood, which threatened ruling authoritarian state power in the region throughout the 2010s. Notably, and unlike most of the civil-society-based actors studied in this book, state-sponsored dialogue initiatives across the region, including DICID, KAICIID, and the Forum for Promoting Peace in Muslim Societies, have promoted a vision of citizenship without explicitly naming democracy as a necessary political framework for achieving that vision.

Thus, as much as interreligious dialogue represents a global and Islamic religious breakthrough which unlocks new combinations of religious ideas and action, it is simultaneously deeply attractive to states seeking to build legitimacy, restore credibility, and extend their rule. The case studies in Part III illustrated a range of ways in which dialogue initiatives have generated important services for authoritarian regimes in the region. On the one hand, state-based dialogue efforts have created international opportunities for states and strengthened their positions in global alliances. As Chapter 9 documented, key dialogue actors sponsored by Qatar, Saudi Arabia, and the UAE have taken star turns at large, new, governmental conferences connecting policymakers and religious leaders, like the US-sponsored Religious Freedom Ministerials, or have been appointed to key positions in international organizations. This includes the secretary general of KAICIID, Faisal bin Muaammar, who co-chairs the UN's Interagency Taskforce on Religion and Development's Advisory Council and is an honorary president of Religions for Peace; Qatar's Nassir Abdulaziz al Nasser, who served as the high representative for the UN's Alliance of Civilizations from 2013 to 2019; and Sheikh Abdallah bin Bayyah, who is a co-moderator of Religions for Peace and has collaborated closely with the UN on a number of occasions, most notably with the UN Office on Genocide Prevention.

These actors and institutions themselves constitute an emerging global religious engagement regime that has formalized new religion-state partnerships for international policy goals. Thus KAICIID, the Forum, the Muslim World League, and al Azhar, operating in partnership with various agencies at the United Nations and the European Union and together with large international religious bodies like Religions for Peace, the World Council of Churches, and the Vatican, have formed a loose but increasingly institutionalized network which has mobilized multireligious collaboration and support for policies like the UN's Sustainable Development Goals,[1] global pandemic relief,[2] and the political rights of religious minorities.[3] These efforts represent important instances of faith-based action in favor of international peace and humanitarian aid, and they highlight the increased role played by transnational religious actors in international institutions. They are also significant exercises in religious soft power (Mandaville and Hamid 2018) by the states which sponsor them, whose credibility has been further bolstered by their adoption of a political discourse in favor of inclusive citizenship.

Endorsing a model of inclusive citizenship without endorsing democracy has also aided states in their capacity to manage the political disaffection of their citizens and to divert the appeals of religiously expressed political movements, like the Muslim Brotherhood, which threaten their rule. Hence, the suspicion of a number of scholars of the counterrevolutionary, post–Arab Spring discourse of bin Bayyah and others and their complicity with authoritarian powers in the region (Quisay and Parker 2019; al Azami

2019; Warren 2021), or of the instrumental use of citizenship discourse by states for a more ambitious but authoritarian model of modernization which requires higher levels of active citizen engagement across multiple domains of society (Masoud 2021; Barbato 2020b). Indeed, as highlighted in Part II, interreligious declarations have often emphasized the prerogative of the nation-state to determine and defend the national moral order as well as the political and religious responsibilities of the citizen to aid and abide by it. These criticisms extend to the international politics of cooperation favored in these declarations. In particular, the Abraham Accords, signed by Israel, the UAE, and Bahrain in September 2020, were understood by various observers to be linked to the UAE's and Saudi Arabia's interreligious engagement strategies which had helped to pave the road for such normalized relationships between these states. This includes the recent outreach described in Parts II and III, of KAICIID, the Forum for Promoting Peace in Muslim Societies, the Muslim World League, and especially the Alliance of Virtue project, to Jewish communities and interfaith leaders. The deal also confirmed the suspicions of the instrumentalization of dialogue efforts by these regimes in authoritarian ways,[4] which did not necessarily reflect the thinking of mainstream Muslim scholars or the desires of Muslim-majority populations.[5]

At the same time, however, in these same declarations, the promotion of national loyalty and the responsibilities of citizens to the state have clearly been proposed on the basis of a contractual understanding of citizenship. As highlighted in the Marrakesh Declaration and reflecting a common interreligious exegesis of the Charter of Medina, the duties of citizens are offered in return for the state's promotion of those citizens' well-being and the protection of their rights. Likewise, the qualified limitations to freedom and rights referenced in Article 29 of the Universal Declaration of Human Rights, which a number of these declarations cite with approval, are justified in the same article of the declaration "for the purpose of securing . . . respect for the rights and freedoms of others" and for "the general welfare in a democratic society." In order to avert what many of these rulers and religious elites defined as disorderly democratic transitions, and to ward off the specter of Islamist movements like the Muslim Brotherhood, these states have supported the development of a substantive model of citizenship and amped up their discourse on individual political rights and religious freedom to do so. As Chapter 5 highlighted, a cumulative, authoritative body of interreligious dialogue work has given this model religious and theological support.

One of the consequences of these initiatives, therefore, is that the development of interreligious engagement in the region has been tied to specific normative content which the barebones geopolitical account of these initiatives often glosses over. Interreligious engagement in the region, as a result, cannot be characterized as only dialogue for the sake of dialogue or public appearances, nor has it enabled infinitely malleable possibilities for states to instrumentalize new religion-state partnerships or policies that flow from its recommendations. Instead, recent interreligious declarations in the region have set out a clear political ideal, what we might refer to as the dignity-freedom-citizenship principle. This principle recognizes that all human beings have been created by God with equal and inviolable dignity, that such dignity requires religious freedom, and that dignity and freedom both require the development of a more inclusive practice of citizenship to be fully realized. As Part II demonstrated, this ideal has been consistently adopted in the public narrative of these religious traditions, is buffered by a strong internal religious logic, and is linked to the changing religious and political desires of society.

This book has framed these interreligious efforts throughout the region as part of a broader search for a third-way alternative between open liberal secular models of politics, on the one hand, and closed authoritarian models, on the other hand, of both religious and secular stripes. In the Catholic European search for the same, religious freedom, dialogue, citizenship, and democracy were all bundled together, catalyzed in democratic contexts in the aftermath of World War II. The "Catholic modern" synthesis codified at Vatican II occurred twenty years after major Christian democratic victories across Europe, including in the Church's Italian backyard, and then radiated out slowly afterward. In this sense, the emergent religious modern embodied in the interreligious efforts studied in this book has been forged in more variable political settings and with more varied political results in terms of democracy. In those contexts where regime rhetoric is officially democratic, including Lebanon, Algeria, Indonesia, and Turkey (especially in the early 2000s), interreligious efforts have clearly linked the dignity-freedom-citizenship principle to democracy. In the countries of the Gulf, however, the same principle has not been openly tied to democracy, and it is unclear whether it will result in a democratic religious modern there or not.

The ambivalence of these major interreligious dialogue declarations and initiatives, especially those emanating from the Gulf countries, about the relationship between the promotion of citizen rights and democratic politics has guaranteed its ongoing relevance for state-led political reform in the region. In part, this model remains dynamic because of the way religious and interreligious leaders have used it to make an appeal to the new religious, political, and social landscape which has crystallized in the region and which is largely supportive of greater democratic politics and greater participation of citizens within them. But it is also dynamic because, as a model, it hews to an ideal of religious partnership with the state, offering it the potential of a positive exit from its current political crises. This ambivalence has also produced strong tensions between the vision within this model and the actual politics of the region. So far, these tensions have not yet been pushed to a place of breaking, where interreligious dialogue initiatives have been perceived to openly challenge, or threaten, rather than collaborate with state plans for political reform. For their part, as seen in Part III, many dialogue activists in the region, including those devoted to democratic models of development, continue to welcome and support the dialogue efforts of Saudi Arabia, Qatar, and the UAE, and see them as critical to the success of dialogue-inspired reform in the region. It is worth recalling, as the DICID and KAICIID cases illustrated, that it was Sheikh Hamad in Qatar and King Abdullah in Saudi Arabia who overrode objections from influential religious authorities, including reformists like al Qaradawi, to insist on the necessity and legitimacy of interreligious dialogue. In both cases this opened up space for broader, public theological engagement on interreligious dialogue by high-level religious authorities who were in a position to build and mobilize Islamic discourse in favor of religious pluralism in the region.

In this light, the recent experience of Turkey offers an important cautionary tale about the future capacity of dialogue efforts to influence more inclusive political development in the Middle East as well as the double-edged sword of support by less than democratic states for religious visions of change. When the AKP-dominated government came to perceive dialogue as a liability, one which challenged its domestic and international legitimacy and questioned its narrative of democratic openness and international cooperation, the Turkish state dramatically altered its preferences, rejecting its investment in dialogue in favor of a more closed authoritarian, nationalist religious discourse and using its state-run religious institutions to do so. It is possible that similar trajectories may be followed by states in the Gulf and beyond. If authoritarian states are pressed to change in what they perceive to be destabilizing ways, support for interreligious dialogue and models of inclusive citizenship may similarly wane as a result.

This research, thus, raises a number of questions which remain to be answered about the future of interreligious engagement and political reform in the region, especially with respect to the role of state power and interests. In particular, the book's findings bring new attention to the nature and sustainability of authoritarian models of modernization which adopt "active citizenship" agendas. Critically, it is not clear whether authoritarian states in the region can convincingly strengthen religious freedom and citizenship rights, as they have promised, without enacting wider democratic-like reforms which enable citizens to exercise those rights and responsibilities to the state and to each other. In other words, will these states be able to satisfy the post-Islamist urges of their people for rights and freedom and piety without enacting meaningful political reform? To what extent, and up until what point, will religious authorities, who have been supported by these same states, demand change of them when/if they fall short of the vision of citizenship and freedom for which they have advocated? Can these states construct and sustain a more inclusive authoritarian politics which satisfies their changing religious and political societies and which is in line with the new religious and theological perspectives explored in this book? To what extent will authoritarian states in the region be able to hold onto power if they do not?

These questions point to the unresolved tensions in ongoing interreligious engagement efforts in the region and the need for more research and data to continue to track and understand their nature and impact on both religious and political life. If interreligious dialogue continues to remain dynamic in the region, it might confirm the strength of its breakthrough as an integral force for political development which combines religious pluralism and religious truth claims in the service of social solidarity and new political equilibria. If, however, dialogue fizzles or fades, it might confirm the State Supreme story of Chapter 1. Or, as contemplated in Chapter 2, it might reflect the collapse of religious forces under the weight of their own accommodations or their refusal to make them, or some combination of both. Above all, this moment of interreligious dialogue in the Middle East represents an important stage in the global development of religion in modernity and its capacity to give meaning to global politics. Interreligious dialogue initiatives have provided an international platform and resources for religious actors and communities to elaborate an interreligious synthesis of modernity, lodge that synthesis in forms of international collaboration, and promote it as a force for more inclusive political development across the Middle East today. The longevity of this model will depend on the commitment of states to enact political reform, the capacity of religious communities to sustain interreligious engagement, and the support and partnership of citizens in doing so. The long-run coherence and enduring strength of interreligious engagement in the region, therefore and the religious-political synthesis it supports, still remain to be seen.

APPENDIX

Interreligious Dialogue Survey Questions

1. Tell me a little bit about your journey and interest in interreligious dialogue. How did you first find out about it? What does it mean to you as a human being?
2. Can you name any change in your thinking or approach towards other persons from different religions as a result of your experience of interreligious dialogue?
3. Has your experience and study of dialogue changed the way in which you relate to or think about religious authority in your own tradition?
4. Has your experience of dialogue affected the way you approach or think about political authority in your country or local context?
5. Tell me a little bit about your hopes for change in your religious community, neighborhood, country, or region.
6. How have your family and neighbors reacted to your interest in interreligious dialogue and extremism?
7. Do you feel that interreligious dialogue and teaching interreligious dialogue to others strengthens religious belief, weakens religious belief, or transforms religious belief? What happens, in your experience?
8. Do you view interreligious dialogue as a force for peace? For reducing extremism? For building democratic societies? Or is dialogue powerless in the face of today's religious violence and extremism?
9. Have you heard about important religious leaders in your community who support interreligious dialogue? Have others heard about them? Have you heard about the "Amman Message" or "A Common Word between Us"?
10. Many states, including Saudi Arabia, the United States, Turkey, Lebanon, and Denmark, are involved in the sponsorship of interreligious dialogue today. Do you think it is appropriate for political representatives to sponsor such religious practices?

Arab Barometer Survey Question Wording

Q516.4   To what extent do you agree or disagree with the following statement? A democratic system may have problems, yet it is better than other systems.
Q602.1   Members of which of the following groups would you not like to have as neighbors? Followers of other religions.
Q605.2   To what extent do you agree or disagree with the following statement? The government and parliament should enact laws in accordance with Islamic law.
Q606.4   To what extent do you agree or disagree with the following statement? Religious practices are private and should be separated from social and political life.
Q608.7   To what extent do you agree with the following statement? Religious minorities have the right to practice their religious ceremonies.
Q610   Do you pray daily?

World Values Survey Question Wording

V9 For each of the following, indicate how important it is in your life: Religion.

V41 On this list are various groups of people. Could you please mention any that you would not like to have as neighbors? People of a different religion.

V140 How important is it for you to live in a country that is governed democratically? On this scale where 1 means it is "not at all important" and 10 means "absolutely important" what position would you choose?

V154 Please tell us if you strongly agree, agree, disagree, or strongly disagree with the following statements: The only acceptable religion is my religion.

V156 Please tell us if you strongly agree, agree, disagree, or strongly disagree with the following statements: People who belong to different religions are probably just as moral as those who belong to mine.

Notes

Introduction

1. Through its establishment in 2012 and promotion of KAICIID, the King Abdullah bin Abdulaliz International Center for Interreligious and Intercultural Dialogue.
2. Through its establishment in 2008 of the Doha International Center for Interfaith Dialogue.
3. Through the creation of diplomatic positions like the Office for Religion and Global Affairs (established in 2013, reorganized under the Office of International Religious Freedom in 2017).
4. Through the creation in 2010 of taskforces and agencies like the UN Inter-agency Taskforce on Engaging Faith-Based Actors for Sustainable Development, which followed a 2008 UN resolution to promote "interreligious and intercultural dialogue, understanding and cooperation for peace."
5. Through the creation in 2016 of positions like the Special Envoy for the Promotion of Freedom of Religion or Belief outside the EU and, in 2019, the European External Action Service's (EEAS) Global Exchange on Religion in Society program launched.
6. Through the creation in 2016 of initiatives like the OIC Center for Dialogue, Peace and Understanding.
7. Through its launching in 2005 of projects like the Alliance of Civilizations Initiative.
8. Through its creation in 2017 of diplomatic positions like the Special Envoy of the President for Interfaith Dialogue.
9. Through its creation in 2013 of positions like the ambassador-at-large for intercultural and interreligious dialogue processes and the support, also in 2013, of its Ministry of Foreign Affairs for the Network for Religious and Traditional Peacemakers.
10. Through its help funding and hosting the International Partnership on Religion and Sustainable Development in 2016.
11. Through its establishment in 2018 of the Observatory on Religious Minorities in the World and on the Respect for Religious Freedom and, in 2022, a Special Envoy for Religious Freedom and Interreligious Dialogue.
12. The Forum for Promoting Peace in Muslim Societies formally changed its name to the Abu Dhabi Forum for Peace at its annual conference in December of 2021. It has also recently tagged itself as the "Muslim Peace Forum." The book refers to the organization throughout as "The Forum for Promoting Peace in Muslim Societies," which was the formal name of the organization throughout the time of research.
13. As Daou (2014a:2) has written in this regard, "It is necessary to save dialogue from a certain utilitarian and pragmatic temptation dominant in our culture, that judges everything on the basis of its effects rather than on the basis of what it is. So before

debating the sociopolitical results of dialogue it is necessary to recognize what it represents, not only a means towards an end which is outside the self, but also an intellectual, spiritual and psycho-social position."

14. In a recent survey of Lebanon, for example, which hosts over fifty interreligious dialogue initiatives, fewer than a handful of these initiatives could be categorized as state-promoted or state-sponsored in any explicit fashion (Driessen et al. 2020).
15. A number of Middle East scholars have taken to defining the widespread protests which gained momentum in the spring of 2011 across the Middle East as the "Arab Uprisings," in part to emphasize the dramatic but variegated political outcomes which those protests instigated and which included a democratic transition in Tunisia, a violent change of regime in Libya, and the beginning of a long, violent civil war in Syria. Throughout the book I retain the popular use of the term "Arab Spring," not in reference to these varied outcomes but in reference to the dynamics which united many of the protesters at the time and to the demands they made for democratic elections.
16. As in the high-end dialogue featured in Abu Dhabi in 2019 between the Grand Imam Sheikh Ahmed al Tayeb of al Azhar and Pope Francis. As subsequent chapters illustrate, the region has also witnessed important dialogue efforts between Muslim communities and other historic Christian communities in the region, including Coptic Churches and Orthodox Christian communities, religious minorities like the Yezidi and Druze, and Jewish communities as well.
17. M. Cenap Aydin (2019), for example, has argued that the etymological roots of "interreligious" (from the latin *religio*) more appropriately signifies dialogue between institutional religions, as opposed to the etymological roots of "interfaith" (from the latin *fides*), which could signify dialogue among more general belief systems.
18. The Roman Catholic Archdiocese of Chicago, for example, defines "interfaith" as pertaining to dialogue among Abrahamic religions, while "interreligious" pertains to dialogue with non-Abrahamic religions. For a discussion, see Gustafson's (2018) review of the use of the terms.

Chapter 1

1. Lee Marsden (2018) and other scholars have argued that this recognition has been especially adopted by policymakers as opposed to secular scholars.
2. From the "Founding Document of the Interreligious Platform for Dialogue and Cooperation in the Arab World," signed by high-level religious leaders and heads of Religious Institutions in Vienna, February 2018, and available at https://www.kaiciid.org/dialogue-knowledge-hub/resources/statements/founding-document-interreligious-platform-dialogue-and.
3. On this point, see Teissier (1998:126). As Chapter 5 will qualify in more detail, Egypt and Turkey, in this sense, both represent more complex cases, given the presence, in particular, of Al Azhar and the Muslim Brotherhood in Egypt and the recent success of Islamist-inspired movements and parties in Turkey.

4. As the King of Morocco is formally designated in the Moroccan constitution.
5. For some political analysis of these visits see, for example, Cook (2013) and Marks (2013).
6. Alongside a number of other Middle East and North African countries, including Bahrain, Yemen, and Mauritania. Saudi Arabia moved to resolve the blockade through the Al'Ula statement in 2021, signed jointly with the emir of Qatar, Sheikh Tamim bin Hamad al Thani.
7. Bin Salman was formally appointed crown prince in June 2017, less than three weeks after the start of the Qatari blockade. He had been minister of defense since 2015 and was active in leading the Saudi military intervention in the Yemeni Civil War.
8. According to a Human Rights Watch (2019) report, Turkey dismissed over 130,000 citizens from their places of employment for alleged links with the plotters of the coup, most of whom were accused of being Gülenists. Whole businesses, universities, and media outlets, including the most-read daily Turkish newspaper, *Zaman*, were also shut down on account of their links to the Gülen movement. The same report estimated that thirty-four thousand Gülenists remained in prison at the end of 2018 under summary charges of terrorism and were subject to politicized trials. It also reported accusations of torture and mistreatment.
9. In the Arab-language press for the event, UAE crown prince Mohammed bin Zayed is featured prominently alongside Pope Francis and Sheikh al Tayeb, appearing to sign some agreement or memorandum between the three. In the international press coverage, the images typically center on Tayeb and Francis signing the actual document (which is issued in their names alone). The UAE, it can be noted, also hosts the Kalam Research and Media Center (established in 2013) and the Hedayah Center (established in 2012), both of which are invested in interreligious dialogue. It also created a Ministry of Tolerance (2017) and proclaimed 2019 the Year of Tolerance.
10. See, for example, Aldrousi (2019).

Chapter 2

1. This, following a relatively brief but destructive interlude of ideological struggle in which fascist and communist models of modernity vied with liberalism as replacements for that traditional order.
2. For two recent reviews of the enduring impact of Huntington's Clash of Civilizations thesis on international relations scholarship, see the edited volumes by Haynes (2019) and Orsi (2018).
3. As this book went to press, the war in Ukraine began. Scholars working on postsecular conflicts in Eastern Europe highlighted the religious dimensions of the conflict and the relationship between the construction of religious nationalism and the perceived weaknesses of liberalism. See especially Stoeckl and Uzlaner (2022).
4. On this point, see also Areshidze (2017), but especially Vatter (2013, 2020).
5. See also Moyn (2015) and Taylor (2020a, 2020b).

6. This principle found its concrete expression in the ideal of subsidiarity, which guided Christian democratic policy preferences for decades.
7. For *Dignitatis Humanae* and other declarations, encyclicals and other official documents of the Catholic Church, the book relies on the texts provided at the vatican.va website.
8. In this Murray writes that the text's recognition of the legitimacy of Church establishment, under certain circumstances, represented a *via media* to the question of religious freedom favored by the Council fathers, in which establishment would be accepted as a historical possibility but not as a necessary consequence of doctrine. The institution of human freedom, he argued, *did* represent a settled matter of doctrine for the Council fathers, and *Dignitatis Humanae* made this position clear.
9. As quoted in Böckenförde 2020 [1967]: 167. Böckenförde described the paradox as the "great gamble" that liberalism makes for the sake of freedom See Künkler and Stein's (2020) edited volume of Böckenförde's writings.
10. Including the author. See Driessen (2012, 2014).
11. The chapter will come back to the parallel between Hallaq's critique of liberalism and MacIntyre's critique of liberalism, noted here by Hallaq himself. On the significance of the *sharia* as a resource for a better project of modernity, Hallaq (2013:13) continues, "Pitting the Shari'a against the Enlightenment obviously does not work for every purpose, but as the central domain of the moral, the Shari'a is not only a match for the Enlightenment and its resultant moral system but is potentially an immeasurably instructive moral font."
12. See especially Deeb (2006), Mahmood (2012), and Khan (2019).
13. Chapter 5 explores NU's embrace of religious humanism and interreligious dialogue more fully through its promotion of the Humanitarian Islam project and the connection it has established with Christian democracy as a tradition and institution.
14. See, among others, Lynch (2005).
15. Cavanaugh (2004: 35) memorably argued that such justifications had been systematically used to legitimize violence against Islamists in the US war on terror in order to "bomb them into a higher rationality."
16. The idea of an Axial Age was constructed as an explicit attempt to mark out a common turning point in the great civilizations of humanity before the advent of Christianity, as evidenced in the common appearance and development of the Upanishads in India, the tradition of the Hebrew prophets in Israel, the work of Confucius and Lao Tse in China, and Platonism in Ancient Greece. For Karl Jaspers, whose work many take as the starting point for Axial Age discourses, the Western intellectual tradition, through to Hegel, mistakenly presented the particularities of Christian modernity as a universal model of modernity. This mistake was the result of a deeply lodged Western, cultural understanding of Christ as *the* axis of history. By recuperating these earlier Axial ruptures, deep-history sociologists and intellectual historians have named more basic, pre-Christian civilizational dynamics which appeared roughly around the same time in human history in the great philosophies and religious systems and which have animated their progress to the present. In this account, the presence, reality, and interpretation of the transcendent are essential.

17. Casanova (2012: 192) asks, "[I]s our modern global secular age the teleological unfolding of potentials implicit in the Axial breakthroughs, namely the full crystallization of axial 'theoretic' culture? Or does modernity constitute a post-Axial secular breakthrough of its own?" The very articulation of the idea of an Axial Age itself poses this question, for in recognizing the dynamics of the Axial Age, its articulation also points to its surpassing.
18. In a different way this is also the position of an atheist philosopher like Žižek, who argues that only by taking the death of god seriously does humanity unlock the potential to full agency, action, and social responsibility. Only as (truly believing) atheists, as opposed to liberal Protestants (or an agnostic materialist) but closer to truth-inspired ascetics of old, can human beings take seriously the awareness of their own divinity, that they become creators, gods-on-this-earth, the source of full agency, action, and construction. See Žižek and Milbank (2011).
19. On this note, the exchange between Lilla and Milbank at a 2008 Georgetown conference is illustrative. Lilla responds to a comment by Milbank by saying, "I actually find common ground with thinkers like John [Milbank]. I think there is recognition on both our sides that there is a significant break in modern thought, and I use the metaphor of the two shores to describe our perspective positions. Theorists like John and theorists like me are standing on opposite shores looking at each other with a mutual disdain for those who think that they can somehow negotiate the middle by developing a liberal theology. I think we agree entirely on that picture" (see the exchange in Kessler 2013:17).
20. Moyn (2015:98) continues, "albeit one equally intended to steer far clear of communism. Indeed, in my view this is the key to placing the document—along with the human rights idea in general—more securely in the ambiance of the war's aftermath, as part of the moral reconstruction of Europe perceived to be necessary to stave off future world crises and conflicts." In this passage Moyn is especially focused on Maritain's personalism and his insistence on thinking about human beings as persons-inserted-in-community as opposed to autonomous individuals.
21. See Driessen (2018) for a review of these scholarly criticisms.
22. He continues, "The loosening of social bonds in nearly every aspect of life—familial, neighborly, communal, religious, even national—reflects the advancing logic of liberalism and is the source of its deepest instability" (Deneen 2019:29). Deneen frequently employs the image of liberalism "drawing down" from the bank of moral virtue. Earlier in *Why Liberalism Failed* he writes, "[L]iberalism has ruthlessly drawn down a reservoir of both material and moral resources that it cannot replenish" (18).
23. He then goes on to quote MacIntyre on the same page, writing, "Rational enquiry and thus ethical values are embedded, MacIntyre rightly observes, 'in a *tradition, a conception* according to which the standards of rational justification themselves emerge from and are part of a history in which they are vindicated'" (Hallaq 2013:6).
24. Mansour criticized al Issa of starting a "new religion." For coverage, see Welby (2020) and Judd and Alfaisal (2020). Parallels can be made here to Milbank's criticism (on Twitter) of Sinead O'Connor as a "civilizational traitress" for having converted to Islam. See Milbank's explanation of his comments on "Christianity, Islam and the

206 NOTES

Self-Betrayal of the West," *ABC Religion and Ethics*, October 13, 2018. There are also parallels with the new religious defenses of nationalism especially prevalent in National Conservativism as a movement. Hazony's (2018) *The Virtue of Nationalism* is illustrative in this sense. See also the "Against the Dead Consensus" manifesto published by *First Things* in 2019. For a review of some of these trends, see Driessen (2021).

25. Taylor (1996:37) writes in "A Catholic Modernity?," "Better, I would argue, after an initial (and let's face it, still continuing) bewilderment, gradually to find our voice from within the achievements of modernity; to measure the humbling degree to which some of the most impressive extensions of a Gospel ethic depended on a breakaway from Christendom; and from within these gains try to make clear to ourselves and others the tremendous dangers that arise in them."

Chapter 3

1. This observation can be extended beyond Christianity and Islam, as the Rissho Kosei Kai movement, a lay Buddhist renewal movement which expanded in the postwar democratic environment of Japan and went on to help establish the Religions for Peace network, attests to (Catalano 2015).
2. Speaking at the World Conference on Dialogue in Madrid in 2008, sponsored by Saudi Arabia. See Premawardhana (2008), then director of the World Council of Churches Program on Inter-religious Dialogue and Cooperation, for a reflection.
3. The organization which eventually grew out of the first World Parliament of Religions, held in Chicago in 1893, and which produced the Global Ethic 100 years later in 1993.
4. As the United Religions Initiative has been described, which began in 1993 in organic relationship to the United Nations and which, as its charter states, seeks to unite religions on an ongoing basis to, among other things, "provide a global opportunity for participation by all people, especially by those whose voices are not often heard" (https://uri.org/what-we-do/charter).
5. See Cambridge Inter-faith Programme's "The CIP Approach to Inter-faith Encounters" at https://www.interfaith.cam.ac.uk/aboutus/cipapproachinterfaithencounters.
6. For discussion, see Cheetham (2007) and Hedges (2008).

Chapter 4

1. Recent international relations scholars, like Scott Thomas, have made a similar interpretation of the early Franciscan visits to the Islamic world, and in particular St. Francis's meeting with Sultan al Kamil. The first visit, to Morocco, did not end well for the early friars, who met their end after what some have described as provocative preaching to their hosts. The second visit, St. Francis's trip to Egypt with the fifth

crusade in 1219, ended differently: al Kamil was curious, wanted to hear more, and then let Francis go back free and unharmed. Thomas (2018:13) has described these meetings as decentering encounters with the peripheries which led the early friars to better understand their vocation in the world. In particular, the meeting with the sultan influenced the insertion of two approaches to mission in the early rule of St. Francis, namely, that of *presence* as well as *preaching*, as in encouraging the option of friars to make themselves "subject to every human creature for God's sake and to acknowledge that they are Christians."

2. The parable of the Good Samaritan is also the central gospel story which Pope Francis chooses to reflect on in his 2020 Encyclical, *Fratelli Tutti*.
3. The full prayer, from the New Revised Standard Version: [20] "I ask not only on behalf of these, but also on behalf of those who will believe in me through their word, [21] that they may all be one. As you, Father, are in me and I am in you, may they also be in us, so that the world may believe that you have sent me. [22] The glory that you have given me I have given them, so that they may be one, as we are one, [23] I in them and you in me, that they may become completely one, so that the world may know that you have sent me and have loved them even as you have loved me."
4. On this point, see particularly Pope Paul VI's (1975) encyclical *Evangelii Nuntiandi* (§53): "The Church respects and esteems these non-Christian religions because they are the living expression of the soul of vast groups of people. They carry within them the echo of thousands of years of searching for God, a quest which is incomplete but often made with great sincerity and righteousness of heart. They possess an impressive patrimony of deeply religious texts. They have taught generations of people how to pray. They are all impregnated with innumerable 'seeds of the Word' [74] and can constitute a true 'preparation for the Gospel,' [75] to quote a felicitous term used by the Second Vatican Council and borrowed from Eusebius of Caesarea."
5. See, for example, Ayoub (2011).
6. The full document, which was subtitled "Declaration on the Unicity and Salvific Universality of Jesus Christ and the Church," also stated, "The Church likewise believes that the key, the center, and the purpose of the whole of man's history is to be found in its Lord and Master" (*Dominus Iesus*, §13).
7. Paul VI (1967) proposed the term in his encyclical *Progressio Populorum*. On the relations between integral human development and interreligious dialogue, see Paul VI, Angelus, May 17, 1970; John Paul II, 2001, "Dialogue between Cultures for a Civilization of Love and Peace," January 1, 2001, World Day of Peace, and Pope Francis, "Address to the Participants in the Conference Organized by the Dicastery for Promoting Integral Human Development, marking the 50th Anniversary of the Encyclical *Progressio Populorum*" (April 4, 2017).

Chapter 5

1. All quotes and references to the Amman Message are taken from the official Amman Message website in English at https://ammanmessage.com/.

2. The Amman Message also includes signatories who were associated with the Muslim Brotherhood, including the director general of the Muslim Brotherhood in Jordan.
3. Former vice president of IUMS and an ECFR member, signatory to and consultant for the Amman Message and A Common Word, president of Forum for Promoting Peace in Muslim Societies, lead organizer of Marrakesh Declaration.
4. Former grand mufti of Egypt and grand imam of al Azhar, signatory to A Common Word and Amman Message, lead author with Pope Francis on the Human Fraternity document.
5. Former president of IUMS, ECFR, signatory to Amman Message, regular participant in Doha's DICID.
6. Signatory to Amman Message and A Common Word, ECFR member.
7. Secretary general of IUMS, ECFR member, regular participant in Doha's DICID, signatory to Amman Message.
8. ECFR member, signatory to Amman Message.
9. Several other important Muslim leaders and intellectuals, such as Hamza Yusuf (USA), Yahya Pallavicini (Italy), Timothy Winter (UK), and Mohammad Sammak (Lebanon), also accompanied all of these declarations while not necessarily participating in the international unions of Muslim scholars listed above.
10. As quoted from Prince Ghazi bin Muhammad's introduction to the Amman Message on the Official Website of the Amman Message at https://ammanmessage.com/introduction/.
11. The address included a reference to an arcane debate about violence from the medieval period, which Benedict used to warn against the adoption of religious absolutism. Benedict argued that such absolutism had dangerously isolated some forms of Islamic thinking from processes of critical reasoning which were capable of challenging the religious and doctrinal appeals that religiously inspired violent actors make on the basis of such absolutism. It is possible that the negative reaction to Regensburg was as much spurred by a general perception of a chilling of official Catholic enthusiasm for dialogue and Islam that Benedict's papacy seemed to embody as by the text of the Regensburg speech itself. It is possible, in fact, to see within the Regensburg Address some similarity with the projects of the A Common Word document, the Marrakesh Declaration, and other recent interreligious dialogue initiatives in the Middle East, namely, that of finding a new, mutually purifying equilibrium between religion and modernity, faith and reason. As Benedict XVI said in the Regensburg Address, and echoing his dialogue with Habermas of the previous year, "The intention here is not one of retrenchment or negative criticism, but of broadening our concept of reason and its application. While we rejoice in the new possibilities open to humanity, we also see the dangers arising from these possibilities and we must ask ourselves how we can overcome them. We will succeed in doing so only if reason and faith come together in a new way, if we overcome the self-imposed limitation of reason to the empirically falsifiable, and if we once more disclose its vast horizons. . . . Only thus do we become capable of that genuine dialogue of cultures and religions so urgently needed today. In the Western world it is widely held that only positivistic reason and the forms of philosophy based on it are universally valid. Yet the world's profoundly

religious cultures see this exclusion of the divine from the universality of reason as an attack on their most profound convictions. A reason which is deaf to the divine and which relegates religion into the realm of subcultures is incapable of entering into the dialogue of cultures." Quotation from Benedict XVI's Regensburg address from the vatican.va website: https://www.vatican.va/content/benedict-xvi/en/speeches/2006/september/documents/hf_ben-xvi_spe_20060912_university-regensburg.html.

12. Prince Ghazi (2012:131) of Jordan, who wrote the first draft, has written that he sought immediate feedback on the draft from several scholars from Al Azhar and from Sheikh Abdallah bin Bayyah before presenting it to a wider audience.
13. In formulating the shared Great Commandments in this way, Prince Ghazi (2012), as he notes in his five-year review of the A Common Word document, drew on his PhD dissertation, which he wrote at Cambridge University on the theme of love in Islam. All references to the A Common Word between Us and You rely on the text of the document from the A Common Word between Us and You website at: https://www.acommonword.com/the-acw-document/.
14. Some have even accused arguments of the type that the A Common Word makes as a covert attempt to declare that the primordial nature of Christians and Jews remains Islamic even if Jews and Christians do not recognize it as such. See Brague (2016).
15. And which has been published as "Religious Minorities in Muslim-Majority Lands: A Legal Framework and a Call to Action" by the Forum for Promoting Peace in Muslim Societies (2016) alongside the unabridged Marrakesh Declaration signed at the same conference.
16. See Warren and Gilmore (2014) on al Qaradawi and Ali Bulaç, and Mumisa (2016) on Rachid Ghannouchi and Ali Gomma. Other scholars, including Hallaq (2013), Fadel (2012), and Winter (2019), have also held up the Charter of Medina as a key text for contemporary Islamic political thought.
17. Who had invited Muhammad to formally mediate between the warring tribes in Medina.
18. See Council of Foreign Relations, "A Conversation with Abdallah bin Bayyah," interview, June 4, 2015, https://www.cfr.org/event/conversation-shaykh-abdallah-bin-bayyah.
19. In his introductory paper to the topic of inclusive citizenship, which approvingly references Habermas's translation proviso, bin Bayyah (2018) observes that among the most important components of citizenship referenced in the Marrakesh Declaration are "the principle of recognizing pluralism and acknowledging religious freedom" and "the principle of mutual duties and equal rights."
20. Who has been looked to as an important twentieth-century father of the *maqasid* approach (Rane 2012–2013; Auda 2008).
21. On the relationship between religious freedom and religious violence and its extension to contemporary conflicts in the Muslim-majority world, see Grim and Finke (2010) and Philpott (2019).
22. As quoted in the abridged version of the Marrakesh Declaration found on the Marrakesh Declaration website at https://www.marrakeshdeclaration.org/files/Bismilah-2-ENG.pdf. References to the unabridged Marrakesh Declaration are taken

from the Marrakesh Declaration published in 2016 in print form by the Forum for Promoting Peace in Muslim Societies (Abu Dhabi).
23. The first point of the 2017 Al Azhar Declaration, for example, states, "[T]he concept of 'Citizenship' has its origin in Islam as it was perfectly applied in the constitutional document of Madinah and the subsequent covenants and treaties in which Prophet Muhammad, peace and blessings be upon him, defined the relationships between Muslim[s] and non-Muslims. The Declaration stresses that citizenship is not just a desirable solution but rather a necessary recalling of the first Islamic application of the fairest system of governance to the first Muslim community in the state of Madinah. The prophet's application of citizenship was totally free of any discrimination against any category of the society at that time; it featured policies based on religious, racial, and social pluralism. Such pluralism could only prosper in an environment of full citizenship and equality under the constitutional document of Madinah. The document stated clearly that all citizens of Madinah must be treated equally in terms of their rights and responsibilities, that they together constitute one nation, regardless of their different races and religions, and that non-Muslims have the same rights given to Muslims and are required to fulfill the same obligations imposed on Muslims." For the English version of the al Azhar declaration, I rely on the Oasis Center's translation from https://www.oasiscenter.eu/en/there-are-no-minorities-only-citizens.
24. See especially the Charter of the New Alliance of Virtue Charter's Article 4, points 1 and 2, "Human Dignity" and "Freedom of Conscience and Religion or Belief." For the recognition of *Dignitatis Humanae,* see the Charter's preamble.
25. See, for example, the Muslim World League's secretary general, Muhammed bin Abdul Karim Al-Issa's 2019 speech on inclusive citizenship, http://www.arabnews.com/node/1464736/saudi-arabia.
26. See, for example, KAICIID's project in favor of citizenship in the Arab World.
27. See, for example, bin Bayyah's 2018 remarks and the Forum for Promoting Peace in Muslim Societies' project "Inclusive Citizenship: A Topic for Research."
28. This experience of toleration was relative (positively so in comparison to Western Europe at the time) and did not imply political equality in its modern liberal usage. Scholars have pointed out how legal definitions of religious minorities across Islamic empires, especially as codified in the status of *dhimmi,* which defined a protected status on certain religious minorities, also created incentives for political repression and marginalization of those minorities in ways that continue to matter for interfaith relations today. Among others, see Scott (2010).
29. Diez (2020) offers a similar analysis on the Islamic appeal to natural law in recent interreligious dialogue texts in the region, especially in the Alliance of Virtue Charter.
30. Emon reads al Ghazali as still writing "in the shadow of classical Greek philosophy," which al Ghazali came to through Ibn Sina (Avicenna), whom, however, al Ghazali famously criticized in his work *The Incoherence of the Philosophers.*
31. In publicizing the importance of the document, the Amman Message specifically mentions the endorsement of several high-level religious authorities by name to signify its authority and resonance, namely, the grand sheikh of al Azhar, Grand

Ayatollah al Sistani of Iraq, and Yusuf al Qaradawi. See the International Islamic Conference's (2005) statement on the Amman Message (presented on the Amman Message official website: https://ammanmessage.com/the-statement-issued-by-the-international-islamic-conference/).

32. The Alliance of Virtue project is also significant for the way it establishes partnerships between Muslim communities in the Middle East and Evangelical and Jewish communities in the United States on the issues of interreligious dialogue and religious freedom. See, for example, Pastor Bob Roberts's statement at the Alliance of Virtue conference in Washington, DC (February 5–7, 2018), as reviewed by the Network of Traditional and Religious Peacemakers: https://www.peacemakersnetwork.org/hundreds-religious-leaders-affirm-rights-religious-minorities-respect-muslims-united-states/.

33. Hamza Yusuf, who has often been referred to as a neotraditionalist, as opposed to an Islamic reformist, has argued that "Renovation" is a better term to use than "Reform." In part, the term allows him to argue that Islam itself is not in need of reform. In part, it allows him to distinguish his project from those favored by recent Islamist parties in the region. See, for example, his 2010 debate with Tariq Ramadan at Oxford, titled "Rethinking Islamic Reform." Ramadan sticks with the term "Reform."

34. On this point, see also Sachedina (2001).

35. See also Esack (1997) on this point.

36. In particular through the 2016 International Summit of Moderate Islamic Leaders Nahdlatul Ulama Declaration, the 2017 Gerakan Penuda Ansor Declaration on Humanitarian Islam, and the 2018 Nusantra Manifesto.

37. A crisis which it identifies with a closed, revolutionary form of political Islam. See especially the 2017 *Declaration on Humanitarian Islam*: "The Islamic world is in the midst of a rapidly metastasizing crisis, with no apparent sign of remission" (25).

38. The Centrist Democrat International (CDI) is the international network of Christian democratic parties and was formerly called the Christian Democratic International. The organization still defines its purpose as supporting "Christian democracy, integral humanism and interreligious dialogue," which is the tagline it uses to describe its activities on its official homepage.

39. In 2019, the Indonesian Nationalist Awakening Party, which is historically associated with NU, became a formal member of CDI. Anggia Erma Rini, the deputy general secretary of the party and also then the chairperson of the NU's young adult women's movement (or Fatayat, with an estimate of 7 million members), presented the resolution for adoption at the meeting in Rome.

40. In developing this model of Humanitarian Islam, NU has also drawn a line to its former chairman, Abdurrahman Wahid, who helped lead a period of major reform within NU and within the government and became the first Indonesian president to be democratically elected by the People's Consultative Assembly. Wahid's grave is marked with the epitaph "Here rests a humanist."

41. The Resolution begins, "Recognizing that the spiritual, philosophical and historical origins of the Centrist Democrat International (CDI) lie in the traditions of Christian humanism, and the response of Christian democratic political movements to the

profound moral and geopolitical crisis that European and Latin American nations faced after World War II . . . [and a]cknowledging the central role of the humanist tradition, and of Christian democratic political movements which helped inspire and secure the adoption of the Universal Declaration of Human Rights." The text of this resolution and other official documents related to Humanitarian Islam can be found at the Bayt Ar-Rahmah website at: https://www.baytarrahmah.org/media/2019/CDI _Resolution-on-ethics-and-values-that-should-guide-the-exercise-of-power.pdf

42. Which has a parallel in Paul's exhortation in Romans 12:10 to "love one another with mutual affection; outdo one another in showing honor."

43. Here Burhani (2011:340) distinguishes between sociological as opposed to theological pluralism. The rank and file of Muhammadiyah, he argues recognize and observe sociological plurality as something "given by God that cannot be rejected." That said, they do not celebrate theological diversity or embrace theological pluralism.

44. On the questions of the political consequences of love and affection in Islam, see Khan's (2019) recent book *Islam and Good Governance: A Political Philosophy of Ihsan*.

45. Even Ahmed al Tayeb, who signed the Human Fraternity document with Pope Francis in 2019, has seemed to justify crucifixion as an appropriate Qur'anic punishment for ISIS fighters and to defend death sentences for apostasy. See, for example, "Al Azhar Calls for Killing, Crucifixion of ISIS Terrorists," *Al Arabiya News*, February 4, 2015.

46. See for example, an earlier fatwa from bin Bayyah which has been roughly translated "Christians in the Hereafter" (https://islamqa.org/w/maliki/binbayyah/29788), as well as Hamza Yusuf's 2007 essay, "Who Are the Disbelievers?" In both texts, an expanded understanding of salvation is evident, even though it is only in and through a full and free recognition of God's oneness that salvation is possible, meaning that fully informed Christians who freely reject Qur'anic claims are in a weak position in the afterlife. Bin Bayyah (2019) has also made it clear that the Forum's support for religious freedom does not imply the abolishment of blasphemy laws.

47. To use a phrase from Soroush (2000:126).

48. The penultimate version of the text's Religious Freedom clause (Article 4.2), circulated to participants at the conference, began with the invocation "there is no compulsion in the religion or belief," and included the following phrase, which was eventually struck out: "people have a right to choose their beliefs and to practice their faith without fear of persecution."

49. The final text of the Charter for Inclusive Citizenship likewise rejected definitions of religious freedom which would have mirrored European and American formulations of freedom of religion or belief. The document details religious freedom as individual freedom from compulsion, freedom to worship, and freedom of conscience but is silent on issues related to apostasy and blasphemy and religious responsibilities to one's religious community. Rather than freedom of religion or belief, the document adopted the formula "religious freedom and the sanctity of human conscience."

50. Esack (1997:174) comments in his work on Islam and pluralism that Islam may maintain its status as an/the ideological leader among religions insofar as it struggles to

construct a society and politics marked by inclusive understandings of justice, liberation, and mercy which would reflect God's command to unity among a God-willed religious diversity.
51. The Marrakesh Declaration states in this regard, "The objectives of the Charter of Medina provide a suitable framework for national constitutions in countries with Muslim majorities, and the United Nations Charter and related documents, such as the Universal Declaration of Human Rights, are in harmony with the Charter of Medina, including consideration for public order."
52. See UAE Federal Decree Law No. 2 of 2015, "On Combating Discrimination and Hatred." In Article 1, blasphemy is defined as "any act of insulting or showing contempt for God, to religions, prophets or messengers, holy books or places of worship according to the provisions of this Decree Law."
53. Bin Bayyah (2018) notes in this regard, "Therefore, the call for the freedom of desecration of the sacred is one of the deluded applications of freedom of expression that incite to violence and hatred, and allows the disturbance of the public order of societies and thus the disruption of social peace."
54. On this point, Glendon (1997), as have others, draws attention to the first part of Article 29, which states, "Everyone has duties to the community in which alone the free and full development of his personality is possible." She comments, "Human beings are said to be 'endowed with reason and conscience,' and they are expected to 'act towards one another in a spirit of brotherhood.' . . . Article 29 tells us that it is in community 'alone' that the 'free and full development of his personality is possible.' Though its main body is devoted to basic freedoms, the Declaration begins and ends with exhortations to solidarity (Articles 1 and 29). Whatever else may be said of him or her, the Declaration's 'everyone' is not a lone bearer of rights" (1172). See also Glendon (2013).
55. Striking a similar tone, Yusuf is also a lead participant in the Religious Freedom Institute's Virtue Project, which "explores ways that classical traditions of virtue, rooted in the transcendent, might serve as a potent antidote to the plummeting consensus in America on what it means to pursue the common good." The Religious Freedom Institute also participated in the drafting of the Alliance of Virtue Charter.
56. Remarks at the Forum for Promoting Peace in Muslim Societies' 2022 conference on Inclusive Citizenship, December 5–7, Abu Dhabi.
57. A vision Quisay and Parker (2019) especially articulate through the work of bin Bayyah's close associate Hamza Yusuf.
58. One who, Warren (2021) argues, has been consistently less supportive of democracy since the Arab Spring than al Qaradawi.
59. See, for example, bin Bayyah's (2019) framework paper, "The Nation State in Muslim Societies," addressed to his association's Third Annual Forum for Promoting Peace in Muslim Societies, in 2016.
60. While the 2011 and 2012 al Azhar declarations, written in the immediate aftermath of the Arab Spring, did advocate for democracy (e.g., the 2012 document declares al Azhar's support for "the mobilisation of the brother Arab peoples for freedom

and democracy"), the 2017 al Azhar declaration on citizenship, like the Marrakesh Declaration, does not mention the term. The 2021 charter for Inclusive Citizenship (originally proposed as the "Charter for Inclusive Citizenship in the Arab World") likewise does not mention the word "democracy" but is more specific than its predecessors in naming the kinds of constitutional rights to participation, representation, and shared decision-making that the exercise of citizenship and religious freedom require. The NU declarations on Humanitarian Islam do mention democracy. The 2018 Nusantara Manifesto, for example, is openly supportive of democracy and warns against authoritarianism in religious terms. Of course, not all declarations in favor of democracy actually talk about democracy. None of the major documents produced at Vatican II, for example, from *Dignitatis Humanae,* to *Gaudium et Spes, Lumen Gentium, Ad Gentes,* or *Nostra Aetate,* mentions the word "democracy," but they do make strong statements which favor its practice, such as in *Gaudium et Spes,* "Praise is due to those national procedures which allow the largest possible number of citizens to participate in public affairs with genuine freedom" (§31), and in the opening lines from *Dignitatis Humanae,* "A sense of the dignity of the human person has been impressing itself more and more deeply on the consciousness of contemporary man, and the demand is increasingly made that men should act on their own judgment, enjoying and making use of a responsible freedom.... The demand is likewise made that constitutional limits should be set to the powers of government, in order that there may be no encroachment on the rightful freedom of the person and of associations." Pope John XXIII's encyclical, *Pacem in Terris,* by contrast, which called for the council, does mention democracy and reads like a Christian democratic manifesto. Similar observations could be made about the Universal Declaration of Human Rights, which mentions democracy only once, ironically in Article 29, which connects democracy to society's needs for moral and public order.

61. Bin Bayyah's Forum for Promoting Peace in Muslim Societies issued a statement in support of the blockade of Qatar shortly after the decision was made to do so by the UAE and other Gulf states. The UAE Fatwa Council, which bin Bayyah also heads, issued a statement agreeing with the UAE's designation of the Muslim Brotherhood as a terrorist organization in 2020.

62. There are important differences in the religion-state arrangements among these states sponsoring interreligious initiatives. Notably, as discussion on the Human Fraternity document indicates, al Azhar's steps at the beginning of the Arab Spring to carve out some independence from the Egyptian state apparatus in its self-organization as a religious body has been important for al Tayeb's work with Pope Francis on the question of citizenship. See Fahmi (2021).

63. Al Sisi had instituted strict new travel regulations for senior state officials just two weeks before the Human Fraternity event, which some interpreted as aimed specifically at containing the influence of al Tayeb. See Brown and Dunne (2021).

64. All references to the Human Fraternity document rely on the English translation from the vatican.va website at https://www.vatican.va/content/francesco/en/travels/2019/outside/documents/papa-francesco_20190204_documento-fratellanza-umana.html.

65. Which, Pope Francis has observed, is distinct from solidarity. See Ferrara (2021).

NOTES 215

66. Various religious leaders in the region and beyond involved in interreligious dialogue lauded the signing of the document. Afterward, for example, NU presented a resolution to CDI formally endorsing the Human Fraternity document and noted its resonance with Humanitarian Islam.
67. Francis invited Judge Mohamed Mahmoud Abdel Salam, who was an advisor to Sheikh al Tayeb and a principal contributor to the Human Fraternity document, to present the encyclical at the official Vatican launch in October 2020, together with a panel that included Cardinal Miguel Ayusho Guixot, the president of the Pontifical Council for Interreligious Dialogue, and Andrea Riccardi, the founder of the community of Sant'Egidio, whose annual International Prayer for Peace had facilitated contacts between the Vatican and al Tayeb. For his part, Sheikh al Tayeb, while not present for the launch, also hailed the encyclical as "an extension of the document on Human Fraternity, [that] reveals a global reality in which the vulnerable and marginalized pay the price for unstable positions and decisions" (quoted in O'Connell 2020). Various Vatican commentators have presented the encyclical as a clear summation of Francis's papacy to date (Spadaro 2020).
68. The Human Fraternity document refers to religious diversity as "willed by God in his wisdom" and as the foundation for religious freedom.
69. Which, like the Human Fraternity document, was issued in al Tayeb's name.

Chapter 6

1. In 2021, Fadi Daou stepped down from his position at Adyan. Nayla Tabbara became president of the foundation, and Elie al Hindy its executive director.
2. Critically, however, and reflecting important differences in the way support for secularism may manifest, Lebanese respondents are the most likely of the four countries to support the teaching of *all* religions in public schools (60% of Lebanese respondents were in favor of public religious education of all religions, compared to only 20% of Algerian respondents and 17% of Qatari respondents).
3. The survey data, in fact, reveal various complexities surrounding what might be loosely labeled conservative versus liberal religious attitudes in the Muslim-majority world and their relationship to political positions. While Qatari respondents, for example, might register as more traditionally/religiously conservative on some measures, on other measures they did not. Thus, Qatari respondents were the most likely of the four to think that neither abortion nor divorce was ever justifiable (76% of Qatari respondents thought neither were ever justifiable. In comparison, 51% of Lebanese respondents thought abortion was never justifiable and 45% thought divorce was never justifiable; 44% of Algerian respondents thought abortion was never justifiable and 51% thought divorce was never justifiable). At the same time, however, Qatari respondents were the most likely to believe that it was never justifiable to beat one's wife (77% of Qatari respondents; 54% of respondents in Lebanon; 39% in Algeria), and the most likely to believe that it was acceptable for women to have more income than their husband (53% of Qatari respondents; only 29% of Lebanese respondents and 26% of Algerian respondents).

Chapter 7

1. Representing 10% of the nearly two hundred Catholic religious in Algeria at the time.
2. See, for example, coverage of the beatifications by Anne-Bénédicte Hoffner, "Martyrs d'Algérie, les enjeux d'une beatification exceptionnelle," *La Croix*, December 7, 2018, and "Mgr Pierre Claverie, les moines de Tibhirine et onze autres religieux et religieuses reconnus martyrs," *La Croix*, January 27, 2018.
3. Interview with author, June 12, 2017, Tlemcen.
4. Interview with author, June 12, 2017, Tlemcen.
5. Interview with author, June 14, 2017, Algiers.
6. Interview with author, June 8, 2017, Oran.
7. Interview with author, June 11, 2017, Tlemcen.
8. Interview with author, June 5, 2017, Algiers.
9. Interview with author, June 14, 2017, Algiers.
10. Interview with author, June 5, 2017, Algiers.
11. Interview with author, June 4, 2017, Algiers.
12. Interview with author, June 14, 2017, Algiers.
13. Interview with author, June 10, 2017, Oran.
14. Interviewed by Donato Chiampi in the film *L'Idéal de L'Unité: Contributions de L'Algérie pour Réaliser la Fraternité Universelle* (2016).
15. Mokrani is himself of Algerian origin and taught for many years at the Pontifical Institute for the Study of Islam and Arabic in Rome before becoming a senior expert at the John XXIII Institute for Religious Sciences research center on the history and doctrines of Islam in Palermo.
16. Interview with author, February 8, 2018, Rome. See also Mokrani (2008, 2017).
17. Interview with author, June 13, 2017, Tlemcen.
18. See also Lemarié (2017) on the efforts to create Islamic meditations on the *Word of Life*.
19. Interview with author, February 7, 2018, Rome.
20. Interview with author, June 14, 2017, Algiers.
21. Interview with author, June 11, 2017, Tlemcen.
22. Interview with author, June 4, 2017, Algiers.
23. Interviewed by Donato Chiampi in the film *L'Idéal de L'Unité: Contributions de L'Algérie pour Réaliser la Fraternité Universelle* (2016).
24. Interviewed by Donato Chiampi in the film *L'Idéal de L'Unité: Contributions de L'Algérie pour Réaliser la Fraternité Universelle* (2016).
25. Interview with author, June 11, 2017, Tlemcen.
26. Interview with author, June 10, 2017, Tlemcen.
27. Interview with author, June 12, 2017, Tlemcen.
28. Interview with author, June 7, 2017 Oran.
29. Interview with author, June 11, 2017, Tlemcen.
30. Interview with author, June 5, 2017, Algiers.
31. The Focolare movement also promotes programs on active citizenship and fraternity for youth through its Politics for Unity Movement.

NOTES 217

Chapter 8

1. Tabbara has subsequently become president of the Foundation.
2. Interview with author, June 13, 2018, Beirut.
3. The literal translation of the original French publication is *Divine Hospitality: The Other in the Dialogue of Christian and Muslim Theologies*. The English translation was published in 2017.
4. Interview with author, June 8, 2014, Beirut.
5. Interview with author, June 13, 2018, Beirut.
6. Interview with author, June 11, 2018, Beirut.
7. Adyan Foundation, *Toolkit for Religious Education on Citizenship Values*, film, 2014.
8. Interview with author, June 13, 2018, Beirut.
9. Interview with author, June 5, 2018, Beirut.
10. Interview with author, June 14, 2018, Beirut.
11. Interview with author, June 7, 2018, Beirut.
12. *Adyan Foundation Biennial Report: 2017–2018*.
13. Interview with author, June 1, 2018, Beirut.
14. Ballout won Lebanon's 2017 Teacher of the Year award and was one of two Middle East teachers shortlisted for the Varkey Foundation Global Teacher of the Year prize in 2018.
15. Interview with author, June 1, 2018, Beirut.
16. Interview with author, June 1, 2018, Beirut.
17. Interview with author, June 13, 2018, Bschammoun.
18. Interview with author, May 31, 2018, Beirut.
19. Survey conducted by author with Adyan participants, August 2014, Broummana.
20. Interview with author, June 8, 2018, Beirut.
21. Interview with author, May 30, 2018, Beirut.
22. Interview with author, June 2, 2018, Beirut.
23. Interview with author, June 13, 2018, Beirut.

Chapter 9

1. Although, as various scholars also point out and as registered in the US State Department's *International Religious Freedom Reports*, in general Saudi Arabia allows the private religious practice of non-Muslims. In part this reflects the inescapable nature of the economy that Saudi Arabia and other Gulf states, including, especially, Qatar, have constructed, which rely highly on imported workers, many of whom are Christians.
2. The Pew Research Center's 2010 estimate for the Christian population of Qatar is slightly higher, at 13% (Pew Research Center 2020). The Religious Characteristics of States Dataset estimated that 9% of the Qatari population was Roman Catholic.

3. Significantly, according to DICID, the conference marked the first time that the Pontifical Council of Interreligious Dialogue formally met as an official group at a public conference with corresponding members of a different faith.
4. In 2005, Abdullah had already helped to support a major conference in Mecca by the Organization of Islamic Cooperation in which the three major points of the Amman Message were formally adopted by an assembly of more than four hundred Muslim scholars and leaders.
5. See coverage by Sandro Magister (2008) in *Chiesa Espresso*. Faisal bin Muaammar, who traveled with the king to the meeting with the pope in 2007, confirmed the details of the visit as the origins of KAICIID (interview with author, October 4, 2018, Vienna).
6. The close relationship that developed between Pope Francis and Grand Imam Sheikh Ahmed al Tayeb, through the Human Fraternity document and subsequent activity associated with it, has shifted the direction of the Vatican's privileged channel for dialogue with the Muslim-majority world.
7. Interview with DICID participants, February 18, 2018, Doha.
8. "Agenda of Doha 3rd Conference of Religions Dialogue," June 29–30, 2005.
9. In 2018, for example, and building on previous editions, DICID ended the conference by publicly signing memoranda of understanding with official delegations from Tajikistan, Jordan, Bosnia, Ukraine, and Germany.
10. Interview with author, February 21, 2018.
11. Interview with author, June 12, 2018, Beirut.
12. Interview with author, June 12, 2018, Beirut. See also Thompson (2014).
13. Interview with author, October 4, 2018, Vienna.
14. In the summer of 2022, KAICIID officially inaugurated its new offices in Lisbon.
15. KAICIID, for example, keeps a 50% gender equity balance on its staff. Currently, women religious leaders make up 25% of its advisory board.
16. Phone interview with author, October 12, 2018.
17. Phone interview with author, October 12, 2018.
18. KAICIID offers dialogue training at World Scouting events and jamborees and helped develop a dialogue merit badge program with the Scouts, one of the largest multireligious youth organizations in the world, with 20 million Scouts in Indonesia alone.
19. See UNESCO and KAICIID coverage of the launch: https://en.unesco.org/news/media-and-information-literacy-training-religious-leaders-and-dialogue-practitioners-0 and https://www.kaiciid.org/node/5546.
20. See KAICIID news coverage of event: https://www.kaiciid.org/news-events/news/prominent-arab-christian-muslim-leaders-kaiciid-conference-promote-coexistence-and.
21. Interview with author, October 4, 2018, Vienna.
22. Interview with author, October 5, 2018, Vienna.

NOTES 219

23. As this book went into publication, in early 2022, al Issa and the Muslim World League hosted a first-of-its-kind interreligious conference physically in Saudi Arabia, which included the participation of rabbis and Buddhist and Hindu leaders and an array of Christian leaders, including Pietro Parolin, secretary of state for the Holy See.
24. Phone interview with author, October 12, 2018.

Conclusion

1. Through, for example, the UN Environment Programme's adoption of the Faith for Earth Initiative in 2017.
2. See, among others, the 2020 "Global Pledge for Action by Religious Actors and Faith-Based Organizations to Address the Covid-19 Pandemic in Collaboration with the United Nations."
3. Through, for example, the UN Office of the High Commissioner for Human Rights' adoption of the Faith for Rights framework from the 2012 Rabat Plan of Action and the 2017 Beirut Declaration.
4. Notably, a declaration of support in favor of the deal released by the Forum for Promoting Peace in Muslim Societies sparked controversy among a number of its high-profile supporters. Two board members resigned following the statement, and a third, Hamza Yusuf, took pains to distance himself from its content. On the event, see Warren (2020) and Farooq (2020). While the Forum's statement was taken down from its website, bin Bayyah released a statement of support through the Emirati Fiqh Council.
5. Shadi Hamid wrote of the deal on his Twitter account (August 13, 2020), "The word 'authoritarian' is worth highlighting here. It's hard to imagine an Arab country, if it were democratic, striking a peace deal with Israel today. Whether that's a strike against—or for—democracy is another question. Of course, it's not exactly an accident that Israel, one of the region's few democracies, prefers that its Arab neighbors not be democratic, and the deal with the UAE is a reminder why." See also Warren 2021.

Bibliography

Charters, Declarations, and Encyclicals

A Common Word between Us and You. 2007. Issued by the Royal Aal Al-Bayt Institute of Islamic Thought. Amman.
The Amman Message. 2004. Issued by King Abdullah II bin al Hussein. Amman.
Beirut Declaration on Faith for Rights. 2017. United Nations High Commissioner for Human Rights. Beirut.
Charter for Inclusive Citizenship. 2021. Wilton Park Dialogues on Inclusive Citizenship. Wilton House.
Charter for Compassion. 2009. Council of Conscience. Washington DC.
Charter of Makkah. 2019. Declaration by Muslim World League Conference. Makkah.
The Charter of the New Alliance of Virtue. 2019. Issued at Forum for Promoting Peace in Muslim Societies. Abu Dhabi.
Declaration on Citizenship and Coexistence. 2017. Al Azhar. Cairo.
Declaration on Fundamental Freedoms. 2012. Al Azhar. Cairo.
Declaration on Humanitarian Islam. 2017. Gerakan Pemuda Ansor. Jombang.
Declaration on the Future of Egypt. 2011. Al Azhar. Cairo.
Declaration on Violent Extremism and Religious Education. 2017. Jakarta.
Declaration towards a Global Ethic. 1993. Parliament of World's Religions. Chicago.
Dialogue and Proclamation: Reflection and Orientations on Inter-religious Dialogue and the Proclamation of the Gospel of Jesus Christ. 1991. Joint Document of the Pontifical Council for Interreligious Dialogue. Rome.
Dignitatis Humanae: Declaration on Religious Freedom. 1965. Promulgated by Pope Paul VI. Rome.
A Document on Human Fraternity: For World Peace and Living Together. 2019. Pope Francis and Sheikh Ahmed al Tayyeb. Abu Dhabi.
Dominus Iesus: On the Unicity and Salvific Universality of Jesus Christ and the Church. 2000. Congregation for the Doctrine of the Faith. Rome.
Ecclesiam Suam: On the Church. 1964. Encyclical Letter. Pope Paul VI. Rome.
Evangelii Nuntiandi. 1975. Apostolic Exhortation. Pope Paul VI. Rome.
Fratelli Tutti: On Fraternity and Social Friendship. 2020. Encyclical Letter. Pope Francis. Rome.
Gaudium et Spes : Pastoral Constitution on the Church in the Modern World. 1965. Promulgated by Pope Paul VI. Rome.
The Marrakesh Declaration on the Rights of Religious Minorities in Muslim-Majority Lands. 2016. Issued by Forum for Promoting Peace in Muslim Societies. Marrakesh.
The Nusantara Manifesto. 2018. Gerakan Pemuda Ansor and Bayt Ar-Rahmah. Yogyakarta.
Nostra Aetate: Declaration on the Relation of the Church to Non-Christian Religions. 1965. Promulgated by Pope Paul VI. Rome.

Universal Declaration of Human Rights. 1948. United Nations. New York.
Plan of Action for Religious Leaders and Actors to Prevent Incitement to Violence that Could Lead to Atrocities. 2017. United Nations Office on Genocide Prevention and the Responsibility to Protect.
Populorum Progressio: On the Development of Peoples. 1967. Encyclical Letter. Pope Paul VI. Rome.
Rabat Plan of Action. 2012. United Nations High Commissioner for Human Rights. Rabat.
Redemptoris Missio: On the Permanent Validity of the Church's Missionary Mandate. 1990. Encyclical Letter. Pope John Paul II. Rome.
Together before God for the Welfare of the Individual and of Society. 1994. Third Pastoral Letter. Eastern Catholic Patriarchs.
Vienna Declaration: From the Interfaith and Inter-Civilization Cooperation to Human Solidarity. 2019. KAICIID. Vienna.
Vienna Declaration: United Against Violence in the Name of Religion. 2014. KAICIID. Vienna.

Books, Journals and Other Media Sources

Abdulla, Husain. 2017. "Bahrain: An Oasis of Religious Freedom in the Middle East?" *OpenDemocracy*. https://www.opendemocracy.net/en/north-africa-west-asia/bahrain-s-international-religious-tolerance-campaign-should-st/.
Abrams, Elliott. 2012. "'Destroy All the Churches': Saudi Arabia's Poor Treatment of Christians." *The Atlantic*, March 18.
Abu-Nimer, Mohammed, amd Renata Katalin Smith. 2016. "Interreligious and Intercultural Education for Dialogue, Peace and Social Cohesion." *International Review of Education* 62(4), 393–405.
Abu-Nimer, Mohammed, Amal Khoury, and Emily Welty. 2007. *Unity in Diversity: Interfaith Dialogue in the Middle East*. Washington, DC: US Institute of Peace.
Accetti, Carlo Invernizzi. 2019. *What Is Christian Democracy? Politics, Religion and Ideology*. New York: Oxford University Press.
A Common Word between Us and You: 5 Year Anniversary Edition. 2012. Amman: Royal Aal Al-Bayt Institute of Islamic Thought.
Adyan Foundation Biennial Report: 2017–2018. 2018. Beirut: Adyan Foundation.
Aldrousi, Mina. 2019. "UAE Is a Trailblazer for Freedom of Religion in the Region, says US Envoy." *The National*, February 24.
Al Saify, Mahmoud and Alexandre Caeiro. 2009. "Qaradawi in Europe, Europe in Qaradawi: The Global Mufti's European Politics." In Bettina Gräf and Jakob Skovgaard-Petersen (eds.), *Global Mufti: The Phenomenon of Yusuf al-Qaradawi*. London: Hurst.
Ajami, Fuad. 1993. "The Summoning." *Foreign Affairs*, September/October, 2–9.
Al Arabiya News. 2015. "Al Azhar Calls for Killing, Crucifxion of ISIS Terrorists." February 4.
Arab News. 2019. "Diversity Is Part of Human Nature, Says Muslim World League chief Al-Issa." March 10.
al Azami, Usaama. 2017. "Gulf Crisis: How Autocrats Use Religious Scholars against Qatar." *Middle East Eye*. https://www.middleeasteye.net/opinion/gulf-crisis-how-autocrats-use-religious-scholars-against-qatar.

al Azami, Usaama. 2018. "The Conflicting Legacies of Hamza Yusuf." *TRT World*, December 17. https://www.trtworld.com/opinion/the-conflicting-legacies-of-hamza-yusuf-22558

al Azami, Usaama. 2019. "Abdullāh bin Bayyah and the Arab Revolutions: Counter-revolutionary Neo-traditionalism's Ideological Struggle against Islamism." *Muslim World, 109*(3).

al Issa, Muhammad Karim. 2019. "Why Muslims around the World Should Remember the Holocaust." Op-ed. *Washington Post*, January 25.

Al Qaradaghi, Ali. 2019. "Statement by Sheikh Ali Al-Qaradaghi, General Secretary of the International Union for Muslim Scholars, for the Occasion of the Visiting of Pope Francis to Abu Dhabi." *International Union for Muslim Scholars*.

Ali Nayed, Aref. 2009. "Growing Ecologies of Peace, Compassion and Blessing: A Muslim Response to 'A Muscat Manifesto.'" Lecture. Cambridge Inter-Faith Programme, Faculty of Divinty, University of Cambridge.

Almond, Gabriel, R. Scott Appleby, and Emmanuel Sivan. 2003. *Strong Religion*. Chicago: University of Chicago Press.

Ansari, Ali S. 2003. "'So That You May Know One Another': A Muslim American Reflects on Pluralism and Islam." *Annals of the American Academy 588*, 40–51.

Appleby, R. Scott. 1999. *The Ambivalence of the Sacred: Religion, Violence and Reconciliation*. Lanham: Rowman and Littlefield.

Appleby, R. Scott, Richard Cizik, and Thomas Wright. 2010. *Engaging Religious Communities Abroad: A New Imperative for US Foreign Policy: Report of the Task Force on Religion and the Making of US Foreign Policy*. Chicago: Chicago Council on Global Affairs.

Areshidze, Giorgi. 2017. "Taking Religion Seriously? Habermas on Religious Translation and Cooperative Learning in Post-Secular Society." *American Political Science Review 111*(4), 724–737.

Arifianto, Alexander R. 2013. "Moral Authority Leadership and Progressive Islamic Discourse: The Gülen Movement and the Nahdlatul Ulama in Comparative Historical Perspective." *Social Science Research Network*.

Arifianto, Alexander R. 2017. "Practicing What It Preaches? Understanding the Contradictions between Pluralist Theology and Religious Intolerance within Indonesia's Nahdlatul Ulama." *Al-Jami'ah: Journal of Islamic Studies 55*(2), 241–264.

Arifianto, Alexander. R. 2021. "From Ideological to Political Sectarianism: Nahdlatul Ulama, Muhammadiyah, and the State in Indonesia." *Religion, State & Society 49*(2), 126–141.

Armstrong, Karen. 2006. *The Great Transformation: The Beginning of Our Religious Traditions*. New York: Anchor.

Asani, Ali. 2002. "Pluralism, Intolerance and the Quran." *American Scholar 71*(1), 52–60.

Auda, Jasser. 2008. *Maqasid al-Shariah as Philosophy of Islamic Law: A Systems Approach*. London: International Institute of Islamic Thought.

Aydin, M. Cenap. 2019. "Francis and the Sultan: Perspectives form an Islamic, Dialogical Approach." Paper presented at European Academy of Religions, Bologna.

Ayoub, Mahmoud. 2011. "9/11 and the Need for a New Paradigm for Interfaith Dialogue." *Muslim World 101*(3), 562–564.

Bailey, Tom, and Michael Driessen. 2016. "Mapping Contemporary Catholic Politics in Italy." *Journal of Modern Italian Studies 21*(3), 419–425.

Bailey, Tom, and Michael Driessen. 2017. "Engaging Post-Secularism: Rethinking Catholic Politics in Italy." *Constellations 24*(2), 232–244.

Bailey, Tom, and Valentina Gentile. 2015. *Rawls and Religion*. New York: Columbia University Press.

Banchoff, Thomas. 2012. "Interreligious Dialogue and International Relations." In Timothy Samuel Shah, Alfred Stepan, and Monica Duffy Toft (eds.), *Rethinking Religion and World Affairs*. New York: Oxford University Press, 204–216.

Bano, Masooda, ed. 2018. *Modern Islamic Authority and Social Change*. Vol. 1: *Evolving Debates in Muslim-Majority Countries*. Edinburgh: Edinburgh University Press.

Barbato, Mariano. 2010. "Conceptions of the Self for Post-secular Emancipation: Towards a Pilgrim's Guide to Global Justice." *Millenium: Journal of International Studies* 39(2), 547–564.

Barbato, Mariano. 2012. "Postsecular Revolution: Religion after the End of History." *Review of International Studies* 28, 1079–1097.

Barbato, Mariano, ed. 2020a. *The Pope, the Public, and International Relations: Postsecular Transformations*. New York: Palgrave Macmillan.

Barbato, Mariano. 2020b. "Postsecular Plurality in the Middle East: Expanding the Postsecular Approach to a Power Politics of Becoming." *Religions* 11(4), 162.

Barbato, Mariano, and Friedrich Kratochwil. 2009. "Towards a Post-Secular Political Order?" *European Political Science Review* 1(3), 317–340.

Barkey, Karen. 2008. *Empire of Difference: The Ottomans in Comparative Perspective*. New York: Cambridge University Press.

Barkey, Karen, Sudipta Kaviraj, and Vatsal Naresh, eds. *Negotiating Democracy and Religious Pluralism: India, Pakistan and Turkey*. New York: Oxford University Press.

Baroudi, Sami E. 2014. "Sheikh Yusuf Qaradawi on International Relations: The Discourse of a Leading Islamist Scholar (1926–)." *Journal of Middle Eastern Studies* 50(1), 2–26.

Barton, Greg. 2014. "The Gülen Movement, Muhammadiyah and Nahdlatul Ulama: Progressive Islamic Thought, Religious Philanthropy and Civil Society in Turkey and Indonesia." *Islam and Christian-Muslim Relations* 25(3), 287–301.

Baskan, Birol. 2011. "The State in the Pulpit: State Incorporation of Religious Institutions in the Middle East." *Politics and Religion* 4(1), 136–153.

Baskan, Birol. 2014. *From Religious Empires to Secular States: State Secularization in Turkey, Iran and Russia*. London: Routledge.

Baskan, Biron, and Steven Wright. 2011. "Seeds of Change: Comparing State-Religion Relations in Qatar and Saudi Arabia." *Arab Studies Quarterly* 33(2), 96–111.

Bayat, Asef. 2013. *Life as Politics: How Ordinary People Change the Middle East*. Stanford, CA: Stanford University Press.

Bellah, Robert N. 2011. *Religion in Human Evolution*. Cambridge, MA: Harvard University Press.

Bellah, Robert N., and Hans Joas. 2012. *The Axial Age and Its Consequences*. Cambridge, MA: Harvard University Press.

Bellah, Robert N., Richard Madsen, William M. Sullivan, Ann Swidler, and Steven M. Tipton. 1985. *Habits of the Heart: Individualism and Commitment in American Life*. Berkeley: University of California Press.

Benedict XVI. 2006. "Faith, Reason and the University: Memories and Reflections." Lecture. Regensburg.

Berger, Peter. 2014. *The Many Altars of Modernity: Toward a Paradigm for Religion in a Pluralist Age*. Berlin: Walter de Gruyter.

Bettiza, Gregorio. 2019. *Finding Faith in Foreign Policy: Religion and American Diplomacy in a Postsecular World*. New York: Oxford University Press.

Bettiza, Gregorio, Fabio Petito, and Davide Orsi. 2018. "Why (Clash of) Civilizations Discourses Just Won't Go Away? Understanding the Civilizational Politics of Our Times." In Davide Orsi (ed.), *The "Clash of Civilizations" 25 Years On: A Multidisciplinary Appraisal*. E-International Relations.

Bilgin, Pinar. 2012. "Civilisation, Dialogue, Security: The Challenge of Post-Secularism and the Limits of Civilizational Dialogue." *Review of International Studies* 38, 1099–1115.

Bin Bayyah, Abdallah. 2016. "A Legal Framework and a Call to Action." In *The Marrakesh Declaration on the Rights of Religious Minorities in Muslim-Majority Lands*. UAE: Forum for Promoting Peace in Muslim Societies, 11–43.

Bin Bayyah, Abdallah. 2018. "Inclusive Citizenship: A Topic for Research." Keynote address. Wilton Park Inclusive Citizenship Dialogues Conference, November 12, Abu Dhabi.

Bin Bayyah, Abdallah. 2019. *The Nation State in Muslim Societies*. Forum for Promoting Peace in Muslim Societies. Abu Dhabi.

Bhargava, Rajeev. 2012. "How Should States Deal with Deep Religious Diversity? Can Anything Be Learned from the Indian Model of Secularism?" In Timothy Shah, Alfred Stepan, and Monica Duffy Toft (eds.), *Rethinking Religion and World Affairs*. Oxford University Press, 73–84.

Bock, Jan-Jonathan, John Fahy, and Samuel Everett, eds. 2019. *Emergent Religious Pluralism*. New York: Palgrave Macmillan.

Böckenförde, Wolfgang. 2020 [1967]. "The Rise of the State as a Process of Secularization." In Mirjam Küknler and Tine Stein (eds.), *Selected Writings*. Vol. 2: *Religion, Law and Democracy*. New York: Oxford University Press.

Bouta, Tsjeard, S. Ayse Kadayifci-Orellana, and M. Mohammed Abu-Nimer. 2005. *Faith-Based Peace-Building: Mapping and Analysis of Christian, Muslim and Multi-Faith Actors*. The Hague: Clingendael Institute.

Bradley, Anthony B., and Greg Forster, eds. 2015. *John Rawls and Christian Social Engagement: Justice as Unfairness*. Lanham, MD: Lexington Books.

Brague, Remi. 2016. "God and Freedom: Biblical Roots of the Western Idea of Liberty." In Timothy Samuel Shah and Allen D. Hertzke (eds.), *Christianity and Freedom*. Vol. 1: *Historical Perspectives*. Cambridge: Cambridge University Press.

Bretherton, Luke. 2014. *Resurrecting Democracy: Faith, Citizenship and the Politics of a Common Life*. Cambridge: Cambridge University Press.

Brodeur, Patrice. 2005. "From the Margins to the Centers of Power: The Increasing Relevance of the Global Interfaith Movement." *CrossCurrents* 55(1), 42–53.

Brookings Institute. 2015. "Experts Weigh In: Is Quietist Salafism the Antidote to ISIS?" https://www.brookings.edu/blog/markaz/2015/04/27/experts-weigh-in-part-10-is-quietist-salafism-the-antidote-to-isis/.

Broomhall, Elizabeth. 2012. "Destroy All Churches in Gulf, Says Saudi Grand Mufti." *Arabian Business*, March 15.

Browers, Michaelle. 2011. "Offical Islam and the Limits of Communicative Action: The Paradox of the Amman Message." *Third World Quarterly*, 32(5), 943–958.

Brown, Nathan, and Michelle Dunne. 2021. "Who Will Speak for Islam in Egypt—And Who Will Listen?" In Frederic Wehry (ed.), *Islamic Institutions in Arab States: Mapping the Dynamics of Control, Co-option and Contention*. Carnegie Endowment for International Peace.

Buehler, Matt. 2018. *Why Alliances Fail: Islamist and Leftist Coalitions in North Africa*. Syracuse, NY: Syracuse University Press.

Burchardt, Marian. 2013. "Faith-based Humanitarianism: Organizational Change and Everyday Meanings in South Africa." *Sociology of Religion* 74(1), 30–55.

Burgat, Francois. 1997. *The Islamic Movement in North Africa*. Trans. W. Dowell. Austin: Center for Middle Eastern Studies, University of Texas.

Burhani, Ahmad Najib. 2011. "Lakum dīnukum wa-liya dīnī: The Muhammadiyah's Stance towards Interfaith Relations." *Islam and Christian–Muslim Relations* 22(3), 329–342.

Butt, Riazat. 2008a. "Leading Clerics Urge Muslims to Learn about Other Faiths in Drive to Promote Harmony." *The Guardian*, June 7.

Butt, Riazat. 2008b. "Mecca Talks Stress Religious Tolerance." *The Guardian*, June 5.

Caeiro, Alexandre. 2011. "The Making of the Fatwa: The Production of Islamic Legal Expertise in Europe." *Archives de Sciences Sociales des Religions* 155, 81–100.

Casanova, José. 1994. *Public Religions in the Modern World*. Chicago: University of Chicago Press.

Casanova, José. 2011. "Cosmopolitanism, the Clash of Civilizations and Multiple Modernities." *Current Sociology* 59(2), 252–267.

Casanova, José. 2012. "Religion, the Axial Age, and Secular Modernity in Bellah's Theory of Religious Evolution." In Robert N Bellah and Hans Joas (eds.), *The Axial Age and Its Consequences*. Cambridge, MA: Harvard University Press, 191–221.

Catalano, Roberto. 2010. *Spiritualità di Comunione e Dialogo Interreligioso: L'Esperienza di Chiara Lubich e del Movimento dei Focolari*. Rome: Città Nuova Editrice.

Catalano, Roberto. 2015. "Gülen, Focolare and Rissho Kosei-kai Movements: Commonalities for Religious and Social Renewal." *Claritas: Journal of Dialogue and Culture* 4(1), 42–61.

Catalano, Roberto. 2017. "Spiritual Friendship and Interreligious Dialogue: The Experience of Chiara Lubich and Nikkyo Niwano." *Claritas: Journal of Dialogue and Culture* 6(1), 6.

Catholic News Agency. 2004. "Qatar Conference on Muslim-Christian Dialogue Ends with 'Great Hope' Vatican Says." June 1.

Bamat, Tom, Nell Bolotn, Myla Leguro, and Atalia Omer (eds.). 2017. *Interreligious Action for Peace: Studies in Muslim-Christian Cooperation*. Baltimore: Catholic Relief Services.

Cavadini, John C., and Donald Wallenfang. 2019. *Evangelization as Interreligious Dialogue*. Eugene, OR: Wipf and Stock.

Cavanaugh, William T. 2004. *The Violence of "Religion": Examining a Prevalent Myth*. Notre Dame: Helen Kellogg Institute for International Studies.

Cavanaugh, William T. 2009. *The Myth of Religious Violence: Secular Ideology and the Roots of Modern Conflict*. Oxford: Oxford University Press.

Cesari, Jocelyne. 2004. *When Islam and Democracy Meet: Muslims in Europe and in the United States*. New York: Palgrave Macmillan.

Cesari, Jocelyne. 2014. *The Awakening of Muslim Democracy: Religion, Modernity and the State*. Cambridge: Cambridge University Press.

Cesari, Jocelyne. 2016. "Disciplining Religion: The Role of the State and Its Consequences on Democracy." *Journal of Religious and Political Practice* 2(2), 135–154.

Cesari, Jocelyne, and S. McLoughlin, eds. 2005. *European Muslims and the Secular State*. Burlington, VT: Ashgate.

Chamedes, Giuliana. 2019. *A Twentieth-Century Crusade: The Vatican's Battle to Remake Christian Europe*. Cambridge, MA: Harvard University Press.

Chappel, James. 2018. *Catholic Modern: The Challenge of Totalitarianism and the Remaking of the Church*. Cambridge, MA: Harvard University Press.

Charter of Makkah. 2019. Declaration by the Conference on the Charter of Makkah. May 27–29. https://www.saudiembassy.net/statements/charter-makkah.
Cheetham, David. 2007. "The 'Global Ethic': Criticisms and the Possibilities of Postsecular Thinking." *Islam and Christian-Muslim Relations 18*(1), 19–32.
Ciftci, Sabri. 2010. "Modernization, Islam, or Social Capital: What Explains Attitudes toward Democracy in the Muslim World." *Comparative Political Studies 43*(2), 1442–1470.
Claverie, Pierre. 1996. *Lettres et Messages d'Algérie*. Paris: Karthala.
Clooney, Francis. 2010. *Comparative Theology: Deep Learning across Religious Borders*. Boston: Wiley-Blackwell.
Cocchiaro, Matilde. 2006. *Nel Deserto Fiorisce la Fraternità: Ulisse Caglione fra i Musulmani*. Rome: Città Nuova.
Coda, Piero. 2003. *Il Logos e il Nulla: Trinità, Religioni, Mistica*. Rome: Città Nuova.
Coda, Piero. 2015. *Il Concilio della Misericordia: Sui Sentieri del Vaticano II*. Rome: Città Nuova.
Community of Sant'Egidio. 2014. "Turning Point for Peace in the Phillippines: Signed the Final Agreement on Mindanao." https://archive.santegidio.org/pageID/3/langID/en/itemID/8489/Turning-point-for-peace-in-the-Philippines-signed-the-final-agreement-on-Mindanao.html.
Cook, Steven A. 2013. "Egypt and Turkey: Nightmares." US Council on Foreign Relations. Blog post, November 25. https://www.cfr.org/blog/egypt-and-turkey-nightmares.
Cornille, Catherine, ed. 2013. *The Wiley-Blackwell Companion to Interreligious Dialogue*. Boston: Wiley-Blackwell.
Dallmayr, Fred. 2010. *Integral Pluralism: Beyond Culture Wars*. Lexington: University Press of Kentucky.
Dallmayr, Fred. 2012. "Post-secularity and (Global) Politics: A Need for Radical Redefinition." *Review of International Studies 38*, 963–973.
Daou, Fadi. 2014a. "La Crise du Dialogue Islamo-Chrétien dans le Contexte des Bouleversements dans le Monde Arabe." Paper presented at the International Conference De la Rencontre des Religions, pour un Renouveau du Dialogue Islamo-Chrétien, Casablanca, Le Collège des Bernadins, La Bibliothèque Nationale du Royaume du Maroc, Rabat, May 2–3.
Daou, Fadi. 2011. "Les Église de l'Orient Arabe face à la Mondialisation du Dialogue Islamo-Chrétien," *Le Dialogue Islamo-Chrétien 19*(2), 89–99.
Daou, Fadi. 2014b. "Les Chrètiens Arabes dans la Tourmente des Bouleversements Règionaux." In Adrien Candiard (ed.), *Dans L'Amitié et la Prière: Hommage au Frère J. J. Pérennés, Op.* Cairo: Institute Dominicain d'Etudes Orientales.
Daou, Fadi. 2017. "Covenants and Revelations." In Fadi Daou and Nayla Tabbara, *Divine Hospitality: A Christian-Muslim Conversation*. World Council of Churches Publications, 35–71.
Daou, Fadi, and Nayla Tabbara. 2017. *Divine Hospitality: A Christian-Muslim Conversation*. World Council of Churches Publications.
Davie, Grace. 1990. "Believing without Belonging: Is This the Future of Religion in Britain?" *Social Compass 37*(4), 455–469.
De Gasperi, Alcide. (1954) 1990. "La Nostra Patria Europa." In *Alcide de Gasperi e la Politica Internazionale*. Vol. 3, 437–440. Rome: Cinque Lune.
De Gasperi, Alcide. 2003. *Lettere della Prigione: 1927–1928*. Rome: Marietti.
Deeb, Lara. 2006. *An Enchanted Modern: Gender and Public Piety in Shi'i Lebanon*. Princeton, NJ: Princeton University Press.

Del Noce, Augusto. 2017. *The Age of Secularization*. Trans. and ed. Carlo Lancelotti. Montreal: McGill-Queen's University Press.

Deneen, Patrick J. 2019. *Why Liberalism Failed*. New Haven, CT: Yale University Press.

Deutsche Presse Agentur. 2005. "Religious Conference in Doha Welcomes Jewish Speakers amid Boycotts." June 29.

Dickinson, Elizabeth. 2010. "A Conversation with Anwar Ibrahim." *Foreign Policy*, February 3.

Diez, Martino. 2020. "The Alliance of Virtue: Towards an Islamic Natural Law?" *Oasis* (March).

Diotallevi, Luca. 2016. "On the Current Absence and Future Improbability of Political Catholicism in Italy." *Journal of Modern Italian Studies* 21(3), 485–510.

Dorsey, James M. 2013. "Wahhabism vs. Wahhabism: Qatar Challenges Saudi Arabia." Working Paper 262. Singapore: S. Rajaratnam School of International Studies.

Dreher, Rod. 2017. *The Benedict Option: A Strategy for Christians in a Post-Christian Nation*. New York: Penguin.

Driessen, Michael D. 2012. "Public Religion, Democracy, and Islam: Examining the Moderation Thesis in Algeria." *Comparative Politics* 44(2), 171–189.

Driessen, Michael D. 2014. *Religion and Democratization: Framing Religious and Political Identities in Muslim and Catholic Societies*. New York: Oxford University Press.

Driessen, Michael D. 2018. "Sources of Muslim Democracy: The Supply and Demand of Religious Policies in the Muslim World." *Democratization* 25(1), 115–135.

Driessen, Michael D. 2021. "Catholicism and European Politics." *Religions* 12(4), 271.

Driessen, Michael D., Anna Maria Daou, Dima Karadsheh, Meira Omerovic, and Faris Ilyas Keti. 2020. "Mapping and Evaluating Interreligious Dialogue Activities in Lebanon, Jordan, Turkey and Iraq." Policy Report. Beirut: Adyan Foundation.

Duderija, Adis, ed. 2014. *Maqasid al-Shari'a and Contemporary Reformist Muslim Thought: An Examination*. New York: Palgrave Macmillan.

Duderija, Adis. 2018. "Qur'ān, Sunnah, Maqāsid, and the Religious Other: The Ideas of Muhammad Shahrūr." In Idris Nassery, Rumee Ahmed, and Muna Tatari (eds.), *The Objectives of Islamic Law: The Promises and Challenges of the Maqāsid al-Sharī'a*. London: Washington, DC: Rowman and Littlefield, 89–109.

Dutru, Isaline Bourgenot. 2018. *L'Empreinte du Paradis: Chiara Lubich et les Premiers Témoins de la Spiritualité de l'Unité*. Paris: Nouvelle Cité.

Eberle, Christopher J. 2002. *Religious Conviction in Liberal Politics*. Cambridge: Cambridge University Press.

Eck, Diana L. 2006. "What Is Pluralism." Pluralism. http://pluralism.org/pluralism/what_is_pluralism.

Eisenstadt, Shmuel N. 2000. "Multiple Modernities." *Daedalus* 129(1), 1–29.

Emon, Anver M. 2010. *Islamic Natural Law Theories*. New York: Oxford University Press.

Emon, Anver M. 2014. "Islamic Natural Law Theories." In Anver M. Emon, Matthew Levering, and David Novak (eds.), *Natural Law: A Jewish, Christian and Islamic Trialogue*. New York: Oxford University Press, 144–187.

Esack, Farid. 1997. *Qur'an, Liberation and Pluralism: An Islamic Perspective of Interreligious Solidarity against Oppression*. Oxford: Oneworld.

Esposito, John L., and Dalia Mogahed. 2007. *Who Speaks for Islam—What a Billion Muslims Really Think*. New York: Simon and Schuster.

Esposito, John L., and Emad El-Din Shahin. 2018. *Key Islamic Political Thinkers*. New York: Oxford University Press.

Esposito, John L., and John Voll. 2003. "Islam and the West: Muslim Voices of Dialogue." In Pavlos Hatzopoulos and Fabio Petito (eds.), *Religion in International Relations: The Return from Exile*. New York: Palgrave Macmillan, 237–271.

Eyadat, Zaid. 2012. "Islams: Between Dialoguing and Mainstreaming." *Philosophy and Social Criticism* 38(4–5), 507–516.

Eyadat, Zaid. 2013. "Fiqh Al-Aqalliyyât and the Arab Spring: Modern Islamic Theorizing." *Philosophy and Social Criticism* 39(3), 733–753.

Fadel, Mohammad. 2012. "Muslim Reformists, Female Citizenship, and the Public Accommodation of Islam in Liberal Democracy." *Politics and Religion* 5(1), 2–35.

Fadel, Mohammad. 2013. "'No Salvation Outside Islam': Muslim Modernists, Democratic Politics and Islamic Theological Exclusivism." In Mohammad Hassan Khalil (ed.), *Between Heaven and Hell: Islam, Salvation and the Fate of Others*. New York: Oxford Unviersity Press, 35–65.

Faggioli, Massimo. 2020. *The Liminal Papacy of Pope Francis: Moving toward Global Catholicity*. Maryknoll: Orbis Books.

Fahmi, Georges. 2021. "Al-Azhar and the Path towards Inclusive Citizenship in Egypt." In Fabio Petito, Fadi Daou, and Michael Driessen (eds.), *Human Fraternity and Inclusive Citizenship: Interreligious Engagement in the Mediterranean*. Milan: Ledizioni, 169–181.

Fahy, John. 2018a. "International Relations and Faith-Based Diplomacy: The Case of Qatar." *Review of Faith and International Affairs* 16(3), 76–88.

Fahy, John. 2018b. "Out of Sight, Out of Mind: Managing Religious Diversity in Qatar." *British Journal of Middle Eastern Studies* 28, 1–23.

Fahy, John, and Jan-Jonathan Bock. 2018. *Beyond Dialogue? Interfaith Engagement in Delhi, Doha and London*. London: Wolff Institute.

Fahy, John, and Jeffrey Haynes. 2018. "Interfaith on the World Stage." *Review of Faith and International Affairs* 16(3), 1–8.

Farooq, Umar A. 2020. "Influential Muslim Scholar Hamza Yusuf Criticised for Backing UAE-Israel Deal." *Middle East Eye*, August 21.

Farquhar, Michael. 2016. *Circuits of Faith: Migration, Education and the Wahhabi Mission*. Stanford, CA: Stanford University Press.

Fealy, Greg, and Sally White, eds. 2008. *Expressing Islam: Religious Life and Politics in Indonesia*. Institute of Southeast Asian Studies.

Ferrara, Pasquale. 2016. *Il Mondo di Francesco: Bergoglio e la politica internazionale*. Rome: San Paolo.

Ferrara, Pasquale. 2021. "Social Friendship and Universal Fraternity." In Fabio Petito, Fadi Daou, and Michael Driessen (eds.), *Human Fraternity and Inclusive Citizenship: Interreligious Engagement in the Mediterranean*. Milan: Ledizioni, 91–107.

Fiedler, Rebekka. 2018. *The Impact of the Interfaith Peace Platform on the Peace Process in the Central African Republic*. Geneva: World Evangelical Alliance.

Firestone, Reuven. 2015. "Can Those Chosen by God Dialogue with Others?" In Paul Hedges (ed.), *Contemporary Muslim-Christian Encounters: Diversity, Developments, Dialogues*. New York: Bloomsbury, 34–50.

Fitzgerald, Michael L. 2000. "Reflection on Pentecost." *Pontifical Council for Interreligious Dialogue*. https://www.vatican.va/roman_curia/pontifical_councils/interelg/docume nts/rc_pc_interelg_20000530_pentecoste-2000-3_en.html.

Foret, François. 2015. *Religion and Politics in the European Union*. Cambridge University Press.

Forlenza, Rosario, and Bjorn Thomassen. Forthcoming. *Italy's Christian Democracy*. Oxford University Press.

Fox, Jonathan. 2002. "Ethnic Minorities and the Clash of Civilizations: A Quantitative Analysis of Huntington's Thesis." *British Journal of Political Science* 32(3), 415–434.

Fox, Jonathan. 2006. "World Separation of Religion and State into the 21st Century." *Comparative Political Studies* 39(5), 537–569.

Fox, Jonathan. 2008. *A World Survey of Religion and the State*. New York: Cambridge University Press.

Fox, Jonathan. 2015. *Political Secularism, Religion and the State: A Time Series Analysis of Worldwide Data*. New York: Cambridge University Press.

Fox, Jonathan. 2016. *The Unfree Exercise of Religion: A World Survey of Religious Discrimination against Religious Minorities*. New York: Cambridge University Press.

Fox, Jonathan. 2019. Civilizational Clash or Balderdash? The Causes of Religious Discrimination in Western and European Christian-majority Democracies. *The Review of Faith & International Affairs* 17(1), 34–48.

Francis. 2017. "Address to the Participants in the Conference Organized by the Dicastery for Promoting Integral Human Development, marking the 50th Anniversary of the Encyclical *Progressio Populorum*." Rome.

Fukuyama, Francis. 1989. "The End of History?" *National Interest* (16), 3–18.

G20 Interfaith Forum. 2018. "Religious Contributions for a Dignified Future: Policy Recommendations." https://www.g20interfaith.org/argentina-2018-3/.

Gabijan, Crescencia C. 2009. "The Spiritual Vision of Chiara Lubich: Pathways of Interreligious Dialogue." *Boletin Eclesiastico de Filipinas* 85(874–875), 518–557.

Ghazi, bin Muhammad bin Talal. 2012. "The Genesis of 'A Common Word.'" In *A Common Word between Us and You: 5 Year Anniversary Edition*. Amman: Royal Aal Al-Bayt Institute of Islamic Thought, 131–135.

GHR Foundation. 2014. "A Starting Point: Evaluating Inter-Faith Dialogue." Minneapolis: GHR Foundation Report.

Gillespie, Michael Allen. 2008. *The Theological Origins of Modernity*. Chicago: University of Chicago Press.

Glendon, Mary A. 1997. "Knowing the Universal Declaration of Human Rights." *Notre Dame Law Review* 73, 1153.

Glendon, Mary A. 2002. *A World Made New: Eleanor Roosevelt and the Universal Declaration of Human Rights*. New York: Random House Trade Paperbacks.

Glendon, Mary A. 2013. "The Influence of Catholic Social Doctrine on Human Rights." *Journal of Catholic Social Thought* 10(1), 69–84.

Göle, Nilüfer. 2000. "Snapshots of Islamic Modernities." *Daedalus* 129(1), 91–117.

Gorski, Philip S., and Ateş Altınordu. 2008. "After Secularization?" *Annual Review of Sociology* 34, 55–85.

Gräf, Bettina, and Jakob Skovgaard-Petersen, eds. 2009. *Global Mufti: The Phenomenon of Yusuf al-Qaradawi*. Hurst.

Griera, Mar, and Alexander-Kenneth Nagel. 2018. "Interreligious Relations and Governance of Religion in Europe: Introduction." *Social Compass* 65(3), 301–311.

Grim, Brian J., and Roger Finke. 2010 *The Price of Freedom Denied: Religious Persecution and Conflict in the Twenty-First Century*. Cambridge University Press.

Gryzmala-Busse, Anna. 2015. *Nations under God: How Churches Use Moral Authority to Influence Policy*. Princeton, NJ: Princeton University Press.

Gülen, Fethullah. 2004. *The Necessity of Interfaith Dialogue: A Muslim Perspective*. The Light.

BIBLIOGRAPHY 231

Gustafson, Hans. 2018. "'Interfaith' is So 1970s! Navigating the Linguistic Quagmire of the 'Interfaith' World." *State of Formation*, April 12.

Gutkowski, Stacey. 2016. "We Are the Very Model of a Moderate Muslim State: The Amman Messages and Jordan's Foreign Policy." *International Relations* 30(2), 206–226.

Habermas, Jürgen. 2006. "On the Relations between the Secular Liberal State and Religion." In Hent de Vries and Lawrence E. Sullivan (eds.), *Political Theologies: Public Religions in a Post-Secular World*. New York: Fordham University Press, 251–260.

Habermas, Jürgen. 2008. "Prepolitical Foundations of the Constitutional State?" In Jürgen Habermas, *Between Naturalism and Religion: Philosophical Essays*, trans. Ciaran Cronin. Cambridge, UK: Polity Press, 101–114.

Habermas, Jürgen. 2011. "'The Political': The Rational Meaning of a Questionable Inheritance of Political Theology." In Eduardo Mendieta and Jonathan VanAntwerpen (eds.), *The Power of Religion in the Public Sphere*. New York: Columbia University Press, 15–33.

Haddad, Yvonne Yazbeck, and Rahel Fischbach. 2015. "Interfaith Dialogue in Lebanon: Between a Power Balancing Act and Theological Encounters." *Islam and Christian-Muslim Relations* 26(4), 423–442.

Haenni, Peter. 2005. *L'Islam de Marché*. Paris: Seuil.

Halík, Tomáš. 2011. "Patience with God: The Story of Zacchaeus Continuing in Us. Author's Response." *Horizons* 38(1), 125–131.

Hallaq, Wael. 2001. *Authority, Continuity and Change in Islamic Law*. New York: Cambridge University Press.

Hallaq, Wael. 2013. *The Impossible State: Islam, Politics and Modernity's Moral Predicament*. New York: Columbia University Press.

Hansen, Henrik Lindberg. 2015. "Interreligious Dialogue and Politics in Revolutionary Egypt." *Journal of Islamic Research* 9(2), 4–27.

Hashas, Mohammed, ed. 2021. *Pluralism in Islamic Contexts: Ethics, Politics and Modern Challenges*. Springer.

Hashemi, N. 2009. *Islam, Secularism, and Liberal Democracy: Towards a Democratic Theory for Muslim Societies*. New York: Oxford University Press.

Hatzopoulos, Pavlos, and Fabio Petito, eds. 2003. *Religion in International Relations: The Return from Exile*. New York: Palgrave MacMillan.

Haykel, Bernard, Thomas Hegghammer, and Stéphane Lacroix, eds. 2015. *Saudi Arabia in Transition*. New York: Cambridge University Press.

Haynes, Jeffrey. 2018a. "Huntington's 'Clash of Civilizations' Today: Responses and Developments." In Davide Orsi (ed.), *The "Clash of Civilizations" 25 Years On: A Multidisciplinary Appraisal*. E-International Relations, 52–63.

Haynes, Jeffrey. 2018b. "The United Nations Alliance of Civilizations and Interfaith Dialogue: What Is It Good For?" *Review of Faith and International Affairs* 16(3), 48–60.

Haynes, Jeffrey. 2019. "Introduction: The "Clash of Civilizations" and Relations between the West and the Muslim World." *Review of Faith & International Affairs* 17(1), 1–10.

Hayward, Susan. 2016. "Understanding and Extending the Marrakesh Declaration in Policy and Practice." Special Report 392 (September). US Institute for Peace. https://www.usip.org/publications/2016/09/understanding-and-extending-marrakesh-declaration-policy-and-practice.

Hedges, Matthew, and Giorgio Cafiero. 2017. "The GCC and the Muslim Brotherhood: What Does the Future Hold?" *Middle East Policy Council* 24(1), 129–153.

Hedges, Paul. 2008. "Concerns about the Global Ethic: A Sympathetic Critique and Suggestions for New Direction." *Studies in Interreligious Dialogue* 18(1), 1–16.

Hefner, Robert W. 2000. *Civil Islam: Muslims and Democratization in Indonesia*. Princeton, NJ: Princeton University Press.

Heneghan, Tom. 2008. "Interfaith Talks on Agenda in Mecca, Rome and London." *Reuters*, June 4.

Heneghan, Tom. 2012. "Saudi Reforms Detour through Vienna Faith Center." *Reuters*, November 23.

Heneghan, Tom. 2018. "Mohammed bin Salman's Reforms Bolster Interfaith Efforts." *Christian Century*, March 13.

Heydemann, Steven. 2007. *Upgrading Authoritarianism in the Arab World*. Saban Center for Middle East Policy at the Brookings Institute.

Heydemann, Steven. 2013. "Tracking the 'Arab Spring': Syria and the Future of Authoritarianism." *Journal of Democracy* 24(4), 59–73.

Hick, John, and Paul Knitter. 2005. *The Myth of Christian Uniqueness: Towards a Pluralistic Theology of Religions*. Eugene, OR: Wipf and Stock.

Hoffner, Bénédict. 2018. "Martyrs d'Algérie, les Enjeux d'une Beatification Exceptionnelle." *La Croix*, December 7.

Hoffner, Bénédict. 2018. "Mgr Pierre Claverie, les Moines de Tibhirine et onze autres Religieux et Religieuses Reconnus Martyrs." *La Croix*, January 27.

Horsfjord, Vebjorn. 2018. "The Marrakesh Declaration on Rights of Religious Minorities: Opportunity or Dead End?" *Nordic Journal of Human Rights* 36(2), 151–166.

Huang, Yong. 1995. "Religious Pluralism and Interfaith Dialogue: Beyond Universalism and Particularism." *International Journal for Philosophy of Religion* 37, 127–144.

Human Rights Watch. 2019. *World Report: Turkey*.

Huntington, Samuel P. 1991. "Democracy's Third Wave." *Journal of Democracy* 2(2), 12–34.

Huntington, Samuel P. 1993. "The Clash of Civilizations?" *Foreign Affairs* 72(3), 22–49.

Huntington, Samuel P. 1996. *The Clash of Civilizations and the Remaking of World Order*. New York: Touchstone.

Hurd, Elizabeth Shakman. 2007. "Theorizing Religious Resurgence." *International Politics* 44(6), 647–665.

Hutchcroft, Paul, ed. 2018. *Mindanao: The Long Journey to Peace and Prosperity*. Signapore: Anvil.

Ibn Ashur, Muhammad al-Tahir. 2006. *Treatise on Maqasid al-Shariah*. London: International Institute of Islamic Thought.

Ignazi, P., and E. Wellhofer. 2013. "Votes and Votive Candles: Modernization, Secularization and the Decline of Religious Voting in Italy: 1953–1992." *Comparative Political Studies* 46, 31–62.

Inglehart, R., C. Haerpfer, A. Moreno, C. Welzel, K. Kizilova, J. Diez-Medrano, M. Lagos, P. Norris, E. Ponarin, and B. Puranen, eds. 2014. "World Values Survey: Round Six—Country-Pooled Datafile Version." JD Systems Institute. https://www.worldvaluessurvey.org/WVSDocumentationWV6.jsp.

Invernizzi-Accetti, Carlo. 2019. *What Is Christian Democracy? Politics, Religion and Ideology*. Cambridge University Press.

Joas, Hans. 2014. *Faith as an Option: Possible Futures for Christianity*. Stanford University Press.

Joas, Hans. 2021. *The Power of the Sacred: An Alternative to the Narrative of Disenchantment*. Oxford University Press.
John Paul II. 1986. *Discorso alla Curia Romana per gli Auguri di Natale*. Rome.
John Paul II. 2001. *Dialogue between Cultures for a Civilization of Love and Peace*. Vatican.
Johnston, Douglas, and Cynthia Sampson, eds. 1995. *Religion, the Missing Dimension of Statecraft*. New York: Oxford University Press.
Joint Learning Initiative on Faith and Local Communities. 2017. "The Evidence Base: Faith, Religion and Humanitarian Action (2010–2015): Annotated Bibliography." https://jliflc.com/wp-content/uploads/2019/02/AnnotatetBibliography_NEW_TRYK-1.pdf.
Judd, Emily, and Leen Alfaisal. 2020. "Muslim World League Chief Responds to Attacks after
Participation in Jewish Forum." *Al Arabiya*, June 17.
Khan, M. A. Muqtedar. 2019. *Islam and Good Governance: A Political Philosophy of Ihsan*. New York: Palgrave Macmillan.
KAICIID. 2015. "Interreligious Directory Report: Methodology and Data Collection." KAICIID Peacemapping Programme.
KAICIID. 2017. "The Vienna Declaration." https://www.kaiciid.org/vienna-declaration-united-against-violence-name-religion.
KAICIID. 2018. "Network of Arab Faculties and Institutes." https://www.kaiciid.org/news-events/news/first-its-kind-meeting-"network-arab-faculties-and-institutes"-took-place-kaiciid.
Kalyvas, Stathis. 1996. *The Rise of Christian Democracy in Europe*. Ithaca, NY: Cornell University Press.
Kalyvas, Stathis, and Kees van Kersbergen. 2010. "Christian Democracy." *Annual Review of Political Science* 13, 183–209.
Katzenstein, Peter J., ed. 2009. *Civilizations in World Politics: Plural and Pluralist Perspectives*. Routledge.
Kayaoğlu, Turan. 2010. "Preachers of Dialogue: International Relations and Interfaith Theology." In John Esposito (ed.), *Islam and Peacebuilding: Gülen Movement Initiatives*. New York: Blue Dome Press, 511–525.
Kayaoğlu, Turan. 2012. "Constructing the Dialogue of Civilizations in World Politics." *Islam and Christian-Muslim Relations* 23(2), 129–147.
Kayaoğlu, Turan. 2015. "Explaining Interfaith Dialogue in the Muslim World." *Politics and Religion* 8(2), 1–27.
Kéchichian, Joseph A. 2013. *Legal and Political Reforms in Saudi Arabia*. New York: Routledge.
Kenyon, Peter. 2008. "Cleric's Remarks Spark Sunni-Shia Tensions." *NPR Morning Edition*, October 13.
Kepel, Gilles. 1994. *Revenge of God: The Resurgence of Islam, Christianity and Judaism in the Modern World*. State College: Pennsylvania State University Press.
Kessler, Michael Jon, ed. 2013. *Political Theology for a Plural Age*. New York: Oxford University Press.
Khalil, Mohammad Hassan. 2012. *Islam and the Fate of Others: The Salvation Question*. New York: Oxford University Press.
Khalil, Mohammad Hassan, ed. 2013. *Between Heaven and Hell: Islam, Salvation and the Fate of Others*. New York: Oxford University Press.
Knitter, Paul. 2005. "Mission and Dialogue." *Missiology: An International Review* 33(2), 200–210.

Knitter, Paul. 2013. "Interreligious Dialogue and Social Action." In Catherine Cornille (ed.), *The Wiley-Blackwell Companion to Interreligious Dialogue*. Boston: Wiley-Blackwell, 133–148.

Koesel, Karrie. J. 2014. *Religion and Authoritarianism: Cooperation, Conflict, and the Consequences*. Cambridge University Press.

Kors, Anna, and Alexander-Kenneth Nagel. 2018. "Local 'Formulas of Peace': Religious Diversity and State-Interfaith Governance in Germany." *Social Compass* 65(3), 346–362.

Krämer, Gudrun, and Sabine Schmidtke, eds. 2006. *Speaking for Islam: Religious Authorities in Muslim Societies*. Vol. 100. Brill.

Krokus, Christian. 2012. "Louis Massignon's Influence on the Teaching of Vatican II on Muslims and Islam." *Islam and Christian-Muslim Relations* 23(3), 329–345.

Krokus, Christian. 2017. *The Theology of Louis Massignon*. Catholic University Press.

Küng, Hans. 2004. *Global Responsibility: In Search of a New World Ethic*. Eugene, OR: Wipf and Stock.

Künkler, Mirjam, John Madeley, and Shylashri Shankar. 2018. *A Secular Age beyond the West*. New York: Cambridge University Press.

Kuru, Ahmet T. 2007. "Changing Perspectives on Islamism and Secularism in Turkey: The Gülen Movement and the AK Party." In Ihsan dalam Yilmaz (coord.), *Muslim World in Transition: Contributions of the Gülen Movement (International Gülen Conference Proceedings)*, 140–151. London.

Kuru, Ahmet T. 2009. *Secularism and State Policies toward Religion: The United States, France, and Turkey*. Cambridge University Press.

Kuru, Ahmet T. 2019. *Islam, Authoritarianism, and Underdevelopment: A Global and Historical Comparison*. Cambridge University Press.

Kurzman, Charles. 1999. "Liberal Islam: Prospects and Challenges." *Middle East Review of International Affairs* 3(3), 11–19.

Kurzman, C., and I. Naqvi. 2010. "Do Muslims Vote Islamic?" *Journal of Democracy* 21(2), 50–63.

Lacroix, Stéphane. 2011. *Awakening Islam*. Cambridge, MA: Harvard University Press.

Lacroix, Stéphane. 2014. "Saudi Arabia's Muslim Brotherhood Predicament." The Qatar Crisis. Project on Middle East Politics. https://pomeps.org/saudi-arabias-muslim-brotherhood-predicament.

Lacroix, Stéphane. 2015. "Understanding Stability and Dissent in the Kingdom: The Double-Edged Role of the *Jama'at* in Saudi Politics." In Bernard Haykel, Thomas Hegghammer, and Stéphane Lacroix (eds.), *Saudi Arabia in Transition*. New York: Cambridge University Press, 167–181.

Lacroix, Stéphane. 2019. "Saudi Arabia and the Limits of Religious Reform." *Review of Faith & International Affairs* 17(2), 97–101.

Lauzière, H. 2005. "Post-Islamism and the Religious Discourse of 'Abd al-Salam Yassin." *International Journal of Middle East Studies* 37(2), 241–261.

Lehmann, K., and A. Koch. 2015. "Perspectives from Sociology: Modeling Religious Pluralism from Inward and Outward." *Journal of Interreligious Studies* 16, 30–40.

Lemarié, Paul. 2017. "To Live Together: Unity in Diversity: The Focolare Movement and Dialogue with Muslims." In Michael Fitzgerald and Biju Michael (eds.), *Christian-Muslim Dialogue: Festschrift in Honour of Prof. Pier Giorgio Gianazza SDB*. Jerusalem: STS Publications.

Lewis, Bernard. 1990. "The Roots of Muslim Rage." *The Atlantic Monthly*, September.

Light, Aimee Upjohn. 2009. "Post-Pluralism through the Lens of Post-Modernity." *Journal of Interreligious Dialogue* 1(1), 71–74.
Lilla, Mark. 2008. *The Stillborn God: Religion, Politics and the Modern West*. Vintage.
"Local Faith Community and Related Civil Society Engagement in Humanitarian Response with Syrian Refugees in Irbid, Jordan." 2015. Report to the Henry Luce Foundation. https://jliflc.com/resources/local-faith-community-and-related-civil-society-engagement-in-humanitarian-response-with-syrian-refugees-in-irbid-jordan-report-to-the-henry-luce-foundation/.
Luissier, D., and S. Fish. 2012. "Indonesia: The Benefits of Civic Engagement." *Journal of Democracy* 23(1), 70–83.
Lynch, Marc. 2005. "Transnational Dialogue in an Age of Terror." *Global Society* 19(1), 5–28.
Lynch, Marc. 2017. "Three Big Lessons of the Qatar Crisis." *POMEPS Brief 31*, 14–16.
MacIntyre, Alasdair. 1981. *After Virtue*. South Bend, IN: University of Notre Dame Press.
Mahmood, Saba. 2006. "Secularism, Hermeneutics and Empire: The Politics of Islamic Reformation." *Public Culture* 18(2), 323–347.
Mahmood, Saba. 2012. *Politics of Piety: The Islamic Revival and the Feminist Subject*. Princeton, NJ: Princeton University Press.
Mahmood, Saba. 2015. *Religious Difference in a Secular Age: A Minority Report*. Princeton, NJ: Princeton University Press.
Magister, Sandra. 2008. "For the Vatican, King Abdullah Matters More Than 138 Muslim Scholars." *Chiesa Expresso*, March 31.
Mamdani, Mahmood. 2002. "Good Muslim, Bad Muslim: A Political Perspective on Culture and Terrorism." *American Anthropologist* 104(3), 766–775.
Mandaville, Peter, and Shadi Hamid. 2018. "Islam as Statecraft: How Governments Use Religion in Foreign Policy." Report. Washington, DC: Brookings Institute.
Mandaville, Peter, and Sara Silvestri. 2015. "Integrating Religious Engagement into Diplomacy: Challenges and Opportunities." Brookings Institute Report. Washington DC.
March, Andrew. 2009. *Islam and Liberal Citizenship: The Search for Overlapping Consensus*. New York: Oxford University Press.
March, Andrew. 2013. "Rethinking Religious Reasons in Public Justification." *American Political Science Review* 107(3), 527–530.
Maritain, Jacques. (1936) 1996. "Integral Humanism." In O. Bird, J. Evans, and R. O'Sullivan (trans.), *Integral Humanism, Freedom in the Modern World and A Letter on Independence*. Notre Dame, IN: University of Notre Dame Press, 143–320.
Markiewicz, Sarah. 2018. "Interfaith on the World Stage: Much Ado about Nothing?" *Review of Faith and International Affairs* 16(3), 89–101.
Markiewicz, Sarah. 2019. "Preaching to the Converted? Interfaith Dialogue vs. Interfaith Realities." in Jan-Jonathan Bock, , John Fahy, and Samuel Everett (eds.), *Emergent Religious Pluralism*. New York: Palgrave Macmillan, 251–278.
Marks, Monica. 2013. "Erdogan Comes to Tunisia." *Foreign Policy: The Middle East Channel*. https://foreignpolicy.com/2013/06/06/erdogan-comes-to-tunisia/.
Marsden, Lee. 2018. "The Golden Rule: Interfaith Peacemaking and the Charter for Compassion." *Review of Faith and International Affairs* 16(3), 61–75.
Marshall, Katherine. 2008. "Religion and Global Development: Intersecting Paths." In Thomas Banchoff (ed.), *Religious Pluralism, Globalization, and World Politics*. Oxford University Press, 195–228.
Marshall, Katherine. 2017. *Interfaith Journeys: An Exploration of History, Ideas and Future Directions*. Georgetown University: World Faiths Development Dialogue.

Marshall, Katherine, and Marisa Bronwyn van Saanen. 2007. *Development and Faith: Where Mind, Heart, and Soul Work Together*. World Bank Publications.

Masoud, Tarek. 2021. "The Arab Spring at 10: Kings or People?" *Journal of Democracy* 32(1), 139–154.

Massad, Joseph A. 2015. *Islam in Liberalism*. Chicago: University of Chicago Press.

Mavelli, Luca. 2012. *Europe's Encounter with Islam: The Secular and the Postsecular: Interventions*. Francis and Taylor.

Mavelli, Luca, and Fabio Petito. 2012. "The Postsecular in International Relations." *British International Studies* 38(5), 931–942.

Menchik, Jeremy. 2016. *Islam and Democracy in Indonesia: Tolerance without Liberalism*. Cambridge University Press.

Michel, Thomas. 2005. "Sufism and Modernity in the Thought of Fethullah Gülen." *Muslim World* 95(3), 341–358.

Michel, Thomas. 2013. *Peace and Dialogue in a Plural Society: Contributions of the Hizmet Movement at a Time of Global Tensions*. New York: Blue Dome Press.

Milbank, John. 2009. "The Double Glory, or Paradox versus Dialectics: On Not Quite Agreeing with Slavoj Žižek." In John Milbank, Slavoj Žižek, and Creston Davis, *The Monstrosity of Christ: Paradox or Dialectic*. Cambridge, MA: MIT Press, 110–234.

Milbank, John, and Adrian Pabst. 2016. *The Politics of Virtue: Post-Liberalism and the Human Future*. Lanham, MD: Rowman & Littlefield.

Miller, Vincent J. 2003. *Consuming Religion: Christian Faith and Practice in a Consumer Culture*. Bloomsbury.

Mohamed, Abdulfatah Said, and Ronald Ofteringer. 2016. "Rahmatan Lil-'alamin: Islamic Voices in the Debate on Humanitarian Principles." *International Review of the Red Cross* 93(897–898), 371–394.

Mokrani, Adnane. 2008. "Il Dialogo del Movimento dei Focolari con i Musulmani." *Islamochristiana* 34, 79–86.

Mokrani, Adnane. 2017. "To Read the Qur'an with the Eye of Mercy." in Michael Fitzgerald and Biju Michael (eds.), *Christian-Muslim Dialogue: Festschrift in Honour of Prof. Pier Giorgio Gianazza SDB*. Jerusalem: STS Publications, 167–183.

Mouline, Nabil. 2015. "Enforcing and Reinforcing the State's Islam: The Functioning of the Committee of Senior Scholars." In Bernard Haykel, Thomas Hegghammer, and Stéphane Lacroix (eds.), *Saudi Arabia in Transition*. Cambridge University Press, 48–67.

Moyaert, Marianne. 2012. "Recent Developments in the Theology of Interreligious Dialogue: From Soteriological Openness to Hermeneutical Openness." *Modern Theology* 28, 1.

Moyn, Samuel. 2008. "Jacques Maritain, Christian New Order, and the Birth of Human Rights." *Social Science Research Network* 1134345.

Moyn, Samuel. 2015. *Christian Human Rights*. Philadelphia: University of Pennsylvania Press.

Muaammar, Faisal bin. 2018. "Opening Remarks." Wilton Park Inclusive Citizenship Dialogues. Abu Dhabi, November 12.

Müller, Jan-Werner. Forthcoming. *Christian Democracy: A New Intellectual History*. Cambridge, MA: Harvard University Press.

Mumisa, Michael. 2016. "The Problem with the Marrakesh Declaration." SOAS Center for Islamic Studies IdeasHub. https://blogs.soas.ac.uk/muslimwise/2016/05/09/ideas-hub-the-problem-with-the-marrakesh-declaration-by-michael-mumisa-shaykh/.

Murphy, Nancy, Brad J. Kallenberg, and Mark Thiessen Nation. 1997. *Virtues and Practices in the Christian Tradition*. Trinity Press.
Murray, John Courtney. 1966. "The Issue of Church and State at Vatican II." *Theological Studies 27*(December), 580–606.
Nassery, Idris, Rumee Ahmed, and Muna Tatari, eds. 2018. *The Objectives of Islamic Law: The Promises and Challenges of the Maqāsid al-Sharīʿa*. London: Roman and Littlefield.
Neufeldt, Reina C. "Interfaith Dialogue: Assessing Theories of Change." *Peace & Change* 36(3), 344–372.
Norris, Pippa, and Ronald. Inglehart. 2004. *Sacred and Secular: Religion and Politics Worldwide*. New York: Cambridge University Press.
Norris, Pippa, and Ronald Inglehart. 2011. *Sacred and Secular: Religion and Politics Worldwide*. 2nd ed. New York: Cambridge University Press.
O'Connell, Gerard. 2020. "First Muslim ever to Present Papal Encyclical Praises *Fratelli Tutti*," *America Magazine*. October 5.
Omer, Atalia. 2017. "Interreligious Action as a Driver for Social Cohesion and Development." In Tom Bamat, Nell Bolotn, Myla Leguro, and Atalia Omer (eds.), *Interreligious Action for Peace: Studies in Muslim-Christian Cooperation*. Baltimore: Catholic Relief Services.
Omer, Atalia, R. Scott Appleby, and David Little. 2015. *The Oxford Handbook of Religion, Conflict and Peacebuilding*. New York: Oxford University Press.
Orsi, Davide. 2018. "The 'Clash of Civilizations' and Realism in International Political Thought." In Davide Orsi (ed.), *The "Clash of Civilizations" 25 Years On: A Multidisciplinary Appraisal*, 5–14. E-International Relations.
Ozzano, Luca. 2014. "Religion, Political Actors and Democratization: The Turkish Case." *Politics and Religion 7*(3), 590–612.
Pabst, Adrian. 2012. "The Secularism of Post-Secularity: Religion, Realism and the Revival of Grand Theory in IR." *British International Studies Association 38*, 995–1017.
Patton, James. 2018. "Including the Exclusivists in Interfaith." *Review of Faith and International Affairs 16*(3), 23–33.
Paul VI. 1970. *Angelus*. Rome.
Pedersen, Kusumita P. 2004. "The Interfaith Movement: An Incomplete Assessment." *Journal of Ecumenical Studies 41*(1), 74–94.
Petito, Fabio. 2011. "In Defence of Dialogue of Civilizations: With a Brief Illustration of the Diverging Agreement between Edward Said and Louis Massignon." *Millennium-Journal of International Studies 39*(3), 759–777.
Petito, Fabio. 2016. "Dialogue of Civilizations in a Multipolar World: Towards a Multicivilizational World Order." *International Studies Review 18*(1), 78–91.
Petito, Fabio. 2018. "Interreligious Engagement Strategies." Project Report. University of Sussex FoRB and Foreign Policy Initiative.
Petito, Fabio, Fadi Daou, and Michael Driessen, eds. 2021. *Human Fraternity and Inclusive Citizenship: Interreligious Engagement in the Mediterranean*. Ledizioni.
Pew Research Center. 2020. "Religious Composition by Country, 2010–2050." Washington, DC. https://www.pewresearch.org/religion/2015/04/02/religious-project ion-table/.
Pew Research Center. 2012. "Most Muslims Want Democracy, Personal Freedoms, and Islam in Political Life." Washington, DC. https://www.pewresearch.org/global/2012/ 07/10/most-muslims-want-democracy-personal-freedoms-and-islam-in-political- life/.

Pew Research Center Report. 2013. "Arab Spring Adds to Global Restrictions on Religion." Washington, DC. https://www.pewresearch.org/religion/2013/06/20/arab-spring-restrictions-on-religion-findings/.

Pew Research Center. 2017. "Muslims and Islam: Key Findings in the U.S. and Around the World." Washington, DC. https://www.pewresearch.org/fact-tank/2017/08/09/muslims-and-islam-key-findings-in-the-u-s-and-around-the-world/.

Philpott, Daniel. 2004. "The Catholic Wave." *Journal of Democracy* 15(2), 32–46.

Philpott, Daniel. 2019. *Religious Freedom in Islam: The Fate of a Universal Human Right in the Muslim World Today*. Oxford University Press.

Pollefeyt, Didier. 2011. "Interreligious Dialogue beyond Absolutism, Relativism and Particularism: A Catholic Approach to Religious Diversity." In Leonard Grob and John K. Roth (eds.), *Encountering the Stranger: A Jewish, Christian, Muslim Trialogue*. Seattle: University of Washington Press.

Premawardhana, Shanta. 2008. "The World Conference on Dialogue: A Reflection." World Council of Churches. https://www.oikoumene.org/resources/documents/the-world-conference-on-dialogue-a-reflexion.

Putnam, Robert D., and David E. Campbell. 2010. *American Grace: How Religion Divides and Unites Us*. New York: Simon and Schuster.

Quisay, Walaa, and Thomas Parker. 2019. "On the Theology of Obedience: An Analysis of Shaykh Bin Bayyah and Shaykh Hamza Yusuf's Political Thought." *Maydan: Islamic Thought*, January 8.

Ramadan, Tariq. 2012. *The Arab Awakening: Islam and the New Middle East*. London: Allen Lane.

Rane, Halim. 2012–2013. "The Relevance of a Maqasid Approach for Political Islam Post Arab Revolutions." *Journal of Law and Religion* 28(2), 489–520.

Reno, R. R. 2016. "Chaplains of Death." *First Things*, December 14,

Reynolds, Gabriel Said. 2019. "Islamic Christology and Muslim-Christian Dialogue." In John C. Cavadini and Donald Wallenfang (eds.), *Evangelization as Interreligious Dialogue*. Eugene, OR: Wipf and Stock, 143–162.

Rist, John. 2016. "Augustine and Religious Freedom." In Timothy Samuel Shah and Allen D. Hertzke (eds.), *Christianity and Freedom*: Vol. 1: *Historical Perspectives*. Cambridge University Press, 103–122.

Roberts, David. 2012. "Understanding Qatar's Foreign Policy Objectives." *Mediterranean Politics* 17(2), 233–239.

Roberts, David. 2014. "Qatar and the Muslim Brotherhood: Pragmatism or Preference." *Middle East Policy* 21(3), 84–94.

Rorty, Richard. 1994. "Religion as Conversation-Stopper." *Common Knowledge* 3(1), 1–6.

Rosati, Massimo, and Kristina Stoeckl, eds. 2016. *Multiple Modernities and Postsecular Societies*. London: Routledge.

Rötting, Martin. 2007. *Interreligiöses Lernen im buddhistisch—Christlichen Dialog, Lerntheoretischer Zugang und empirische Untersuchung In Deutschland Und Südkorea*. St. Ottilien: Eos.

Roy, Olivier. 1994. *The Failure of Political Islam*. Cambridge, MA: Harvard University Press.

Roy, Olivier. 2004. *Globalized Islam*. New York: Columbia University Press.

Roy, Olivier. 2010. *Holy Ignorance: When Religion and Culture Part Ways*. New York: Columbia University Press.

Roy, Olivier. 2012. "The Transformation of the Arab World." *Journal of Democracy* 23(3), 5–18.

BIBLIOGRAPHY 239

Roy, Olivier. 2020. *Is Europe Christian?* New York: Oxford University Press.

Sachedina, Abdulaziz. 2001. *The Islamic Roots of Democratic Pluralism.* New York: Oxford University Press.

Sachs, Jeffrey D. 2013. "Sowing the Future: How the Church Can Help Promote Sustainable Development Goals." *America Magazine.*

Sachs, Jeffrey D. 2015. "A Call to Virtue: Living the Gospel in the Land of Liberty." *America Magazine.*

Said, Edward. 2001. "The Clash of Ignorance." *The Nation* 273(12), 11–13.

Saiya, Nilay. 2017. "Religious Freedom, the Arab Spring and US Middle East Policy." *International Politics* 53, 43–53.

Salem, Ola, and Abdullah Alaoudh. 2019. "Mohammed bin Salman's Fake Anti-Extremist Campaign." *Foreign Policy,* June 13.

Salenson, Christian. 2012. *Christian de Chergé: A Theology of Hope.* Collegeville: Liturgical Press.

Salvatore, Armando. 2007. *The Public Sphere: Liberal Modernity, Catholicism, Islam.* Springer.

Salvatore, Armando. 2016. *The Sociology of Islam: Knowledge, Power and Civility.* John Wiley and Sons.

Salvatore, Armando, and Dale Eickelman. 2004. *Public Islam and the Common Good.* Leiden: Brill.

Schmidt-Leukel, Perry. 2017. *Religious Pluralism and Interreligious Theology: The Gifford Lectures—An Extended Edition.* Orbis Books.

Schwedler, Jillian. 2006. *Faith in Moderation.* New York: Cambridge University Press.

Scott, Rachel M. 2010. *The Challenge of Political Islam: Non-Muslims and the Egyptian State.* Stanford, CA: Stanford University Press.

Shafiq, Muhammad, and Mohammed Abu-Nimer. 2011. *Interfaith Dialogue: A Guide for Muslims.* London: International Institute of Islamic Thought.

Shannahan, Chris, and Laura Payne. 2016. "Faith-Based Interventions in Peace, Conflict and Violence." A Scoping Study. Coventry University.

Shireen Hunter. 2018. "How Effective Is Interfaith Dialogue as an Instrument for Bridging International Differences and Achieving Conflict Resolution?" *The Review of Faith & International Affairs* 16(3), 102–113.

Sinn, Simone, and Tong Wing-Sze. 2016. *Interactive Pluralism in Asia: Religious Life and Public Space.* Leipzig: Lutheran World Federation.

Sirry, Mun'im. 2009. "'Compete with One Another in Good Works': Exegesis of Qur'an Verse 5.48 and Contemporary Muslim Discourses on Religious Pluralism." *Islam and Christian-Muslim Relations* 20(4), 423–438.

Smith, Christian, and Melinda Lundquist Denton. 2005. *Soul Searching: The Religious and Spiritual Lives of American Teenagers.* New York: Oxford University Press.

Soroush, Abdolkarim. 2000. *Reason, Freedom and Democracy in Islam: Essential Writings of 'Abdolkarim Soroush.* Ed. and trans. Mahmoud Sadri and Ahmad Sadri. Oxford University Press.

Spadaro, Antonio. 2020. "Fraternity and Social Friendship." *La Civilta Cattolica* 14(10).

Steinberg, Guido. 2014. *Leading the Counter-Revolution: Saudi Arabia and the Arab Spring.* Berlin: Stiftung Wissenschaft und Politik.

Stensvold, Anne, and Ingrid Vik. 2018. "Religious Peacemakers on the International Scene: Hopes and Motivations." *Review of Faith & International Affairs* 16(3), 9–22.

Stepan, Alfred C. 2000. "Religion, Democracy, and the "Twin Tolerations." *Journal of Democracy* 11(4), 37–57.

Stoeckl, Kristina. 2014. *The Russian Orthodox Church and Human Rights*. London: Routledge.

Stoeckl, Kristina. 2016. "The Russian Orthodox Church as Moral Norm Entrepreneur." *Religion, State and Society* 44(2), 132–151.

Stoeckl, Kristina, and Dmitry Uzlaner. 2022. "Russia Believed the West Was Weak and Decadent. So it Invaded." *Washington Post,* April 15.

Swidler, Leonard. 2013. "The History of Inter-Religious Dialogue." In Catherine Cornille (ed.), *The Wiley-Blackwell Companion to Interreligious Dialogue*. Boston: Wiley-Blackwell, 1–19.

Swidler, Leonard. 2015. "Dialoguing with a Dialogue Pioneer: A Brief Interview with Leonard Swidler." *Journal of Inter-religious Studies* (March 31).

Tabbara, Nayla. 2017. "Islam and Other Religions." In Fadi Daou and Nayla Tabbara, *Divine Hospitality: A Christian-Muslim Conversation*. World Council of Churches Publications, 71–109.

Tabbara, Nayla. 2018. *L'Islam Pensé par une Femme*. Paris: Bayard.

Tabbara, Nayla, and Jeusha Lamptey. 2016. "Feminism, Muslim Theology and Religious Pluralism." *Religions 1*, 37–55.

Taylor, Charles. 1996. "A Catholic Modernity?" *Marianist Award Lectures*, 10. https://ecommons.udayton.edu/uscc_marianist_award/10.

Taylor, Charles. 2007. *A Secular Age*. Cambridge, MA: Harvard University Press.

Taylor, Leonard Francis. 2020a. "Catholic Cosmopolitanism and the Future of Human Rights." *Religions 11*(11), 566.

Taylor, Leonard Francis. 2020b. *Catholic Cosmopolitanism and Human Rights*. Cambridge University Press.

Teissier, Henri. 1984. *Eglise en Islam: Médidation sur l'Existence Chrétienne en Algérie*. Paris: Centurion.

Teissier, Henri. 1991. *Histoire des Chrétiens d'Afrique du Nord: Libye, Tunisie, Algérie, Maroc*. Desclée.

Teissier, Henri. 1998. *Lettres d'Algérie*. Paris: Bayard Editions/Centurion.

Teissier, Henri. 2002. *Chrétiens en Algérie: Un Partage D'Espérance*. Desclée de Brouwer.

Teti, Andrea, Pamela Abbott, and Francesco Cavatorta. 2019. "Beyond Elections: Perceptions of Democracy in Four Arab Countries." *Democratization* 26(4), 645–665.

Tezcür, Güneş Murat. 2010a. "The Moderation Theory Revisited: The Case of Islamic Political Actors." *Party Politics* 16(1), 69–88.

Tezcür, Güneş Murat. 2010b. *Muslim Reformers in Iran and Turkey: The Paradox of Moderation*. Austin: University of Texas Press.

Thomas, Scott M. 2003. "Taking Religious and Cultural Pluralism Seriously." In Pavlos Hatzopoulos and Fabio Petito (eds.), *Religion in International Relations: The Return from Exile*. New York: Palgrave Macmillan, 21–53.

Thomas, Scott M. 2004. "Faith and Foreign Aid: How the World Bank Got Religion and Why It Matters." *Brandywine Review of Faith & International Affairs* 2(2), 21–29.

Thomas, Scott M. 2005. *The Global Resurgence of Religion and the Transformation of International Relations: The Struggle for the Soul of the Twenty-First Century*. Springer.

Thomas, Scott M. 2010. "Living Critically and 'Living Faithfully' in a Global Age: Justice, Emancipation and the Political Theology of International Relations." *Millennium* 39(2), 505–524.

Thomas, Scott M. 2018. "St. Francis and Islam: A Critical Appraisal for Contemporary Muslim-Christian Relations, Middle East Politics and International Relations." *Downside Review* 136(1), 3–28.

Thomas, Scott M. 2019. "The Encounter between Francis of Assisi and al-Malik al-Kāmil and Its Relevance for Muslim-Christian Relations and Contemporary International Relations." *The Muslim World* 109(1–2), 144–168.
Thompson, Mark. 2011. "Assessing the Impact of Saudi Arabia's National Dialogue: The Controversial Case of the Cultural Discourse." *Journal of Arabian Studies* 1(2), 163–181.
Thompson, Mark. 2014. *Saudi Arabia and the Path to Political Change*. London: I. B. Tauris.
Tieszen, Charles. 2018. ed. *Theological Issues in Christian-Muslim Dialogue*. Pickwick.
Tobin, Sarah A. 2016. *Everyday Piety: Islam and Economy in Jordan*. New York: Cornell University Press.
Toft, Monica, Dan Philpott, and Timothy Shah. 2011. *God's Century: Resurgent Religion and Global Politics*. New York: W. W. Norton.
Turner, Bryan S. 2011. *Religion and Modern Society: Citizenship, Secularisation and the State*. New York: Cambridge University Press.
Turner, Bryan S. 2013. *The Religious and the Political: A Comparative Sociology of Religion*. Cambridge University Press.
Turner, Bryan S., and Rosario Forlenza. 2016. "The Last Frontier: The Struggle over Sex and Marriage under Pope Francis." *Rassegna Italiana di Sociologia* 57(4), 689–710.
Uddin, Asma. 2016. "Marrakesh: Rites of Passage." *Newsweek*, April 20.
UN High Council on Refugees. 2015. "Partnership Note on Faith Based Organizations, Faith Communities and Faith Leaders." https://www.unhcr.org/protection/hcdialogue%20/539ef28b9/partnership-note-faith-based-organizations-local-faith-communities-faith.html.
UN Office on Genocide Prevention and the Responsibility to Protect. 2017. "Plan of Action for Religious Leaders and Actors to Prevent Incitement to Violence That Could Lead to Atrocities." https://www.un.org/en/genocideprevention/documents/Plan%20of%20Action%20Advanced%20Copy.pdf.
United Religions Initiative. 2016. "Data Gathering and Narrative Based Impact Assessment through Story Telling and Story Collection." https://jliflc.com/resources/data-gathering-narrative-based-impact-assessment-story-telling-story-collection/.
Urbinati, Nadia. 2010. "Laïcité in Reverse: Mono-Religious Democracies and the Issue of Religion in the Public Sphere." *Constellations* 17(1), 4–21.
US Department of State. 2008. "Report on International Religious Freedom—Saudi Arabia." https://2001-2009.state.gov/g/drl/rls/irf/2008/108492.htm.
US Institute of Peace. 2004. *What Works? Evaluating Interfaith Dialogue Programs*. https://www.usip.org/publications/2004/07/what-works-evaluating-interfaith-dialogue-programs.
Vader, Jennie. 2015. "Meta-Review of Inter-Religious Peacebuilding Program Evaluations." CDA Collaborative Learning Projects and Alliance for Peacebuilding.
Vatter, Miguel. 2013. "Politico-Theological Foundations of Universal Human Rights: The Case of Maritain." *Social Research: An International Quarterly* 80(1), 233–260.
Vatter, Miguel. 2020. *Divine Democracy: Political Theology after Carl Schmitt*. Oxford University Press.
Volf, Miroslav. 2011. "Pluralism as a Political Project for Exclusivist Christians and Muslims." *Review of Faith and International Affairs* 9(3), 51–62.
Wainscott, Ann Maire. 2017. *Bureaucratizing Islam: Morocco and the War on Terror*. New York: Cambridge University Press.

Warner, Carolyn. 2000. *Confessions of an Interest Group: The Catholic Church and Political Parties in Europe*. Princeton, NJ: Princeton University Press.

Warren, David H. 2020. "The Modernist Roots of Islamic Autocracy: Shaykh Abdullah Bin Bayyah and the UAE-Israel Peace Deal." *Maydan*, August 27.

Warren, David H. 2021. *Rivals in the Gulf: Yusuf al Qaradawi, Abdullah Bin Bayyah, and the Qatar-UAE Contest over the Arab Spring and the Gulf Crisis*. London: Routledge Focus.

Warren, David H., and Christine Gilmore. 2014. "One Nation under God? Yusuf al-Qaradawi's Changing Fiqh of Citizenship in the Light of the Islamic Legal Tradition." *Contemporary Islam 8*, 217–237.

Weithman, Paul. 2002. *Religion and the Obligations of Citizenship*. Cambridge: Cambridge University Press.

Welby, Peter. 2020. "There Is No Betrayal in Interfaith Relations," *Arab News*, July 5.

Wikileaks. 2008. "Saudi King on Madrid Inter-Faith Conference." July 6. https://wikileaks.jcvignoli.com/cable_08RIYADH1035?hl=Saudi%20King%20on%20Madrid%20Inter-Faith%20Conference.

Wilson, Erin K., and Manfred B. Steger. 2013. "Religious Globalisms in the Post-Secular Age." *Globalizations 10*(3), 481–495.

Winter, Tim. 2013. "Realism and the Real: Islamic Theology and the Problem of Alternative Expressions of God." in Mohammad Hassan Khalil (ed.), *Between Heaven and Hell: Islam, Salvation and the Fate of Others*. New York: Oxford Unviersity Press, 122–152.

Winter, Tim. 2019. "In Search of a Contemporary Shari'a Discourse of Pluralism." In Jocelyne Cesari (ed.), *EuARe Lectures*. European Academy of Religion, 95–133.

Wittrock, Björn. 2005. "The Meaning of the Axial Age." In Johann P. Arnason, S. N. Eisenstadt, and Björn Wittrock (eds.), *Axial Cvilizations and World History*. Brill, 51–85.

Wittrock, Björn. 2012. "The Axial Age in Global History: Cultural Crystallizations and Societal Transformations." In Robert N. Bellah and Hans Joas (eds.), *The Axial Age and its Consequences*. Cambridge, MA: Harvard University Press, 102–125.

Wolff, Sarah. 2017. "Religious Engagement in the Southern Mediterranean: Much Ado about Nothing?" *Mediterranean Politics 23*(1), 161–181.

Wolterstorff, Nicholas. 1997. "The Role of Religion in Decision and Discussion of Political Issues." In R. Audi and N. Wolterstorrf (eds.), *Religion in the Public Square: The Place of Religious Convictions in Political Debate*. Lanham, MD: Rowman and Littlefield, 67–120.

Woodrow, Peter, Nick Oatley, and Michelle Garred. 2017. "Faith Matters: A Guide for the Design, Monitoring & Evaluation of Inter-Religious Peacebuilding." CDA Collaborative Learning Projects and Alliance for Peacebuilding. https://www.cdacollaborative.org/publication/faith-matters-guide-design-monitoring-evaluation-inter-religious-action-peacebuilding/.

Yang, Fenggang. 2014. "Agency Driven Secularization and Chinese Experiments in Multiple Modernities: Response to Peter Berger." In Peter Berger, *The Many Altars of Modernity: Toward a Paradigm for Religion in a Pluralist Age*. Berlin: Walter de Gruyter.

Vendley, William. 2021. "New Alliance of Virtue Dialogue." Panel presentation at *Inclusive Citizenship: From Mutual Coexistence to Shared Conscience*, at the 8th Assembly of the Abu Dhabi Forum for Peace, Abu Dhabi, December 5–7.

Yilmaz, Ihsan. 2011. "Beyond Post-Islamism: Transformation of Turkish Islamism toward 'Civil Islam' and Its Influence in the Muslim World." *European Journal of Economic and Political Studies 4*(1), 245–280.

Yilmaz, Ihsan, and James Barry. 2018. "Instrumentalizing Islam in a Secular State: Turkey's Diyanet and Interfaith Dialogue." *Journal of Balkan and Near Eastern Studies* 22(1), 1–16.

Yuhel, Salih. 2013. "Muslim-Christian Dialogue: Nostra Aetate and Fethullah Gülen's Philosophy of Dialogue." *Australian eJournal of Theology 20*(3), 197–206.

Yusuf, Hamza. 2008. "Who Are the Disbelievers." *Seasons* (Spring), 31–51.

Yusuf, Hamza. 2016. "Foreword." In *The Marrakesh Declaration on the Rights of Religious Minorities in Muslim-Majority Lands*. : The Forum for Promoting Peace in Muslim Societies.

Yusuf, Hamza, and Tariq Ramadan. 2010. "Rethinking Islamic Reform." Conference debate hosted by the Oxford University Islamic Society, May 26.

Zaman, Muhammad Qasim. 2010. *The Ulama in Contemporary Islam: Custodians of Change*. Princeton, NJ: Princeton University Press.

Zeghal, Malika. 2008. "Reformismes, Islamismes et Liberalismes Religieux." *Revue des Mondes Musulmans et de la Mediterranee 123*, 17–34.

Žižek, Slavoj, and John Milbank. 2011. *The Monstrosity of Christ: Paradox or Dialectic?* Cambridge, MA: MIT Press.

Index

For the benefit of digital users, indexed terms that span two pages (e.g., 52–53) may, on occasion, appear on only one of those pages.

Figures are indicated by *f* following the page number

9/11, 23–26, 30, 83, 123, 168–70

Abduh, Muhammad, 111–12
Abdullah, King, 170–72, 178, 183–84, 196
Abraham Accords, 193–94
accomodationism, 52–53
A Common Word, 26–27, 28, 31*f*, 81–82, 101, 103–6, 108, 116–17, 118, 170–71, 188–89
  criticism, 28, 105–6, 116–17
  origins, 102–4
  political theology, 103–5, 118, 121–22
  relationship to Holy See, 171–72
Adyan Foundation, x–xi, 130, 134–35, 152–66
  citizenship advocacy, xi–xii, 156–58, 189–90
  criticism, 165
  education efforts, 156–57, 159, 162–64
  interreligious activity, 160–61, 162
  interreligious spirituality, 164–65, 187–88
  origins, 152–54
AKP, 6–7, 36–37, 196–97
Al Azhar, 99–100, 122, 158–59, 171, 174
  declarations, 110, 125, 210n.23, 213–14n.60
Algeria
  Catholic Church, 82–83, 92, 137, 146–47
  dark decade, 56, 139
  democratization, 131–34, 195
  demography, 131
  independence, 137
  official Islam, 97
  political Islam, ix, 56, 139
  protests, 190–91
  religious change, 143–44, 148

Alliance of Civilizations (United Nations), 31*f*, 99–100, 175–76, 192–93
Alliance of Virtue, 109–10, 116–20, 176–77, 193–94
Al Issa, Mohammed, 37, 182, 183–84
Al Jazeera, 35, 173
Al Qaeda, 83, 170, 192
Al Qaradaghi, Ali, 102–3, 174–75, 176–77
Al Qaradawi, Yusuf, 34–35, 112–13, 173–75, 177–78
Al Sisi, Fattah, 35, 122, 214n.63
Al Sistani, Grand Ayatollah Ali, xii, 102–3
Al Tayeb, Ahmed, 37, 122, 158–59, 174–75, 212n.45, 214n.63, 215n.67
  views on inclusive citizenship, 158–59
  work on the Human Fraternity Document, 37, 122
Al Thani, Hamad bin Khalifa, 168–69
Al Thani, Tamim bin Hamad, 203n.6
Alwan clubs, 153–54, 156–57, 162–63
Amir al Mu'minin, 31
Amman Message, 25–26, 31*f*, 81–82, 99–100, 101–4
  criticism, 29–30, 116–17
  political theology, 101–3
  origins, 154–55
Appleby, Scott, 74
Arab nationalism, 6–7, 32–33, 35–36
Arab Spring, 4–5, 26, 34–38, 100, 125, 175–76, 188–91
  political aftermath, 26, 35–37, 190–91
  impact on interreligious dialogue, 4–5, 6–7, 100, 154
  terminology (v. Arab Uprisings), 202n.15
Armstrong, Karen, 86–87

Article 29 (Universal Declaration of Human Rights), 118–20, 191–92, 194–95, 213n.54
Assisi, 82–83, 90–91
atheism, 116–17
authenticated Islam, 57–58, 62, 144
authenticity, 48, 57–58, 97
autonomy, 52–53, 68–69, 117
Axial Age, 65–69, 73, 80–81, 84–87, 103–4, 118–19, 124–25
　definition, 65–66
　relationship to liberal modernity, 66
　interreligious interpretations, 80–81, 84–85, 86–87, 103–4

Babel (Tower of), 95
Badawi, Raif, 178–79
Bahrain Declaration on Religious Freedom, 28
Bayat, Asef, 55–56, 59, 60–61
Beirut Declaration, 100
Benedict Option, 69
Benedict XVI, Pope, 103–4, 208–9n.11
Beslan Theater attacks, 25–26
Bin Bayyah, Abdallah, 25–26, 37, 106–13, 118–22, 159–60, 192–94
　criticism, 118, 120–21, 193–94
　interreligious partners, 37
　political theology, 106–8, 109, 121–22
　support for inclusive citizenship 118, 158–59, 182
　views on Habermas, xii, 106–7
　work on Marrakesh Declaration, 106–7
Bin Muaammar, Faisal, 37, 178–79, 181–84, 192–93
Bin Salman, Muhammad, 35–36, 182–84
blasphemy, 116–19, 212n.46, 212n.49, 213n.52
Böckenförde paradox, 55

Caglioni, Ulisse, 138–39, 150–51
Casanova, José, 66, 86–87
Catholicism, 9–10, 89–98, 186
　Catholic Church (Algeria), 83, 137
　Catholic Church (Global), 49–54, 89–90, 91
　Catholic modernity, 47–55, 195

Catholic political parties (*see* Christian democracy)
Catholic politics, 59, 61
Charter of Medina, 106–8, 191, 194–95
Christendom, 50–51
Christian democracy, x–xi, 50, 53–56, 68, 75–76, 196
Christian humanism, 50–51, 115, 211n.35
Christian Nationalism, 46–47
Christian rock music, 73
civilizational traitress, 205–6n.24
clash of civilizations, 25–26, 42–47
Coda, Piero, 89, 91, 93, 96–98, 149
Commission on Unalienable Rights, 119–20
communitarianism, 50–51, 68, 75–76, 119–20
consumerism, 41–42
consumer religiosity, 62, 71
cosmopolitanism, 45, 58
　everyday cosmopolitanism, 61
　rooted cosmopolitanism, 70
Council of Muslim Elders, 37
covid pandemic, xiii–xiv, 193–94

Daou, Fadi, 92–93, 130, 152–55, 158, 165
Dar es Salam, 137–41
dawa, 32–33
de Chergé, Christian, ix, 92, 139
deliberative democracy, 63
democratization, 10, 74–75, 79
Deneen, Patrick, 11, 68–69
dhimmi, 113–14, 210n.28
dialogue among civilizations, 31f, 41, 45, 99–100, 103
Dialogue and Proclamation, 95
dialogue of life, 142
Dignitatis Humanae, 49–52, 109
Diyanet, 36–37, 102–3
Doha International Center for Interfaith Dialogue (DICID), 13,
　al Qaradawi boycott, 173–74
　diplomacy efforts, 173–75
　origins, 167–71
　sponsorship by Qatar, 17, 167–68, 176–77, 196
Dominus Iesus, 96
Dreher, Rod, 69

Druze, 159

Ecclesiam Suam, 91
emancipation, 52, 57–58, 68, 71
epistemic humility, 48–49, 52
epistemology, 81–82
Erdoğan, Recep Tayyip, 6–7, 33–37
establishment (religious), 51
European Council for Fatwa and Research, 102–3
European Union, 1–2
exclusivism, 84–85
Ex ecclesiam nulla salus, 91, 111–12
expressive individualism, 71–72

Focolare community, xi, 54, 93, 134–35
Focolare community in Algeria, 137–41
  ideals, 54, 93, 138, 139–40
  interreligious activity, 139–41, 144–45, 149–51
  interreligious spirituality, 141–42, 143–44, 146–47, 149
  origins, 137–40
Forum for Promoting Peace in Muslim Societies, xiii, 2, 37, 113–14, 134–35, 192. *see* also Bin Bayyah, Abdallah
  relationship to UAE, 2, 37, 134–35, 192
  support for inclusive citizenship, 110, 158–59, 184
  vision of peace, 4–5, 119–20
Francis of Assisi (Saint), 207n.4
Francis, Pope, xii, 37, 122–24, 176–77
  work on Human Fraternity document, xii, 37, 122
  views on interreligious dialogue, 124
Fratelli Tutti, 124
fraternity. *See* Human Fraternity
Freedom of Religion or Belief (FORB), xiii, 212n.49
Front Islamique du Salut (FIS), 139
Fukuyama, Francis, 42
fullness, 84–85, 94, 144–45

G20 interfaith forum, 180–81
Ghannouchi, Rachid, 74, 102–3, 106–7
Global Ethic (The), 66, 87
Global Islam, 32–33, 112
Global Salafism, 35–36

globalization, 25–26, 43, 73–75
Godly Nationalism, 116–17
Good Samaritan, 92
Gülen community, 6–7, 36–37, 60–61, 114–15
Gülen, Fethullah, 115

Habermas, Jürgen, xii, 47–52, 54–55, 94
hadith, 58, 111–12, 147–48
Hallaq, Wael, 58
Hezbollah, 162–63
holiness, 94, 144–45
Holocaust, 82–83, 183–84
Holy Ignorance, 73–74
Holy Spirit, 90–91, 95
human dignity, 53, 68–69, 89–90, 106–7, 108–9, 119–20, 191–92
  in Marrakesh Declaration, 106–7, 108–9
  in Universal Declaration of Human Rights, 119–20, 191–92
  in Vatican II, 51, 53, 89–90. *see also Dignitatis Humanae* and *Nostra Aetate*
Human Fraternity, 122–25, 176–77
humanism, 96–97, 115. *See also* religious humanism
humanitarian Islam, 83, 99–100, 114–16
Huntington, Samuel, 42–46

illiberal tolerance, 116–17
Imago Dei, 89–90
immanence, 62–63, 66, 86–87
inclusion moderation (debate), 55–56
Inclusive Citizenship, xiii, 110, 118, 120, 156–58, 184, 189–90, 193–94
  Adyan Foundation usage, 156, 157–59
  Forum for Promoting Peace usage, xiii, 99–100, 106–7, 117, 118
  National Charter for Education on Living Together in Lebanon, 157
  Wilton Park Charter Process, xi–xii
inclusivism, 84–85, 87, 131
inculturation, 94–95, 141–42, 146–47
individualism, 50, 54–55, 68, 97, 123–24. *See also* expressive individualism
individualization, 10–12, 57–59, 129–30, 148–49
Indonesia, 33–34, 60–61, 102–3, 195

instrumentalization, 1–2, 38
integral human development, 97–98, 110, 207n.7
integral humanism, 50–51
International Religious Freedom Reports, 26, 172, 217n.1
International Union of Muslim Scholars, 102–3, 173
interreligious engagement, 15–16, 180–81, 189, 195–97
intersubjectivity, 97–98, 149
Iran, 35–37, 56
ISIS, 25–26, 154, 165, 192
Islamic civility, 58
Islamic modernism, 111–12, 121
Islamic reform, 6–7, 12–13, 33–34, 100, 111–12, 114, 186
Islamic Vatican II, 12–13, 81–82
Islamist movements, 33–35, 55–56, 100, 139

jihad, 112–13
John Paul II, Pope, 82–83, 90–91
Jordan, 25–26, 31, 99–100, 171
Judaism, 82–83, 90–91, 105–6

King Abdullah bin Abdulaliz International Center for Interreligious and Intercultural Dialogue (KAICIID), 167–68
  in international institutions, 180–81, 192–93
  organizational structure, 179–80
  origins, 37, 167–68, 170–71, 178–79
  sponsorship by Saudi Arabia, 26–27, 177–78, 182–84
  support for citizenship, 110, 179, 181–83
Küng, Hans, 85

Lebanon
  demography, 131
  interreligious dialogue initiatives, 155, 202n.14
  Ministry of Education, 159–60
  Protests, 190–91
  Religious Change, 131–34, 160–61, 165
  War, 152
liberalism, 40–43, 50–52, 58, 67–69, 112
low intensity religion, 72, 73

Lubich, Chiara, 93–94, 139–40

MacIntyre, Alasdair, 67–69
Mahmood, Saba, 9–10, 26–27, 56–59, 148–49
Makkah Charter, 99–100, 121–22, 183–84
Malaysia, 33–34
maqasid al sharia, 103–8, 111–14
mariapoli, 139, 140–41, 145–46
Maritain, Jacques, 50–52, 68
Marrakesh Declaration, 25–26, 31f, 106–10, 189–91
  authors, 103
  criticisms, 116–17, 121–22
  origins, 25–26, 83
  political theology, 106–10, 112–13, 118, 121–22
Marxism, 33
maslaha, 103, 111–15
Massignon, Louis, 92
materialism, 50, 123
Middle East Council for Churches, xi–xii, 154–55, 159
Milbank, John, 69–70
Millet (Ottoman Empire), 44, 81
Ministerial to Advance Religious Freedom, 37
moral therapeutic deism, 149
Morocco, 31, 175–76
Morsi, Mohamed, 34–35
Muhammadiyah, 33–34, 60–61, 114–16
multiple modernities, 9–10, 46, 56–57, 70
Murray, John Courtney, 50–51
Muslim Brotherhood, 34–37, 162, 175–76, 192
Muslim Democracy, x–xi
Muslim World League, 32–33, 182–83
mutual learning, 14, 48–49, 62–63

Nahdlatul Ulama, 33–34, 60–61, 114–15
National Charter for Education on Living Together in Lebanon, 157
natural law, 52, 112
no compulsion in Islam, 104–5, 107–9, 118
Nostra Aetate, 52–55, 81–83, 90–91, 94–95
Nursi, Seyyed, 114–15
Nusantara Manifesto, 100

Organization of Islamic Cooperation, 1–2, 33
orthodoxy, 16, 85–86, 188–89
Ottoman Empire, 43–44

Parliament of the World's Religions, 86–87
Pentecost, 95
personalism, 205n.20
personalization, 10, 47–48, 71–73, 148–49
Petito, Fabio, x–xi, 15–16, 26–27, 44–45
Philpott, Dan, 1, 49
piety (politics of), 57–59, 148–49
pluralism, 12, 41–42, 52, 75–76, 80–81, 84–86, 100–1, 113–14, 116–17, 131–34
political Islam, 32–34, 56
political theology, 17, 53–54, 66–67, 124–25
Pompeo, Mike, 38, 119–20
Pontifical Council for Interreligious Dialogue, xi–xii, 94–95, 141–42
postdogmatic mentalities, 62–64
post-Islamism, 7–12, 55–62, 72–73, 75
  conceptualization by Bayat, 55, 59
  critiques of, 55–56, 58–59, 62–63
  post-Islamism and religiosity, 8, 56–57, 72–73, 75
  relation to democracy, 59, 60
postliberalism, 11, 68–69
postsecularism, 7–8, 11, 46–49, 54–55, 62, 70, 75, 186
  conceptualization by Habermas, 7–8, 47, 48–49, 54–55
  critiques of, 62, 63–64, 71
  in international relations scholarship, 46–47
  normative claims, 47, 75
  postsecular religiosity, 13, 47–48
public diplomacy, 24–25

Qatar
  demography, 168–69
  politics, 167–68
  Qatar blockade, xvii, 121–22
  role in Arab Spring, ix–x, 175–77
  treatment of religious minorities, 168–69, 174–75

visions of modernity, 168–69
worldcup, 175–76

Ramadan, 144, 146–47, 149–50, 161, 165
Ramadan, Tariq, 102–3, 117, 175–76
realism, 40
Regensburg speech, 103–4, 170, 208–9n.11
relativism, 69–70, 95–96
Religions for Peace, 93–94, 192–93
religionwashing, 28
religiosity, 41–42, 48–49, 53–54, 56–60, 72–73, 129–34, 143–44, 148–49, 160–61, 186, 188. *See also* consumer religiosity
religious choice, 10, 47–48
religious freedom, xiii, 37, 49–53, 59, 89–92, 101, 107–8, 117–20, 121–22, 159–60
religious humanism, 114–15, 116, 142
religiously expressed violence, 4–6, 46–47, 135–36, 158
religiously friendly democracy, 4–5
religious market, 72–73
religious minorities, 108–9, 113–14, 189–91
religious modernity, 41, 55–56, 79, 188–89
religious pluralism, 12–13, 74–75, 80–81, 85–87, 94, 100, 105–6, 116–17, 131–34, 143, 144–45, 159–60, 189
Religious Public Affairs (Adyan course), 162
religious renewal, 109, 122–23, 186
Religious Resurgence, 1
religious social responsibility, 156–59, 166
revelation, 86–87, 112
Rida, Rashid, 111–12
Rissho Kosei-kai, 93–94, 179
Roy, Olivier, 10, 11–12, 56, 72–73, 74–75
Royal Institute for Interfaith Studies, x–xi, 134–35, 158–59, 166

Salafism, 35–36, 149
salvation, 73, 91, 94–96, 100–1, 110–12, 149, 164
Samaritan (the Good), 92, 207n.2
Sant'Egidio (community of), ix, 54, 116, 134–35

Saudi Arabia
   citizenship politics, 182, 193–94
   demography, 131–34
   global religious outreach
   politics, 6–7, 26, 32–33, 35, 170
   reaction to Arab Spring, 6–7, 35, 37
   religious identity, 167–68, 172
   treatment of religious minorities, 172, 177–78, 182–83
   visions of modernity, 182–84, 193–94
Schmidt Leukel, Perry, 80–81, 84–87
Secular Age (The), 57, 66, 86–87
sharia, 16–17, 58, 60, 68–69, 108, 111–13, 131. See also *maqasid al sharia*
Social cohesion, 97–98, 100–1, 120–21, 124–25
social mobilization, 11, 17, 186
soft power (religious), 32–33, 192–93
spirituality, 73, 139–45, 154–55, 164, 189
   interreligious, 92, 146–47, 167–68
   passive, 73
spiritual solidarity, 12–13, 108–9, 115, 145, 153–54, 155, 189
strong religion, 74
subsidiarity, 204n.6
supersessionism, 110–11
syncretism, 95–96, 97, 146

Tabbara, Nayla, 107–8, 130, 152–55
Tauran, Cardinal Jean-Louis, 168–71, 176
Taylor, Charles, 57–58, 66, 70, 71, 206n.25
Teissier, Henri, ix, 82–83, 137, 146–47
telos, 67, 112
Thomas, Scott, 1–2, 13, 45–46, 70, 206–7n.1
Tibhirine (monks of), ix, 92, 139
Tlemcen, 137–41, 145–46, 149
tolerance, 24–25, 81, 108, 116–17, 155, 190–91
   illiberal, 116–17 (*see also* illiberal tolerance)
   Ministry of (Tolerance), 203n.9

totalitarianism, 50–51, 95
traditionalism, 47–48, 57, 62, 68–69, 157–58, 188–89
   neotraditionalism, 71, 120–21, 208–9n.11
transcendence, 64, 65–67, 69–70, 86–87, 97, 103–4, 117, 124, 148–49, 186
Treaty of Westphalia, 42–44, 108
Trump, Donald, 37, 119–20
truth claims, 48, 49–52, 62–63, 64, 80–81, 84–87, 89–91, 94, 103, 124–25, 142, 187–88
Tunisia, x–xi, 31, 34–35, 175–76

United Arab Emirates, xi–xii, 2, 31*f*, 35–37, 118–22, 176–77, 192–93
United Nations, 1–2, 179–81, 192–93
   Alliance of Virtue, 99–100
   Office on Genocide Prevention, 180–81, 192–93
   Universal Declaration of Human Rights, 68, 115, 118, 119–20, 191–92, 194–95
Unity prayer, 93
US Ambassador for Religious Freedom, 37, 119–20. *See also* International Religious Freedom Reports

Vatican II (Second Vatican Council), 52, 54, 59, 89–90, 195, 213–14n.60
veiling, 73, 147–48, 149, 161, 163, 165
virtue ethics, 67, 70, 112, 118–19, 120, 186

Wahhabism, 34–35, 167–69, 173
war on terror, 25–26, 30
wasatiyya, 34–35
weak religion, 74
Word of Life (Focolare), 139, 144–45

Yezidis, xi–xii, 202n.16
Yusuf, Hamza, 37, 102–3, 109, 119–20

Zawiyas, 144